ASP.NET 2.0
FOR
DUMMIES®

by Bill Hatfield

WILEY

Wiley Publishing, Inc.

ASP.NET 2.0 For Dummies®

Published by
Wiley Publishing, Inc.
111 River Street
Hoboken, NJ 07030-5774
www.wiley.com

Copyright © 2006 by Wiley Publishing, Inc., Indianapolis, Indiana

Published by Wiley Publishing, Inc., Indianapolis, Indiana

Published simultaneously in Canada

For general information on our other products and services, please contact our Customer Care Department within the U.S. at 800-762-2974, outside the U.S. at 317-572-3993, or fax 317-572-4002.

For technical support, please visit www.wiley.com/techsupport.

Wiley also publishes its books in a variety of electronic formats. Some content that appears in print may not be available in electronic books.

Library of Congress Control Number: 2005927624

ISBN-13: 978-0-7645-7907-3
ISBN-10: 0-7645-7907-X

Manufactured in the United States of America

10 9 8 7 6 5 4 3 2 1

1O/SY/RR/QV/IN

WILEY

About the Author

Bill Hatfield is the best-selling author of numerous computer books, including *Active Server Pages For Dummies*, *Creating Cool VBScript Web Pages*, and *Windows XP in 10 Easy Steps or Less* (all from Wiley). He is also the editor of *Visual Studio .NET Developer*, a monthly technical journal from Pinnacle Publishing. He's a Microsoft Certified Trainer (MCT), a Microsoft Certified Solution Developer (MCSD) and Co-Founder of the Indianapolis .NET Developers Association. He works as a corporate instructor for New Horizons in Indianapolis, Indiana, where he also loves to spend time with his family.

Dedication

This book is dedicated to the best kids in the world: Bryce and Zoe. You two have given me the greatest gift anyone can receive — the ability to love someone else more than myself. Before you were in my life, I couldn't imagine having kids. Now, I can't imagine how impoverished my life would have been without the two of you in it. Thanks for making me a better person. And for being so much fun to pal around with!

Author's Acknowledgments

Thanks to Katie Feltman, acquisitions editor: your kindness, patience and dedication to the quality of this book are the best an author could ask for! To Ken Cox, my technical editor, for great feedback and thoughtful suggestions. To copy editor Virginia Sanders for helping me come across more clearly. Thanks also to all the rest of the Wiley staff that helped make this book possible.

To my wife: Thank you so much for your support with this and my many other projects and activities. It isn't easy dealing with a sometimes (only sometimes?) moody daddy. And thanks most of all for your endless love and care for the best kids in the whole world. I think we make good babies...

Thanks to mom and dad, now more commonly known as mamaw and papaw. Now that I have a little bit better idea what you went through, I think I have a lot to apologize for!

Thanks to my good friends: Brad, Mike, Curtis and Dee, Wayne and TaKiesha. You guys are a lot of fun — a welcome refreshment from a crazy world. And to my buddy Steve, a sophisticated mind that never fails to appreciate the baser things in life!

Publisher's Acknowledgments

We're proud of this book; please send us your comments through our online registration form located at www.dummies.com/register/.

Some of the people who helped bring this book to market include the following:

Acquisitions, Editorial, and Media Development

Project Editor: Mark Enochs

Acquisitions Editor: Katie Feltman

Copy Editor: Virginia Sanders

Technical Editor: Ken Cox

Editorial Manager: Leah Cameron

Media Development Specialist: Kit Malone

Media Development Coordinator: Laura Atkinson

Media Project Supervisor: Laura Moss

Media Development Manager: Laura VanWinkle

Editorial Assistant: Amanda Foxworth

Cartoons: Rich Tennant (www.the5thwave.com)

Composition Services

Project Coordinator: Kathryn Shanks

Layout and Graphics: Carl Byers, Denny Hager, Joyce Haughey, Stephanie D. Jumper, Barbara Moore, Barry Offringa, Lynsey Osborn, Heather Ryan, Julie Trippetti

Proofreaders: Leeann Harney, Jessica Kramer, Carl William Pierce, TECHBOOKS Production Services

Indexer: TECHBOOKS Production Services

Special Help
Kelly Ewing, Laura Miller, Blair Pottenger, Heidi Unger

Publishing and Editorial for Technology Dummies

    Richard Swadley, Vice President and Executive Group Publisher

    Andy Cummings, Vice President and Publisher

    Mary Bednarek, Executive Acquisitions Director

    Mary C. Corder, Editorial Director

Publishing for Consumer Dummies

    Diane Graves Steele, Vice President and Publisher

    Joyce Pepple, Acquisitions Director

Composition Services

    Gerry Fahey, Vice President of Production Services

    Debbie Stailey, Director of Composition Services

Table of Contents

Introduction

● ●

*W*elcome to *ASP.NET 2.0 For Dummies,* the book that shows you how to make your Web pages come alive and interact with the people who visit your Web site. And, best of all, you can do it without dedicating a large portion of your life to your Web site!

I Know Who You Are . . .

Because you've picked up this book off the shelf and you're flipping through it, I can make some pretty good guesses about the kind of person you might be. You might . . .

- ✔ Be a Web site or intranet developer working for a company.
- ✔ Have a personal or small-business Web site.
- ✔ Be someone with experience in ASP.NET and who is curious about what's new in 2.0.
- ✔ Be a Classic ASP developer who's been waiting for Microsoft to "get it right" before you make the plunge.
- ✔ Be one of those folks who just *has* to get in on all the hot, new technologies.

In any case, you're probably looking for ways to make your job easier and your Web site a lot cooler. I'd guess that . . .

- ✔ You know how to use Windows 2003, Windows 2000, or Windows XP, and you know how to use Internet Information Server (IIS), at least well enough to get around. (Or, the company that hosts your Web site takes care of all that.)
- ✔ You're familiar with HTML.
- ✔ You have at least a little experience with a scripting language like JavaScript, VBScript, or Perl.
- ✔ Perhaps you've actually done some programming in Visual Basic, Java, C/C++, or COBOL.

But don't worry if you aren't a programmer or an HTML guru. This book and ASP.NET 2.0 make interactive Web pages easy.

About This Book

The book you're holding in your hands is your key to the world of ASP.NET 2.0. It unlocks the secrets of the easy-to-use Visual Basic 2005 programming language to make your Web pages more intelligent. It helps you transform your pages from a lecture format into a two-way conversation. You'll engage your visitors by making them part of the action!

Although ASP.NET 2.0 is a relatively simple technology, many books and magazines would have you believe that it's only for people with Ph.D.s in Computer Science. They use buzzwords and complex descriptions. They make lots of assumptions about what you already know.

This book is different. It's designed for you. It uses plain English to explore all the exciting features of ASP.NET 2.0 with an eye toward creating practical and fun pages that will keep your visitors coming back to your site again and again. No jargon, no big assumptions, and no distractions — I promise!

About ASP.NET 2.0

Your Web pages are simple and informative, but not very exciting. You'd like to make them more interactive. Maybe add a survey, a trivia question, a game, or perhaps something more serious like a mortgage payment calculator. Maybe you could even retrieve information from the corporate database to make your pages a truly valuable resource.

Unfortunately, you can't do all that nifty stuff with HTML alone. Of course you're interested in exploring new technologies, but you don't want to spend months and months figuring out complex programming languages and esoteric relational database concepts. As quickly as possible, you want to get a handle on all the stuff you need to start making those cool ideas buzzing around in your head a reality.

ASP.NET 2.0 makes it possible. With this book, you can start creating interesting pages right away. And the more you discover, the more you can do. With ASP.NET 2.0, your creativity is the only limit to the kinds of pages you can create!

How This Book Is Organized

This book is divided into several parts, and each part is divided into several chapters. The book first explores the basics and then moves on to the tougher stuff.

Here's a brief rundown of the book's parts and what each part covers.

Part 1: Getting Started

In this part, you find out how to set up your computer so that you can start creating your own Web pages and trying them out right away. You even create your very first ASP.NET page.

Part I also gives you a deeper understanding of ASP.NET and its place in the world of Web development. In this part, I define some terms that you're bound to hear tossed around all the time by developers, books, and magazines. I also give you a context for understanding how ASP.NET fits into the big picture.

Part II: Introducing ASP.NET 2.0

If you've done some ASP.NET programming in the past, you're probably going to want a quick rundown of what's new in ASP.NET 2.0. You can find that here. If you're new to ASP.NET, you can skip Chapter 3 — it probably doesn't matter much to you if a feature is new in this version or if it's been around a long time.

You can use any editor you want (including Notepad) to practice ASP.NET 2.0 with this book. But for those of you who are interested in Microsoft's new Visual Web Developer 2005 Express, I also provide a chapter in this part to get you started with it.

Part III: Speaking the Language

¿Habla Visual Basic 2005? You will after you read the chapters in this part! Through numerous examples and plain-English descriptions, you discover all the essential aspects of programming with Visual Basic 2005 to create cool ASP.NET 2.0 Web pages.

Part IV: Classy Objects and Methodical Properties

Object-oriented programming is one of those buzzwords that can send chills down your spine. No need to fear — it isn't nearly as difficult as everyone tries to make you think it is. In this part, you discover not only *what* it is, but what *good* it does for you in your Web page development. You also find out how to use a few of the built-in objects in ASP.NET 2.0 to do some very cool stuff.

Part V: Creating Interactive Web Applications

Making your pages interactive means giving the user a chance to chime in. That's exactly what you do in this part. Uncover the controls that enable your users to enter information and find out how to make your page respond intelligently to that information.

You also explore advanced controls that look slick and do all the drudgery work for you. Imagine a complete monthly calendar with all the standard functions built into one control — and no coding necessary!

Finally, you uncover ways to easily *validate* the data your users type in — to help them find typos and things they forgot to fill in before they send the data to you.

Part VI: Casting a Wider ASP.NET

When you have the basics down, it's time to dive in! Fortunately, the water is deep, and you're just beginning to discover all the possibilities that ASP.NET offers.

In this part, you build on your knowledge of objects and find a toy box full of functionality in the .NET Framework Class Library. Find out how you can make your applications do all kinds of neat tricks.

You discover various options for enhancing your applications to make them more powerful and flexible. And you find out how to configure Web server settings that apply to your application alone — and all without a system administrator anywhere in sight!

Part VII: Tapping the Database

From users of corporate intranets to home-shopping customers, everyone needs access to information stored in a database. And Part VII takes you from where you are now to turbo-guru in no time. You find out how to retrieve information and display it in a variety of ways. You also discover how to add, update, and delete database information directly from your own ASP.NET 2.0 pages.

Part VIII: Exploring New ASP.NET 2.0 Features

ASP.NET 2.0 adds many new interesting features to your toolbox. In this part, I specifically select the features I think will benefit you the most and explore them.

Master Pages allow you to define your site's layout (location and contents of your header, footer, and so on) in one place and then automatically mirror that throughout your site. Building on this is another new feature called Themes, which allows you to define a look for your HTML tags using CSS files and a look for your server controls using skin files. Then you can apply these themes to your pages or to an entire site with one setting.

Security is another feature that has been enhanced with a whole new set of Login server controls. Now you can literally drag and drop security into your application and begin securing access to pages based on logins or roles.

Finally, as more and more users become Web-savvy, they also begin to demand more from Web user interfaces. High on that list of demands is user customization. Users want to control, not merely the look and feel, but also the actual content presented and its arrangement. Answering this need is the Web portal application. In this part you'll find out how another new ASP.NET 2.0 feature called Web Parts makes portal development much easier than you would ever have thought possible.

Part IX: The Part of Tens

There's so much to explore! Find out all the places you can go to get more information about ASP.NET 2.0, including the top ten ASP.NET 2.0 Web sites. Flipping to The Part of Tens before you read the rest of the book is a little like eating dessert before the main course. I highly recommend it!

Appendix

The CD located in the back of this book includes all the source code for all the major examples in this book — and lots of the smaller examples, too! It also includes useful software from various developers — some demo versions, shareware, and freeware.

You can read all about the CD's contents, the system requirements, and the installation instructions in the appendix.

Napoleon Bonus Part (Get It?) — On the CD

Well, bad pun or no, you can't beat *free* — and that's exactly how much this power-packed Bonus Part costs! If you think something can't be worth much if you get it for free, think again.

In this part, you get detailed, blow-by-blow descriptions on how each page of the Café Chat Room and Classy Classifieds applications works. You also get a Guestbook application and a detailed description of how that application is constructed. In all, you get more than 80 pages of information showing you all the tricks you need to make ASP.NET 2.0 sing.

But wait! There's more! I don't have mail-order knives, but I do have a chapter for those who want more VB 2005 functions to play with. Bonus Chapter 4 hits some of the most important string, date, and time manipulation functions you're likely to need in your applications.

Looking for more validation power? Building on the concepts in Chapter 15, Bonus Chapter 5 shows you some of the more advanced validation controls you can use to assure your users don't try and sneak anything past you.

Bonus Chapter 6 is written specifically for Classic ASP developers. If you've worked with ASP 1.0, 2.0, or 3.0, this is the place to start. Dive into this chapter to get a fast-paced overview of all the key changes you need to consider. Then use this bonus chapter as a roadmap that shows you what you can skip and what you need to pay attention to.

Finally, in case you've never worked with a database before or you need a quick refresher, I provide one for you in Bonus Chapter 7. It's a great stop before you tackle Chapters 19, 20, and beyond.

You sure got your money's worth with this book, didn't you?

Conventions Used In This Book

You should know a few facts about the way I format the text in the book and exactly what I mean when I use special formatting.

When I want to show you the HTML from a Web page or some source code for an example, it will look something like this:

```
<html>
<head>
<title>Hello and Welcome Page</title>
</head>
<body>
. . .
```

Sometimes, I refer to something from a page or a source code listing or something that you see on the screen. When I do, I set it off by using a monofont typeface, like this:

Set the `Budget` variable to the value 25.

When I need you to fill in some detail, I also add italics to the typeface, like this:

Go to `www.`*`yourdomainname`*`.com`.

Suppose I need to refer to items on a menu bar. I want to say, for example, that you should click to pull down the Edit menu and then choose the option called Cut. Here's how I do that: Choose Edit ➪ Cut.

Icons Used In This Book

Throughout this book, I use icons to set off important information. The following icons are the usual *For Dummies* fare:

When you see this icon, read the text carefully and tuck the information away in a safe place in your brain where you can easily find it later. You'll need it.

Sometimes I go off on a tangent about some technical bit of trivia that is completely unessential to the topic at hand. But don't worry. If I do, I label it with this icon so that you know you can safely skip over it, if you want.

This icon highlights a quick idea or technique that will make your life a little better.

If you see this icon, always read and follow the accompanying directions. This information can keep you from having a very bad day.

This icon points to features you can find on the companion CD.

I also include several special icons that are a little more unique. These will help guide you toward the material that is of most interest to you and make the book faster and easier to digest:

If you already have some ASP.NET experience under your belt, keep an eye out for this icon. It points out features and capabilities that are new to ASP.NET 2.0.

Microsoft's Visual Web Developer 2005 Express is a great development environment for beginners in ASP.NET. I don't assume that you're using it in this book (you can use any editor you like — even Notepad), but if you are using it, keep an eye out for this icon — it identifies tips and notes that will help you make the best use of this tool.

If I'm exploring a new topic, I always enjoy it more if I can actually try it out while I'm reading. So I include lots and lots of little examples throughout the book for you to try. When you see this icon, don't just read it — do it!

Sometimes things just don't work the way any normal, rational person would expect them to work. And it's those goofy things that trip you up every time. When you see this icon, watch for weirdness ahead.

Where to Go from Here

Using this book is quite simple, really: You read the first page, then proceed to the second, and go on like that until there are no more pages.

What?! You don't read books from cover to cover? You skip around? Egad! All right, I guess it's just a fact of life. Some people (you know who you are) prefer not to read books from front to back. But if you're going to skip around, let me help you out a bit.

I cover the core stuff you need to know in Chapters 1 to 11. With those topics under your belt, you can begin creating dynamic, interactive Web applications to do all sorts of stuff. Another good spot to hit is Chapter 17, which explores the .NET Framework Class Libraries. You can find all kinds of fun stuff there.

How quickly you can spin through those first few chapters depends heavily on how much programming and Web development experience you have. If you don't have much experience, that isn't a problem — this book starts at the beginning. If you have a little or a lot of development experience, that's great! (For those of you familiar with the previous version of ASP.NET, the next section provides a guide for using this book to come up to speed quickly with 2.0.)You can move through some of these chapters at a brisk pace. But be careful skipping any of the early chapters entirely — ASP.NET 2.0 offers many unique features that you might never have seen before.

Beyond that, it's up to you. Do you want to find out more about Visual Basic 2005? Check out Chapter 16. Do you want to create richer user interfaces? See Chapters 12, 13, and 14. Want to play with features that are new in ASP.NET 2.0? That's exactly what Chapters 21 through 24 cover. Are you interested in working with a database? Chapters 19 and 20 are key. By the way, if you've never worked with a database before, be sure to check out Bonus Chapter 7 (on the CD) before you tackle the other database chapters.

Regardless of your experience level, do yourself a big favor: Don't just read the examples — *try them out!* This book is a lot more fun that way, and you'd be amazed at how much more you absorb by playing around with the examples than you do when you just read about it.

Finally, when you've exhausted this book and you're thirsty for more, head to Chapters 25 and 26. They point you in the right direction.

ASP Me, 1 Might Answer

If you want to send me feedback about the book, I'd love to hear from you! My e-mail address is:

```
BillHatfield@EdgeQuest.com
```

My Web site is:

```
www.edgequest.com
```

And for a Web site completely dedicated to this book, check out:

```
www.aspdotnetfordummies.com
```

Here you find cool ASP.NET 2.0 applications, the latest book corrections, news, and links to other great ASP.NET 2.0 sites.

Help! It Doesn't Work!

In case you run into any problems while reading this book, go to the Web site dedicated to this book and look for the Frequently Asked Questions section:

```
www.aspdotnetfordummies.com
```

At the site, you find reader questions and answers to all sorts of ASP.NET 2.0 and book-related issues.

If you still need more help, Chapter 25 lists the "Ten Best Places to Get Answers." From books and magazines to newsgroups, user groups, and ASP.NET nerds, you have lots of options out there!

Part I
Getting Started

The 5th Wave   By Rich Tennant

"Just how accurately should my Web site reflect my place of business?"

In this part . . .

You're off to a running start as you discover the wonders of creating Web applications with ASP.NET 2.0 technology. You begin by figuring out the computer requirements and setup you need to get going with ASP.NET 2.0. I walk you through every step in the process of creating, running, and testing your first page. That way, you can read the rest of the book with your fingers on the keyboard, trying out—and tearing apart—every example you see!

But getting set up to create pages is just half of it. You don't have to look at too many articles and books on Web development before the hodge-podge of buzzwords and confusing technologies makes your head spin! But don't worry. In this part, I set your mind at ease by giving you some *context* —a quick tour of the Web technologies and an understanding of how ASP.NET 2.0 fits in the puzzle.

Chapter 1

ASP.NET 2.0 — Just Do It!

*M*ost books (especially about .NET, it seems) give you lots of concepts and theories and detailed, boring analysis before they ever let you jump in and play with the stuff. Don't expect that here, though; I turn the traditional philosophy of chapter-order sequence on its head. In this book, I start by getting your server and development environment configured and set up so that you can create your first ASP.NET page in *this* chapter. There's no teacher like experience!

If questions pop up in your mind as you're going through this chapter, hang on! I probably address them in Chapter 2, where I take a step back and put what you've seen into context. There, I show you how ASP.NET came about and how it differs from other technologies you might have heard about.

Do I Need a Development Environment?

To work with most computer languages, you use a *development environment*. Usually this involves an editor that you use to write the source code and to access the utilities that make your development and debugging go faster and more smoothly. These environments put at your fingertips every tool you need to write, run, and test applications that you create.

ASP.NET is different. It's a development technology that is built into the .NET Framework. You can easily create great ASP.NET 2.0 applications with nothing more than Notepad or your favorite editor.

Of course, some integrated development environments (IDEs) *are* available for creating ASP.NET applications. The most prominent is Microsoft's own

Visual Studio 2005. This professional tool is full of features to aid in developing medium- and large-scale development projects. But it can be more than a little intimidating when you're first getting to know .NET.

Because of this, Microsoft has created an entry-level product that is much less intimidating and much more affordable: Microsoft Visual Web Developer 2005 Express Edition. This tool is relatively inexpensive and provides a lot of the best features of Visual Studio without all the stuff you don't care about when you're getting started or when you're working on smaller applications.

A variety of other development tools have been created and made available for free or for sale by other companies. A quick search of Google for "ASP.NET" and "IDE" is probably the fastest way to get an up-to-date list.

Because I don't know what development environment you're using — if any — I don't make any assumptions in this book. You can easily use Notepad or any other editor to enter, save, and test the examples throughout this book.

In the end, though, you don't need lots of complex tools and mystical icons to make ASP.NET work. ASP.NET is a simple language combined with standard HTML. What could be more elegant?

Everything You Need to Get Started

ASP.NET isn't a software package that you can just pick up at your local software store. ASP.NET is a *technology,* which is a fancy way of saying it's a cool feature that's built into some *other* piece of software. That other piece of software, in this case, is the .NET Framework. The .NET Framework is a free Microsoft product. It's the foundation for a new approach to software development, and ASP.NET is a key component of that. For more information on the .NET Framework, see Chapter 2.

To set up a machine for creating and testing ASP.NET 2.0 pages, you need three things:

- ✔ **An operating system that supports Internet Information Server (IIS):** For example, Windows 2003 Server, Windows XP Professional, or Windows 2000 Server/Professional.

- ✔ **IIS:** Windows 2003 Server and Windows 2000 Server install IIS automatically, by default. Windows XP and Windows 2000 Professional might not install IIS by default, but you can install it from the Windows installation discs.

- ✔ **The .NET Framework 2.0 Software Development Kit (SDK):** The .NET Framework 2.0 is available from Microsoft at no charge. You can download it at http://msdn.microsoft.com/netframework. You can also find instructions there telling you all you need to know about downloading and installing the .NET Framework 2.0.

The hosting option

If you don't want to go through the hassle of setting up your own Web server, you might want to find a Web site hosting service that supports ASP.NET 2.0.

Hosting services are companies that provide room on their Web server for you to place your site. You can even get a domain name (like www.mywebsite.com) that jumps right to your hosted site.

However, hosting services aren't all created equal. So, be sure to ask about everything that's important to you:

✔ **Does it host on Windows 2003/2000 machines?** Many hosting services use some form of UNIX operating system and, at least for now, ASP.NET 2.0 doesn't run on UNIX.

✔ **Does it support ASP.NET 2.0 development?** If the service says it supports ASP, it might be referring to Classic ASP or ASP.NET 1.*x*. Be sure to ask specifically about ASP.NET 2.0.

✔ **Does it provide Microsoft Access or SQL Server database support?** Most hosts allow Access databases, since there's no real setup necessary for the hosting service. However, most charge a setup fee and a monthly fee for the use of a SQL Server database.

A hosting service might charge a setup fee and then usually a monthly fee of anywhere from $10 up to hundreds of dollars, depending on what you want. Most services offer various packages at increasing price/feature levels. In some cases, you can add features *à la carte* for an added setup fee and monthly rate.

Lots of hosting services are out there, and shopping around can pay off. In fact, if you just want a simple ASP.NET site to practice on, you might find a few that offer minimal space (5MB or 10MB) for free!

For a list of ASP.NET 2.0 hosting options, go to www.aspdotnetfordummies.com/ hosting.

You don't need an active Internet connection to create and test ASP.NET pages. IIS can also process and serve Web pages to you locally on the server itself or over a local area network (LAN).

After you have the operating system, IIS, and the .NET Framework installed, you're ready to start developing your own ASP.NET pages!

Visual Web Developer Express simplifies your "what you need" list. You can use any Windows XP, Windows 2003, or Windows 2000 operating system. You don't need IIS installed because Visual Web Developer Express has its own Web server for testing built right in. Just install Visual Web Developer Express, and you're ready to get started!

Watch Your Language!

Before you begin your ASP.NET journey, you need to decide which programming language you want to use for creating ASP.NET pages. Microsoft provides Visual Basic 2005, C#, C++ and others. Third-party companies have developed even more languages for .NET.

I've chosen to use Visual Basic 2005 for this book. It's easy to learn, easy to use and it will get you up to speed as quickly as possible. It's also the most popular computer language ever created!

Understanding the Development and Testing Process

In this section I cover a variety of topics that you need to understand before you begin actually creating ASP.NET pages. Among them: choosing the Web server you want to work with, understanding where IIS looks for your pages, where and how to save your pages and how testing works.

Choosing an ASP.NET Web server

Figure out what server you will use to test the pages you create. You might use an existing server at your company, set up your own server, or use a hosting service.

If you use an existing server at your company, there are probably procedures in place regarding how you can add new pages, where you can and cannot put test pages, and so on. Be sure you fully understand and follow those guidelines.

If you set up your own system at work or at home, you're responsible for installing everything and getting it up and running. You're in complete control, but it can be a big task, requiring knowledge of server operating systems and IIS.

Perhaps the easiest solution is to use a Web hosting service that supports ASP.NET. The host gives you the information you need to know to create new folders on your site, send files you create to the site, and test those files. And best of all, the hosting service handles all the installation and maintenance for you! For more information on this option, see the sidebar titled "The hosting option," in this chapter.

Understanding where IIS looks for your pages

If you're working directly with the Web server (*not* through a hosting service), you need to know a little about IIS and where it looks for its pages.

IIS creates a folder on the server's hard drive with the default name inetpub. The inetpub folder contains a subfolder called wwwroot. The wwwroot folder is the root for the Web site.

If you place a new Web page in wwwroot or any of its subfolders, your Web server has access to the page, and you can link to it from other pages on your site.

So when you begin a new project, create a folder under wwwroot for your application, and then, within that folder, create the pages you need. If you have lots of pages, you might want to create subfolders inside your application's folder to help organize things.

The process for creating, saving, and testing pages in Visual Web Developer Express is a little different from doing it in Notepad or a simple editor (and quite a bit simpler). If you like, you might want to jump ahead to Chapter 4, which focuses on Visual Web Developer Express.

Saving your page with the .aspx extension

All ASP.NET page filenames must end with the `.aspx` extension. That's how the Web server knows it should process the page as an ASP.NET page.

If you use Notepad as your editor to create ASP.NET files, be aware that Notepad almost *insists* that you name your files with a `.txt` extension. In fact, if you try to create a new file and save it as `test.aspx`, the file's name ends up `test.aspx.txt`. (Notepad pulls this trick only if you're creating new pages. When you edit and save an existing page, Notepad always saves the page with the extension it had originally.) Here's how you fix that problem: When you type in the filename, put it in quotes — for example, enter **"test.aspx"**. Notepad saves the file with exactly the filename you give it.

If you accidentally save a file with the wrong extension, just go into Windows Explorer and rename the file.

Many versions of Windows, by default, hide known extensions from you. This can be a problem if Notepad saves your file as `test.aspx.txt` because the file might show up in Explorer as `test.aspx` (hiding the `.txt` extension). It looks right, but the `.txt` extension prevents your Web server from recognizing it as an ASP.NET page. Of course, this can be very confusing. To show extensions in Windows Explorer, choose Tools⇨Folder Options. Then click the View tab and scroll down until you find the option labeled Hide File Extensions for Known File Types. Make sure that check box is *not* selected.

Testing your pages

To test your ASP.NET pages, open a browser window, type the address of the page into the Address bar, and press Enter. That makes the browser request the page from the server and gives the server the opportunity to process the ASP.NET code on the page.

If your previous experience is primarily with HTML pages and JavaScript code, you may need to break some old habits when you create and test your ASP.NET pages. In the past, when testing pages, you might have opened the page by simply dragging and dropping it onto the Internet Explorer browser. Or you might have used the browser's File⇨Open command to open the page. You can't use either of those techniques for testing ASP.NET pages. Both techniques open up the page directly without any Web server involvement, so the server has no opportunity to process the server-side code in the page and nothing happens! Because ASP.NET works on the server side, you have to let the server find the page, run the code, and then send the results to the browser.

Getting Your ASP in Gear: Creating an ASP.NET Page

When you have your editor or IDE selected and a Web server where you'll test your pages, you can create your first ASP.NET page:

1. **Create a folder under wwwroot and give it a name.**

   For my examples, I use a folder by the name of hello.

   If you're using a hosting service, you don't see wwwroot. Just create a folder in your root directory. Again, your hosting service can tell you how to do this.

2. **Create a new page in Notepad or the editor of your choice.**

   Most HTML editors work fine, as long as they let you work with the raw HTML tags and don't try to hide them from you. If you're using Visual

Web Developer Express, click the Source tab. If you're using Microsoft FrontPage, click the HTML tab. If your editor puts any tags or other stuff in the page automatically, delete all that so you start with a blank slate.

3. **Enter the code in Listing 1-1.**

Listing 1-1:   The Hello and Welcome Page

```
<%@ Page Language="VB" Debug="True" %>
<html>
<head>
<title>Hello and Welcome Page</title>
</head>
<body>
<center>
<% Dim TextSize As Integer %>
<% For TextSize = 1 To 7 %>
<font size = <%=TextSize%>>
Hello and Welcome!<br>
</font>
<% Next %>
</center>
</body>
</html>
```

Carefully type the code as it is listed. Don't worry about whether something is entered in upper- or lowercase. It will work either way.

4. **Save the page in the folder you created earlier under wwwroot. Give it a filename with the extension `.aspx`.**

   For my examples, I name the file `welcome.aspx`.

   If you're using Notepad, put quotes around the name so that Notepad doesn't add the `.txt` extension.

   If you're using a hosting service, save the file to a spot on your local hard drive, and then send the file to the server.

5. **Open your browser, and then open the page you created by typing** http://localhost/*foldername*/*filename* **into the Address bar at the top of the browser. (Fill in *foldername* and *filename* with the folder and filename you gave these items when you created them.)**

   If you aren't working on the Web server machine that's running your page, access your page by simply typing the intranet URL. Usually, you just type the name of the server in place of `localhost`, as in `http://bigserver/hello/welcome.aspx`.

   If your Web site is on a hosting service, use the address the service gave you or your own domain name to access the page, as in `http://www.mydomain.com/hello/welcome.aspx`.

   You should see the page you created in the browser. It looks a lot like Figure 1-1.

Figure 1-1:
The
welcome.
aspx page.

If you don't see this page, go back and check to make sure you entered the code exactly as it appears in Step 3.

Understanding How This Example Works

In the preceding section, I show you how to create a Web page so that you can understand the *process* for creating and testing pages. Unless you already know Visual Basic 2005 or are a proficient programmer, you probably don't know exactly how the page works just by looking at it. I explain exactly what the code in Listing 1-1 does here.

The programming commands always appear inside <% and %> symbols. Those symbols are called *delimiters.* They keep the commands separate from the HTML tags.

The very first line in Listing 1-1 is a page header:

```
<%@ Page Language="VB" Debug="True" %>
```

A page header isn't required, but including it at the top of any ASP.NET page is a good idea. It does two things: It specifies that the ASP.NET language used in this page is Visual Basic 2005, and it sets Debug to True. The Debug setting helps by providing more detailed error messages for you if you make a mistake.

The first Visual Basic 2005 command on the `welcome.aspx` page is `Dim`. You use the `Dim` command to create variables. Here, it creates a variable named `TextSize`:

```
<% Dim TextSize As Integer %>
```

A *variable* is a place to store information to be used later. The `As Integer` clause at the end of that line indicates that this variable will hold whole numbers. No information is put into the variable, yet. (For more information on using DIM to declare variables, see Chapter 5.)

The next line identifies the beginning of a `For...Next` loop. A *loop* provides a way to repeat the same commands (or HTML) over and over again. This loop repeats the lines between the `For` line and the `Next` line. These lines (shown here in bold) are called the *body* of the loop:

```
<% For TextSize = 1 To 7 %>
<font size = <%=TextSize%>>
Hello and Welcome!<br>
</font>
<% Next %>
```

When does a loop stop looping? Well, different kinds of loops exist, but a `For` loop decides when it's done by counting. In this case, it counts from 1 to 7. The loop sets the value of the `TextSize` variable to 1 the first time through the loop. Then, the body of the loop is executed. The `Next` statement identifies the end of the loop, so the code jumps back up to the top again. The second time through the loop, `TextSize` is set to 2; the third time, it is set to 3; and so on through 7, when the loop ends. (For more information on the `For` loop, see Chapter 6.)

In the body of the loop, the `<font>` tag sets the size of the text. The size is set equal to `<%=TextSize%>`. What's that? The `<%` and `%>` are the normal delimiters, but there are no commands inside! Just an = sign followed by the `TextSize` variable name. This special syntax gets at the *value* of the variable. So the first time through the loop, the HTML `<font>` tag that's generated looks like this: `<font size = 1>`. The second time through, it looks like this: `<font size = 2>`. Each time through the loop, the font size is set to the value of `TextSize`.

Then, `Hello and Welcome!` is displayed on the page. Because the font size is set to a bigger number each time the loop executes, the same line is printed again and again in increasingly larger sizes. And that's exactly what you see in Figure 1-1, shown earlier.

If you choose View⇨Source from the Internet Explorer menu while looking at this page, you see the following HTML:

```
<html>
<head><title>Hello and Welcome Page</title>
</head>
<body>
<center>
<font size=1>
Hello and Welcome!<br>
</font>
<font size=2>
Hello and Welcome!<br>
</font>
. . .
<font size=7>
Hello and Welcome!<br>
</font>
</center>
</body>
</html>
```

As you can see, there's no indication of a loop in the HTML that was sent. In fact, you don't see any programming code at all — just pure HTML. One of the beauties of ASP.NET is that the code is executed on the server and *produces* the HTML that is sent to the browser.

Don't feel like you need to completely understand this example before you go on. You get a better understanding of ASP.NET itself in Chapter 2, and I cover Visual Basic 2005 commands in Chapters 5, 6, and 7. For now, just make sure you understand the process for creating and testing an ASP.NET page.

Modifying, Retesting, and Creating Pages

The information in this chapter and the steps described in the previous section give you the information you need to create and run the examples in this book. However, if you make a mistake, you'll need to know how you can make a change to a page and then retest it to see if you fixed the problem. In addition, there are a few other common tasks that you'll need to understand as you begin creating your own ASP.NET pages. In this section I'll provide some steps you can use to accomplish these goals.

Modifying and retesting pages

If you want to modify a page and then test it again, follow these steps:

1. In your preferred editor, open the page file and make your changes.

2. **Save the file. Save the file. Don't forget to save the file.**

3. **Go to your browser window.**

4. **Click Refresh in the browser window.**

   The page is requested from the server and executed. The results are then displayed in your browser. If they still aren't what you expected, just lather, rinse and repeat.

Creating new pages

Whenever you want to create a new ASP.NET page, follow these steps:

1. **Create the page in your editor and save it with the `.aspx` extension to the appropriate folder.**

   Put quotes around the name if you're saving from Notepad!

2. **Type the page's address into the browser's Address bar and then press Enter.**

   The server retrieves and processes the page, and the results are sent to your browser.

Converting HTML pages to ASP.NET pages

Later, when you're ready to start working on your own Web site, you'll probably want to convert some of your existing HTML pages into ASP.NET pages. That's easy:

1. **Find the file on your server's hard drive by using Windows Explorer.**

2. **Rename the file. Change the `.htm` or `.html` extension to `.aspx`. (Or you could copy the file and give the copy the `.aspx` extension. This allows you to keep the old HTML file, if you like.)**

3. **Edit the page in your editor and add any Visual Basic 2005 commands you like, and then save the page.**

The only difference between normal HTML files and ASP.NET files is the extension. The extension tells the Web server how to process the pages. If you find that your code isn't executing, make sure you set the extension to `.aspx`!

Chapter 2

Putting ASP.NET 2.0 in Its Place

*I*n Chapter 1, I demonstrate how to set up your environment and then create and test an ASP.NET 2.0 page. In this chapter, I step back a moment and put ASP.NET 2.0 into context for you.

ASP.NET 2.0 makes dynamic, interactive Web pages easy to create and maintain. It provides a complete environment for creating everything from simple brochure sites to complex e-commerce and intranet application sites.

In this chapter, I give you a bird's-eye view of the more important technologies that have transformed the Web from a document-viewing technology into something more interactive. My goal in this chapter is to give you a framework for understanding the purpose for ASP.NET 2.0, where it fits in the industry, and what all those buzzwords mean!

Understanding Simple, Static HTML

In this section and the next couple of sections, I'll walk through the process of exactly what happens when you retrieve a static HTML page, when you retrieve an HTML page that includes JavaScript and when you retrieve a page that includes ASP.NET code. As I do, I'll point out the similarities and differences among these different approaches so that you'll see exactly how ASP.NET works.

To begin, think about how a simple Web page works. It works like this:

1. In your browser's address bar, you type your favorite site's name.

   Perhaps the site is called ASP.NET For Dummies. The URL associated with it is

   ```
   www.aspdotnetfordummies.com/default.htm
   ```

2. Your browser sends out a request to the `aspdotnetfordummies.com` server, asking for the page named `page1.htm`.

3. The server finds that page on its hard drive and sends it back to your browser.

4. After your browser gets the page, it looks at what's inside. The browser reads all the HTML tags and then converts them into a beautifully formatted page. The page also might have links to other pages. If you click one of those links, the process starts all over again.

This example shows how the World Wide Web was originally conceived. In its earliest form, the Web provided a very easy way to access and navigate information made of text and pictures. Today, this type of page is referred to as *static HTML*.

Exploring How JavaScript Makes Your Pages More Interactive

So how do you make your Web pages more interactive? The most common way involves using JavaScript alongside your HTML to respond to the users when they enter information or click buttons.

You can use JavaScript in your Web pages to do *client-side scripting. Client-side* refers to the browser and the machine running the browser, as opposed to *server-side,* which refers to the Web server software running on the server machine.

Client-side scripting works like this:

1. You choose a Favorite or click a link in your browser to go to an HTML page that includes client-side scripting code.

2. The Web server locates the page and sends it back to your browser.

3. The browser interprets the HTML tags and, at the same time, executes some client-side JavaScript code that it encounters.

   Some code doesn't execute immediately. Instead, it waits until you do something — such as clicking a button — before it runs.

Client-side scripting gives you the ability to write scripts that make your page more interactive. In client-side scripting, the code appears right alongside the HTML so that everything is in one place. It's also relatively easy to grasp — a scripting language is typically not as complex as a programming language, so you can become productive with it quickly.

However, client-side JavaScript has a few downsides:

- ✔ **Script theft:** The script is downloaded as part of the page, and anyone who wants to can view the source of the page and see your script. Consequently, others can steal the code you worked so hard to develop, and they can use it on their own sites!

- ✔ **Limited browser support:** A client-side script can run only on browsers that support scripting. And if the browser supports scripting but has that support turned off for security reasons, the script fails dismally.

- ✔ **Limited capabilities:** Most importantly, the client-side script is limited (for security reasons) in what it can do. It can't access a database, retrieve files from your hard drive, or many other useful things.

So How Does ASP.NET Work? How is it Different?

So what's the alternative? Why, ASP.NET 2.0 — of course! Here's a little run-down of how an ASP.NET page is processed:

1. You click your favorite site's name in your browser's Favorites or Bookmarks menu.

   Imagine the URL associated with it is

   ```
   www.aspdotnetfordummies.com/default.aspx
   ```

2. The browser sends out a request to the aspdotnetfordummies.com server, asking for the page named page1.aspx.

3. The Web server receives the request, locates the page, and looks at it. Because the filename has an .aspx extension at the end, the server understands that this page is an ASP.NET page.

4. The server checks to see whether it has a compiled version of this page. A Web server can't run an ASP.NET page until that page is compiled, so if the server doesn't have a compiled version, it compiles the page.

5. The server executes the compiled version of the page, running the source-code parts of the page and sending the HTML parts of the page to the browser. None of the source code itself is sent. Only pure HTML is returned to the browser, where the formatted page is displayed.

6. The server saves the compiled version of the page for use next time someone requests the page.

This arrangement has lots of advantages:

✔ **Simplicity:** As with client-side script, ASP.NET pages are easy to write and maintain because the source code and the HTML are together.

✔ **Flexibility:** The source code is executed on the server, so your pages have lots of power and flexibility. Also, your pages aren't limited by the security constraints of the client. They can be configured to freely access the server's files and to access databases.

✔ **Execution speed:** Execution is fast because the Web server compiles the page the first time it is requested, sends the page to the browser and then saves the compiled version of the page for future requests. This means your ASP.NET pages continue to work well even when the server has lots of traffic.

✔ **Code Security:** Only the HTML *produced* by the page is returned to the browser, so your proprietary application source code can't be easily stolen.

✔ **Browser Friendly:** Because only pure HTML is sent back, your ASP.NET pages work with any browser running on any computer. You can even design your applications to work well with PDAs and SmartPhones.

The ASP.NET advantage — faster, simpler, smaller

Microsoft introduced the first version of ASP.NET in January 2002 as the Web component of a comprehensive new development platform. It provides many advantages, including

✔ Drastically reducing the amount of code required to build large projects.

✔ Simplifying working with the user by introducing *server controls*. Server controls make it possible to ignore (for the most part) the fact that the forms are on the client and then submitted to the server for processing. Instead, the developer can pretend that everything is happening on the server. This dramatically simplifies the whole process.

✔ Making retrieving and changing database information a snap.

✔ Providing an easy approach to deployment. When you're done creating your application, it's easy to move it to the real Web server that will host it. All you have to do is copy the files. No need to worry about registering components or dealing with other setup issues.

✔ Running faster and scaling to larger volumes of users without hurting performance.

And now, presenting ASP.NET 2.0

Although ASP.NET was a significant advance, nothing could be perfect. After investing more than three years of effort in listening to developers talk about what works, what doesn't, and what could be improved, Microsoft has responded with the next release: ASP.NET 2.0. Among its benefits:

✔ Once again, it dramatically reduces the amount of code required to develop applications. This is made possible by providing over 50 new server controls, which automate and simplify common programming tasks.

✔ It provides an approach for site layout that allows you to specify common elements, such as headers, footers and menus, in one place and yet display them appropriately on every page.

✔ It includes a framework for easily creating portal-like applications.

✔ Pre-built security membership and personalization capabilities can be flexibly integrated into your applications with very little effort.

The Bigger Picture: The .NET Framework

Of course, ASP.NET 2.0 isn't an island unto itself. It's a part of the *.NET Framework*. The .NET Framework is a large library of code that Microsoft makes available for developers to build on.

Imagine you're a real estate developer building two-dozen houses on a few acres of land that you just bought. You want to build various types of homes to meet the needs of different families.

Now suppose a company comes along and provides a very flexible foundation system. You could use this same foundation and adapt it for almost any kind of home you'd like to build. Are you interested? Of course! If you don't have to think about the foundation for each home, you're that much farther ahead of the game. You can build 'em faster and with less expense than your competitors!

That's what the .NET Framework does for software developers. It's a very flexible foundation on top of which you can build business applications that do all kinds of things. It provides unprecedented support for software development. In fact, it doesn't just lay the foundation, it does the software equivalent of the plumbing and electrical work, too!

Here are some of the benefits of using the .NET Framework:

- **User interface tools:** A complete set of tools for creating user interfaces for use in creating both standard Windows applications and Web applications.

- **Database tools:** A set of libraries helps you access and manipulate data in almost any database.

- **New technologies:** The .NET Framework makes working with XML (Extensible Markup Language) and other new technologies pretty simple.

  New languages: The .NET Framework also enables you to work in almost any programming language you like! It comes with several commonly used languages, like Visual Basic 2005, C# (pronounced *see-sharp*) and C++. In addition to these languages, the Framework's flexibility allows third-party developers to create new languages that just plug right into the .NET Framework. In fact, dozens of such languages are available now, like APL, Haskel, COBOL, SmallTalk and many, many more.

And because ASP.NET 2.0 is built on top of this framework, you can create ASP.NET pages using any of the built-in languages or any of those created by third parties. And you have access to all the features and capabilities of the .NET Framework with no additional work required.

Part II
Introducing
ASP.NET 2.0

The 5th Wave   By Rich Tennant

"This new Help program has really helped me get organized. I keep my project reports under the PC, budgets under my laptop and memos under my pager."

In this part . . .

ASP.NET is growing up! Here I focus on some of the new features introduced in ASP.NET 2.0. The first chapter is specifically for you if you've worked with ASP.NET before and you want to come up to speed quickly with what's new and different.

The second chapter is for those of you interested in using Microsoft's new, inexpensive development tool called Visual Web Developer 2005 Express. It's an editor, a debugger, and a whole lot more—and it can make your Web development faster and easier.

Chapter 3

Exciting New ASP.NET 2.0 Features

In This Chapter

▶ Scoping out the brand new features and capabilities

▶ Checking out features that have been enhanced with the new release

▶ Exploring the new navigation controls

*I*n this chapter, I provide you with a quick overview of the new features in ASP.NET 2.0, beginning with those that are completely new, then covering the ones that have been improved or enhanced. It would take a library of books to describe all these features in detail, so I hit just the highlights here.

However, if you're new to ASP.NET, this chapter is *not* for you. I strongly encourage you to skip it. For you, the best plan is to pick up with Chapter 4 (*if* you plan on using Visual Web Developer 2005 Express Edition — if not, go to Chapter 5) and continue from there. You discover ASP.NET 2.0 from the ground up without worrying about what is new in 2.0 and what is not.

By the way, if you're a Classic ASP developer with no experience in ASP.NET, I've written a chapter just for you. It's on the CD — look for Bonus Chapter 6.

Discovering the Big, New Features

In this section, I focus on features that are completely new to ASP.NET, providing you with the ability to do things that were either impossible or very difficult in the first version of ASP.NET.

Being the master of your domain with the Master Pages feature

One of the most glaring omissions in ASP.NET 1.0/1.1 was any way to create a standard look-and-feel and the ability to reproduce that look-and-feel throughout the site with very little development or maintenance trouble. User controls came closest to filling the bill, but they were limited in their effectiveness and couldn't control the design and layout of the entire page.

Microsoft has answered this need very effectively with a new feature called *Master Pages.* A master page is a page with the extension .master. It provides a definition of the layout elements you want to share across the pages of your site, like headers, menus and footers. Then you add special *placeholder* controls in specific locations on the page. *Content pages,* then, are your usual .aspx pages and they are used to provide the specific content for each page. They do this by playing fill-in-the-blank. Instead of providing HTML, server controls, and code to display the entire page, your .aspx pages now simply identify themselves with the master page and then provide the content that plugs into each placeholder identified on its master. You can have as many placeholders on a master page as you like, and you can even define default information in the placeholder so that if the content page doesn't fill in that particular blank, the blank will automatically be filled in with the default information.

Master Pages work something like the visual inheritance capabilities provided for Windows Forms. Master Pages can inherit their user interface from other Master Pages. However, a Master Page can never be displayed directly. Only an .aspx page can be displayed.

For more information on creating and using Master Pages, see Chapter 21.

Using themes and skins

Looking for a way to make your site beautiful that doesn't require you to visit each and every page when you want to update that look? ASP.NET 2.0 themes and skins are your answer.

A *theme* is a folder that contains .skin files, Cascading Style Sheets (CSS), graphics and other resources for making your site beautiful. You can apply a theme to a page by specifying the theme's name in the @ Page directive. Or you can apply the theme to the entire site in the web.config.

When a theme is applied, the CSS defines the look and feel of the HTML tags on your page. Whereas the .skin files define the look and feel of the ASP.NET server controls. A `.skin` file is nothing more than a file containing server controls that have specific properties (such as `Font`, `BackColor`, `ForeColor`, and so on) set, so that they define what the default values for that control should be when the theme is applied.

When you want to update your site's look, you can simply create a new theme folder, fill it with the appropriate CSS, `.skin` files, and so forth, and then change the theme name in the `web.config`.

Parts is Web Parts

You've probably seen sites such as MSN and Yahoo! that offer you the ability to customize your own home page. You can indicate which kinds of news reports, stock quotes, cartoons, and so on that you want to appear on your customized page. You can often move the various sections of the page by dragging and dropping them. These personalized portal sites have become a very popular approach for building Web applications — especially for intranet applications shared among the members of a department or a whole company. By putting Web information or applications into small, reusable units, the users can select and organize them as they see fit — maximizing the benefit for everyone.

You could build applications like this with ASP.NET 1.0/1.1. In fact, a very popular open-source ASP.NET application called .NET Nuke did just that. But ASP.NET 1.0/1.1 had no built-in features (other than the user control) to make the process easier.

ASP.NET 2.0 introduces a feature called Web Parts. The developer implements the functionality and information presentation into small pieces implemented as a Web Part. The user can then select, customize, and arrange the parts. ASP.NET 2.0 keeps track of user customization and preferences. It also provides features that make it easy for the users to do their customization — including drag-and-drop arrangement on the page. For an introduction to this exciting new feature, see Chapter 24.

Exploring the Faster, Better Features

This section focuses on the features that existed in ASP.NET but have been enhanced in 2.0. Some of these features include new components, such as new controls that enhance previously existing features. (For completely new features, go to "Discovering the Big, New Features" earlier in this chapter.)

ASP.NET 1.0/1.1 was a solid foundation that had some very real strengths. For the 2.0 release, the ASP.NET team built on the existing strengths to make them even better.

Dancing with the database

If you write business applications in ASP.NET, you probably spend a lot of your time dabbling in databases with ADO.NET. So it's no surprise that Microsoft decided to put some extra effort into making this task easier. In fact, one of the major driving goals for the ASP.NET 2.0 release was to reduce the amount of repetitive code required to do common tasks. And the ASP.NET team had a lot of opportunity here. If you've ever written an application that makes extensive calls to stored procedures that each have many parameters, you know what I mean.

With this second version of the .NET Framework, Microsoft has introduced a new set of ASP.NET server controls called *data source* controls. These controls provide easy access to data in a variety of forms so that you can bind your user interface controls to the data source directly. There's a data source control for accessing XML files, business objects, and of course, SQL databases.

The `SQLDataSource` control rolls up the `Connection`, `Commands` and `DataAdapter` objects all into one neat little package. You can simply specify the `Connection` string and a `SelectCommand`, bind the data source to a grid and you've got data! And this control doesn't fall down when things get complicated. It has the capabilities you need to pass complex query parameters and update the database, all with a tiny fraction of the code needed for the same tasks in ASP.NET 1.0/1.1.

New server controls make your user interface sing!

With the original introduction of ASP.NET, Microsoft introduced a whole new way to interact with the user — Web Forms and Server Controls. The approach was so intuitive that it made creating highly interactive applications fun! So it's no surprise that the folks at Microsoft decided to build on this strong foundation. In fact, they built and built and built! ASP.NET 2.0 has more than 50 new server controls. In this section, I hit the high points.

Two important server controls complement the new `SQLDataSource`, which I discuss in the preceding section, very nicely: `GridView` and `DetailsView`. `GridView` is a new, souped-up `DataGrid`. With zero lines of code, you can bind the grid to a `SQLDataSource` and make it both sortable and pageable. It also has built-in support for displaying drop-down lists and images within the cells of the grid. `DetailsView` takes the opposite approach — it displays all the columns of a single row of data. These controls can work very nicely together.

A very handy user interface device added this time around is the `MultiView`. This container control allows you to put any number of controls on one of several pages or *views.* Only one view is displayed at a time, but you can change which page appears by changing a property. This flexible approach makes it easy to implement tab controls as well as dynamic forms.

Inheriting from the `MultiView` is another new control called `Wizard`. It makes building wizard-type pages to walk the user through a process (using the familiar Next and Previous buttons) almost automatic.

Increased security that doesn't require you to remove your shoes

Although the previous version of ASP.NET allowed you to set up security for your applications by using forms authentication, it didn't really help out much with the heavy lifting. You still needed to write your own code to store and update user accounts, create login forms, and validate login information.

ASP.NET 2.0, on the other hand, is a champion weightlifter. It provides server controls that provide an interface for new users to register and for existing users to enter their login information. The controls automatically validate the user with an internally maintained database. The ultimate result is that you can do it all with few or no lines of code — instead of several hundred! For more information on the new login controls and creating a secure Web site, see Chapter 22.

ASP.NET 2.0: The configurator!

Configuration and administration of Web sites was made much simpler (and easier to deploy) in ASP.NET 1.0/1.1 than it was in Classic ASP. Between the `machine.config` file and the various `web.config` files, all you needed was Notepad and a little knowledge of XML (Extensible Markup Language) and you could configure to your heart's content.

However, I'm sure it occurred to you at one time or another that it wouldn't have taken much work for the Microsoft folks to put a visual front-end on these `.config` files. And if they did, maintenance would be a whole lot simpler.

As you might expect, they got it right in ASP.NET 2.0. In the Internet Information Services Manager utility (available under the Control Panel's Administrative Tools), simply right-click the virtual folder of the Web site that you want to configure and choose Properties. In this dialog, you'll find a new tab called *ASP.NET.* From there you can access all of the configuration settings that the application's `web.config` makes available.

Are you away from the host machine? Do you need a way to do your configuration at a distance? No problem. ASP.NET 2.0 includes a Web-based configuration tool that allows you, with the appropriate permissions, to administer all your site settings.

Navigating the Choppy Seas of Your Web Site

Several new controls have been added specifically to help your users more easily navigate your site and see exactly where they are. All of these controls work with a site map that you define. The site map can be provided to the controls in a variety of ways, but the easiest (and the default) way is to create a simple XML file that defines the sections and subsections where pages appear on your site. Once the controls understand what your site looks like, they automatically configure themselves to provide access to it — quickly and easily. Here's a description of each of the controls and what they can do for you:

✔ **TreeView:** The TreeView control works like a listbox, but presents its items hierarchically. That is, each item can have items within it and can be expanded or collapsed to view them. When associated with your site map, the sections, subsections and pages are presented as a hierarchical list of links that can be clicked to navigate to the appropriate page. This allows you to use a TreeView as your primary site navigation tool.

✔ **Menu:** Pop-out menus are a popular navigation device on Web sites. They allow you to select an item and see a pop-out menu that shows the sub-items. This is typically done with JavaScript, but this server control generates all the HTML and JavaScript necessary — no hand-coding is necessary on your part.

✔ **SiteMapPath:** This control provides a feature that's commonly referred to as *bread-crumbs*. The current section, subsection and page are displayed in the control allowing the users to immediately see where they are on the site. In addition, the sections can provide links that allow visitors to go back up the hierarchy, if they like.

Chapter 4

Introducing Visual Web Developer 2005 Express

. . . .

In This Chapter

▶ Getting to know Visual Web Developer 2005 Express

▶ Creating an application

▶ Exploring the windows

▶ Understanding single-file and code-behind pages

. . . .

Read this chapter *only if* you plan to use Visual Web Developer 2005 Express to create your ASP.NET 2.0 pages. Visual Web Developer 2005 Express isn't required for developing ASP.NET pages, and it isn't required to get the most out of this book. You can choose to use your favorite editor or even Notepad to create your pages and just skip this chapter.

However, if you *are* using Visual Web Developer 2005 Express to create your pages, this chapter introduces you to the product and describes its important features and how to use them. This chapter also shows you how to work with the examples in this book when using Visual Web Developer 2005 Express.

In this chapter, I walk you through the process of creating a Web application in Visual Web Developer 2005 Express (VWDE). You can follow along and try it out for yourself. Along the way, I describe the various windows and the options they provide. I certainly don't hit every detail, but by the time you're done reading the chapter, you should know your way around well enough to use VWDE to create, run, and test the examples in this book.

Visual Web Developer 2005 Express: What Is It (Besides a Mouthful)?

Visual Web Developer 2005 Express is notable, not only because it has the longest name of any Microsoft product, but also because it makes developing

Web pages using ASP.NET 2.0 fast, easy, and cheap. It marks the first time that Microsoft has made the vast majority of the cool features in Visual Studio .NET available at such a reasonable price — which makes the product more accessible to small companies and to everyday developers working individually.

Visual Web Developer 2005 Express (which I refer to as VWDE in this chapter to save ink) also has the potential to help simplify the development of your Web applications. With a bit of practice, you'll soon find yourself bouncing around the various windows like a pro. And when you are, you'll find that creating, debugging, and testing your Web applications takes a lot less work than it used to.

Accessing Resources from the Start Page

Whenever you open VWDE, you see the Start Page, as shown in Figure 4-1. The Start Page is a Web page that provides you with a springboard to begin your development. From here, you can create a new project, open an existing project, read news relating to .NET development, search the online help, or use online discussion forums to find the answer to a question. Here's a rundown of the various sections of the Start Page and what they provide:

- **Recent Projects:** This section is in the upper-left corner, and it is (arguably) the most important. Here, with a single click, you can open any of the last dozen or so projects you've worked on. The links at the bottom of this section allow you to open other projects or create a new one.

- **MSDN Visual Studio 2005:** It's the most prominent section on the Start Page and provides you with a list of articles and news items related to .NET development. This information is retrieved from the MSDN Web site when VWDE launches (assuming there's an open Internet connection). So the news is always fresh. This is a great way to keep up to date and find new articles as soon as they're posted.

- **Getting Started:** It's located directly below the Recent Projects section. In it, the first few items — they start with "Create a . . ." — automatically create new projects based on particular *templates*. You can think of a template as a pre-configured set of pages and other files that gives you a running start toward creating your own site. The rest of the items in this section link to various help topics and Web pages you're likely to find interesting as you begin your projects.

- **Visual Web Developer 2005 Express:** This is located below the Getting Started section. It contains a single link that takes you to a page on the Microsoft site where you can submit suggestions or bug reports.

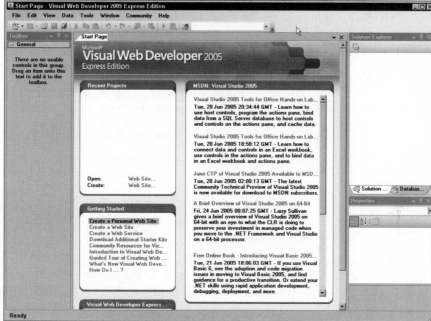

Figure 4-1:
The Visual
Web
Developer
2005
Express
Start Page.

Creating a New Web Site

The first thing you're likely to want to do after surveying the Start Page is to begin creating a new Web site. And, as you might have guessed, the Getting Started section on the Start Page is the place to do that.

Click the Create a New Web Site link. Or, if you prefer, you can choose File↝ New Web Site. Either way, the New Web Site dialog box appears, as shown in Figure 4-2.

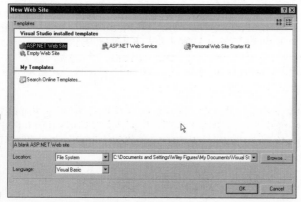

Figure 4-2:
The New
Web Site
dialog box.

Choosing a template

When you begin a new Web site, you need to make decisions regarding three things:

- ✔ **What template you want to use**
- ✔ **Where you want to save the project**
- ✔ **What programming language you prefer to work with**

The New Web Site dialog box prompts you to make these decisions.

Here you can choose from the templates that are installed on your machine. As I mentioned previously, a template is a pre-configured set of pages and other files that gives you a running start toward creating your own site. At a minimum, you see:

- ✔ **ASP.NET Web Site:** Probably the choice you'll pick most often. This template allows you to create a simple setup with a single page, ready for you to begin developing your masterpiece.

- ✔ **ASP.NET Web Service:** Sets you up to begin creating your own *Web services.* A Web Service is an object you can create with methods that can be called from another machine on your network or even from across the Internet. Web Services use a standard way to communicate, so even different machines running different operating systems can communicate well by using Web Services. Web Service is a hot topic and is a very exciting technology. Unfortunately, I don't have room in this book to cover it! If you're interested in finding out more on creating a Web Service you can find out more from the .NET Framwork 2.0 online help documentation — just choose Help Index and search for "Web Services."

- ✔ **Personal Web Site Starter Kit:** Comes with VWDE when you buy it. It's a complete, functioning, personal Web site ready for you to customize to your use.

- ✔ **Empty Web Site:** This option provides you with the ability to create a Web site without creating all the standard files you get automatically with the ASP.NET Web Site template. If you want to start with a clean slate and add each item yourself, this is the way to go.

You might see other templates and starter kits in your dialog box, and you can download more from the Microsoft Web site. Starter kits are a great way to speed up your development. They are simply a project with standard pages that already work well together to accomplish a specific task. They act as a springboard to get you going toward developing certain kinds of applications. All you have to do is customize their look, content, and functionality to your specific needs.

So you can follow along with the examples in the next sections, select the ASP.NET Web Site template (refer to Figure 4-2).

Selecting the location and language

Once you've selected the template you want to use, it's time to select a location, name and language for your site.

Regardless of the template you choose, there are a few more options on this New Website dialog that you need to specify:

✔ Location identifies where your new application will be placed. You can save your Web applications on your local hard drive or on another server through HTTP or FTP. The default location is on your hard drive in your `My Documents\Visual Studio 2005\Web Sites` folder. You can browse for a different location, or if you choose HTTP or FTP, you can enter the address.

✔ The Language option allows you to select the programming language of your choice. This drop-down defaults to whatever was last selected. The options typically include Visual Basic, C# and any other .NET languages you have installed on your machine.

Go with the default Location and be sure that Visual Basic is selected for the Language. Click OK. The main window of VWDE appears, as shown in Figure 4-3.

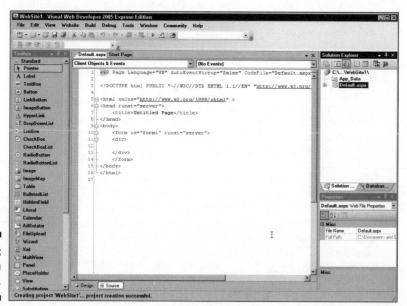

Figure 4-3:
The main
window.

Getting to Know Your Workspace

After you create a new Web site, as I explain in the earlier section, "Creating a New Web Site," VWDE displays a primary window, which contains many smaller windows within it. Most of those smaller windows are *docked* (attached) to the sides or bottom of the primary window. You can resize and move the smaller windows as you like, based on your preferences or your task at the time.

Opening, closing, and hiding windows in VWDE is pretty straightforward. Many windows are opened and docked to a default location along the sides or bottom of the primary window when you begin. To open a window that isn't on the primary window, select that window's name from the View menu. To close a window, click the X in the upper right corner of a window.

Beside the X in the upper right corner of most windows is a picture of a tiny pushpin. This icon allows you to turn the *Auto Hide* feature on and off. When Auto Hide is on, the window slides back and disappears along the side or bottom of the primary window when you are finished working with it (based on the location of your mouse pointer), and a tab replaces it. You can click the tab to see the window and work with it, but when you're done, it will slide away again. This feature is handy when you need a window only every now and then.

However, if you are regularly using a window, you'll probably want to keep it visible and available all the time. In this case, it's better to turn Auto Hide off. To do this, simply click the pushpin icon again. This pins the window open and usually means other windows (especially the Document window) have to shrink a little to make room.

In the following sections, I describe some of the common windows, their default locations, and their functions.

The Toolbox window

The Toolbox, along the left side of the primary window, provides a vast list of items that you might want to add to your pages. HTML controls, server controls, and other components all have a place here. To organize the dozens of entries, the Toolbox is divided into sections, each with its own header, including Standard, Data, Validation, and so on. Each of these section headers has a little + or – icon beside it. These icons indicate that you can click the + (if it's there) to open up the section to display its options; or you can click the – (if it's there) to collapse the section to hide its options. This arrangement allows you to view the kind of entries you want to work with and hide the entries you don't need at the moment.

The Standard section is the section of the Toolbox that you're likely to work with most. This contains all the standard server controls, which you use to create your pages. Server controls provide the primary user interface components in ASP.NET. I describe what server controls are in more detail and how they work in Chapter 10.

To add a server control to your page

1. **Click to select Design view tab in the lower-left corner along the bottom of the Document window.**

2. **Pin the Toolbox open by clicking its pushpin icon (which turns off the Auto Hide feature).**

3. **Open the Standard section of the Toolbox by clicking the plus-sign beside the Standard header and then double-click on the Label control.**

   When you do, a label control appears on the page, selected.

If you prefer, you can drag and drop the control from the Toolbox to the page. This allows you to place it where you like among any other controls that are already on the page. You can also drag and drop a server control on your page when the Document window is in Source view (see the following section for more information). Doing so causes the server control's tag to appear when you drop it within the document.

The Document window

The Document window dominates the most screen real estate — it's that vast area in the center of the primary window. When you first open the application, it contains the Start Page; when you create a Web site, it contains the page you're working on.

A series of tabs appear at the top of the Document window. These tabs let you know what pages are open in the editor (VWDE, that is). They also allow you to quickly switch the page you are working on. If the tab for the page you want to work on doesn't appear in the Document window, just double-click that page in the Solution Explorer window. The page opens in the Document window, and its tab is added.

You can look at a page in the Document window in two different views:

✔ **Source view:** You see the HTML for the page.

✔ **Design view:** You see something more akin to what the page will look like in the browser. (You might be more comfortable with Design view if raw HTML tends to get stuck in your craw.)

To switch back and forth between the Design and Source views, you use the set of tabs in the *lower-left* corner of the Document window.

The Document window, whether in Design view or Source view, is where you'll do most of your work. When you work in Design view, you can type in text and format it much like you would in a word processor. You can drag and drop *server controls* from the Toolbox (discussed in Chapter 10) and arrange them to look exactly as you want.

Finally, the Document window allows you to edit VB 2005 code that you write to respond to various events on the page. I show you how to do that later in this chapter in a section titled, "Writing Code in Response to Events."

The Solution Explorer window

Your anchor is the Solution Explorer. It's in the upper-right corner of the primary window, by default. This is where you can get a bird's-eye view of your project, its folders, and its files. When you first create a new site, there's not much in the Solution Explorer — just the site folder at the top, an App_Data folder below it, and a `Default.aspx` page below that. But as you add more pages and components to your site, they'll appear in this window. And if you ever want to work with a page, you can simply double-click the page in this window to open it in the Document window.

The Properties window

The Properties window, by default, appears in the lower-right corner, under the Solution Explorer window. It allows you to change the properties of whatever server control is currently selected. For example, when you add the Label control to a page, the label is automatically selected. If you do this when the Properties window is visible on your screen, the Properties window shows all the properties for the Label control. You can change these properties by simply scrolling up or down to find the right property, clicking on it, and then entering a new property value. You can change some values by simply typing in text; others you change by selecting from a drop-down list, while still others have their own dialogs that pop up allowing you to specify their values. At the very top of the Properties window is a drop-down list that shows what is currently selected and, therefore, what object's properties you are setting.

You can change how the Properties window organizes its list. By default, the properties are categorized into sections labeled Accessibility, Appearance, Behavior, and so on. You can open and collapse these sections by clicking the + or –, as appropriate. However, if you prefer, you can do away with the categories and look at the properties in one long alphabetic list. You control this organization with two buttons near the top of the Properties window on the left. The first button is called Categorized, and the second is called Alphabetical. Click whichever you prefer.

The Task window

The Task window appears along the bottom of the primary window. It provides a simple to-do list that you can use to keep track of tasks you need to do as you are working on your Web site. Just click in the Description column and type in a note or reminder.

When VWDE finds errors in your code (and it *will* happen!), the errors are listed here in the task window. You can double-click the error message and the Document window jumps to the location of the error so that you can fix it.

Adding Pages to Your Site

When you select the ASP.NET Web Site template to create your new site, VWDE automatically creates a single page for you to begin working with. But most sites require more than a single page! In this section I describe how you add and name new pages.

You start by choosing Website➪Add New Item. Now you see the Add New Item dialog box, as in Figure 4-4.

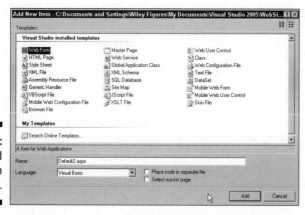

Figure 4-4:
The Add
New Item
dialog box.

Obviously there's a lot more than just Web pages that you can add to your project! A Web Form is what VWDE calls a page — and this is the first entry, and it's selected by default.

Use the Name text box at the bottom of the dialog box to give the new page a name.

For my purposes in this chapter, I call it `DogAge.aspx`. (I use `DogAge.aspx` as an example in some of the sections that follow in this chapter.)

Be sure the Language is set to Visual Basic.

There are also two check boxes at the bottom of the Add New Item dialog box:

   ✔ **Place Code in Separate File.** I discuss the use of this check box later in this chapter, in the "Single-File Versus Code-Behind Pages" section.
   ✔ **Select Master Page.** I discuss the use of this check box in Chapter 21.

For now, just be sure both check boxes are deselected.

Click the Add button. VWDE creates the page in the Solution Explorer window and opens it in the Document window in Source view.

Creating Your User Interface with Server Controls

In this section, I show you how to add and modify server controls on a page to create your user interface. The example you create in this section is the same as the one in Chapter 10. So for more information on what server controls are and how they work, that's where you should look. For more specific information on the server controls used in this section — the Label, Textbox, and Button — see Chapter 12.

Adding server controls

The first step is to use the Toolbox to select the controls you'll need, add them to the page, and then arrange them appropriately.

If the Document window isn't already in Design view, put it in Design view by clicking the Design tab in the lower left of the Document window, along the bottom. Also, if the Toolbox window isn't already pinned open, pin it open by clicking the pushpin icon (which turns the Auto Hide feature off). Open the Standard section of the Toolbox.

Add four server controls to the page: a Label, a Textbox, a Button, and another Label. You can do this by double-clicking the controls in the Toolbox or by dragging and dropping the controls on the page. By default, these controls all end up beside each other at the top of the page. Carefully place your cursor between them and press Enter. This creates a line break and moves any controls positioned to the right of the cursor from that line to the next line. Keep moving your cursor and pressing Enter until each control appears on its own line, as shown in Figure 4-5.

Setting control properties

Now that you have the controls that you want to work with on the page, you can customize how they look and work by setting each control's properties.

1. **Click to select the first Label.**

2. **In the Properties window, find the Text property.**

    It's in the Appearance section if your Property window is categorized. (See the section "The Properties window" earlier in this chapter for details.)

3. **Type this value:** Enter Your Age:

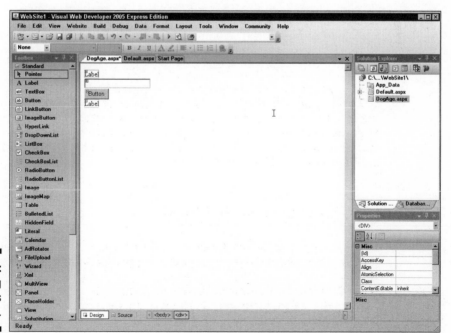

Figure 4-5:
Organizing the controls on a page.

4. **Click to select the Textbox on your page.**

5. **Find the (Id) property in the Properties window.**

   This is the property that you use to name your controls. You don't need to name all your controls, but if you plan to work with a control in your code, it's a good idea to give it a recognizable name. It makes your code more readable.

   The (Id) property is hard to find, whether your Property window is categorized or alphabetic. If it's categorized, (Id) is at the bottom of the list under the Misc category. If it's alphabetic, (Id) is near the top of the list (not in the I's where you'd expect it).

6. **After you find the (Id) property for this Textbox, change its value to Age.**

7. **Click the button to select it. Set the button's (Id) to OK and its Text to OK.**

8. **Click the second label to select it. Set its (Id) to Message and clear out its Text property so that it is blank.**

   When you do so, the name of the label appears inside it on the page. Design view does this because a blank label would be easy to lose otherwise!

When you drop controls on the page and set properties, you are really just creating tags behind the scenes. To see the tags that are created, click the Source tab in the lower left of the Document window along the bottom to change to Source view. The body of the page should look something like this:

```
<body>
    <form id="form1" runat="server">
    <div>
        <asp:Label ID="Label1" runat="server"
          Text="Enter Your Age:"></asp:Label>
        <br />
        <asp:TextBox ID="Age"
          runat="server"></asp:TextBox>
        <br />
        <asp:Button ID="OK" runat="server" Text="OK" />
        <br />
        <asp:Label ID="Message"
          runat="server"></asp:Label>

    </div>
    </form>
</body>
```

As you can see, adding the controls from the Toolbox in Design view causes these server control tags to generate in the body of your page. In addition, the settings you make in the Properties window adds properties, as appropriate, to these server control tags. You can modify these properties here in Source view, and then when you switch back to Design view, the appropriate properties are modified in the Properties window.

Writing Code in Response to Events

Creating a user interface is only part of the battle. The real work of creating dynamic, interactive, intelligent Web applications comes in writing the code that executes in response to events in the user interface. In this section I'll show you how VWDE supports your efforts to do just that.

Beyond default events

Every control has a default event — the one you're most likely to want to write code for. (For example, the default for the Button control is the Click event.) You write code for a control's default event by simply double-clicking the control in Design view. However, if you want to write code for one of the other events, you use the drop-down lists at the top of the Document window when you're in Source view. Here's how:

1. **At the top of the Document window, in Source view, notice the two drop-down lists. Click to select the one on the left.**

   You see that the list is divided into two parts: *Server Objects and Events* and *Client Objects and Events*. The part you're interested in is Server Objects and Events. There you'll see the names of all the server controls you've added to the page.

2. **From the drop-down list on the left, select a control.**

   For example, you might select Age, the text box.

3. **Now click to open the drop-down list on the right.**

   Here you see all the events available for the text box. You can write code to react to any one of these events.

4. **From the drop-down list on the right, select an event.**

   For example, if you select Age in Step 2, you can select TextChanged for Step 4. A new event subroutine called `Age_ TextChanged` is created, and now you can write code for that event, which occurs when the user changes the text in a text box and then tabs away.

In Design view, double-click the Button control.

You immediately go back to Source view. But this time your cursor is up near the top of the page within the `<script runat="server">` tag. VWDE has created an *event handler* for you:

```
Protected Sub OK_Click(ByVal sender As Object, _
    ByVal e As System.EventArgs)

End Sub
```

The code you write here will execute when the user clicks the OK button you created. Add this code:

```
Dim UserAge, DogAge As Integer
UserAge = Age.Text
DogAge = UserAge / 7
Messages.Text="If you were a dog, you'd be " & _
    DogAge & " years old."
```

Debugging, Compiling, and Running Your Web Application

Once you've created your page and written code for its events, you'll want to compile, run and test your application. In this section I demonstrate the steps necessary to do that.

1. **Choose View⇨Other Windows⇨Output.**

    This opens a window that gives you a peak behind the scenes as VWDE compiles your Web site. A window appears at the bottom of the primary window, overtop of the Task window.

2. **Choose Build⇨Build Web site (or press Ctrl+Shift+B).**

    If you entered the code *exactly* as it is in the "Writing Code in Response to Events" section of this chapter, you will see the Error window come forward showing that there is an error in your code: `Name 'Messages' is not declared`. If you double-click the error message, `Messages` in your code is highlighted to let you know where the problem is.

3. **Take the s off the end of `Messages` and try building the site again.**

The error messages go away, but did it compile correctly? You should now see two tabs below the Task window: the Error List tab and the Output tab.

4. Click the Output tab.

You should see a message there that says: `Build: 1 succeeded or up-to-date, 0 failed, 0 skipped`. It worked!

Now you want to see what your page looks like in a browser.

1. Identify the startup page in the Solution Explorer window.

2. Right-click the name of the startup page (`DogAge.aspx`, in my example in this chapter) and choose Set As Start Page.

Now when you run this site, it knows to display that page first.

3. Choose Debug➪Start Debugging or click the Start Debugging button on the toolbar (it looks like a Play button on a tape recorder).

You should see a dialog box that looks like the one in Figure 4-6.

To run an ASP.NET application from VWDE, and use its debugging capabilities, you must first create a `web.config` file and add an entry that allows the application to be debugged.

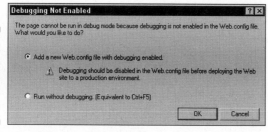

Figure 4-6:
The
Debugging
Not Enabled
dialog box.

4 Select Add a New `Web.config` File with Debugging Enabled (if it isn't already selected). Click OK.

VWDE adds the new `web.config` file for you. Ain't technology grand?

A notification window pops up to let you know that the built-in Web server is running.

Finally, you see a browser with your page in it. Enter your age and check out the result, as in Figure 4-7.

Figure 4-7:
The results
of the
DogAge
page.

Using VWDE to Run the Examples in This Book

In the other chapters of this book, I assume that you're using a simple text editor to create your ASP.NET pages. Therefore, I show the server control tags and their properties as you'd see them in VWDE in the Source view. If you want to work in Source view and simply type in the examples, you can do that and they'll work fine. If you'd prefer to use Design view, drag and drop your controls, and set their properties using the Properties window; that works, too. You can even jump over to Source view when you're done and make sure the page looks more or less like the example in the book. (It won't likely look exactly like the example in the book, since VWDE typically includes a `<!DOCTYPE>` directive and an `<html namespace>` attribute among other things. You can safely ignore these differences.)

If you ever have trouble getting an example to work, you can always select Source view, choose Edit⇨Select All and then press the Delete key. This erases the entire page. Then you can type in the example in Source view exactly as it appears in the book.

This shouldn't be necessary. Usually, you should be able to add appropriate controls to the page, type in code for their events, and get the example to work just as it is described in the book. However, if you can't get that to work, the technique described in the previous paragraph is always available.

Single-File Versus Code-Behind Pages

One important feature that VWDE makes available might trip you up, so I wanted to make sure to let you know. It's called *code-behind pages*.

Code-behind pages is a feature that allows you to separate the code you write for your events from the page that has the HTML and server controls in it. The idea is that if you can put the code into a separate file, you can write the code at the same time someone else is working on the design elements and put them together in the end. In medium- to large-scale projects, this can often prove to be a big benefit.

But for smaller projects, especially when you're first getting started, code-behind pages can create extra complexity with no real benefit. The alternative is single-file pages — ones where your code shares the same file as the HTML and server controls. All the examples in this book are single-file pages, to keep things simple.

VWDE allows you to use either approach. You can even have both single-file and code-behind pages in the same Web site.

When you want to create a new page for your Web site, you choose Website⇨ Add New Item to display the Add New Item dialog box (as described earlier in this chapter in "Addign Pages to Your Site"). When working with the examples in this book, always make sure that the check box labeled Place Code in Separate File is *deselected.* That's what determines whether the page you're creating will use the code-behind feature. Deselected indicates that you want *single-file* pages.

In Solution Explorer, you can always tell whether a page in your Web site is a code-behind page because it will have a + beside it. For example, if a page named `Default.aspx` is in Solution Explorer with a + beside it, you can click the + and see another page appear below it called `Default.aspx.vb`. This is the code-behind page. Single-file pages don't have the + beside them and don't have a separate `.aspx.vb` file for their code. They have both the tags and the code all in the `.aspx` file.

Part III
Speaking the Language

The 5th Wave   By Rich Tennant

VISUAL WEB DEVELOPMENT TEAM

"Give him air! Give him air! He'll be okay. He's just
been exposed to some raw HTML code. It must have
accidently flashed across his screen from the server."

In this part . . .

ASP.NET 2.0 provides a powerful programming language to use when building your Web applications:
Visual Basic 2005. But to harness that power, you first have
to speak the language. Don't worry—it's easy to pick up.
That's why it's the most popular programming language
ever written!

In this part of the book, you find out how programs store
and shuffle information around. Although that might not
sound very exciting, it's probably the most important thing
that computer programs do. You also explore the different
ways Visual Basic 2005 can make decisions, repeat parts
of its code, and organize its code into manageable pieces.
This is where programming gets interesting.

Every page is full of examples, so take your keyboard and
mouse in hand and get ready to have some fun!

Chapter 5

Juggling Information and Firing Off Functions

ASP.NET enables you to combine your HTML with code you write in a simple programming language. Although you can use any language supported by the .NET Framework in your ASP.NET pages, Visual Basic 2005 is an excellent choice if you're just getting started. It is the most popular programming language for ASP.NET and, in fact, the most popular programming language ever created — primarily because it's so productive and easy to use.

In this chapter, you begin to explore the Visual Basic 2005 language and discover how to put it to use creating ASP.NET pages. Visual Basic 2005 has a vast array of commands and capabilities. Fortunately, you don't have to know them all to create useful pages. In this chapter, Chapter 6, and Chapter 7, I show you the key elements you'll use most often in this language.

Using ASP.NET provides you with many powerful capabilities. But when you're first discovering Visual Basic 2005 in the context of ASP.NET, your programs are somewhat limited by how much you know. For example, the applications you create in this chapter and the next aren't very interactive. I show you how to use server controls to accept input from the user in Chapter 10. If I tried to present everything at once, it would be very confusing!

So, as you read this chapter, some of the examples might seem a little simplistic. These commands and their powers become much clearer as you discover more about ASP.NET.

Getting Started with Programming

If you have very little or no computer programming experience, check out the next couple of sections. They define some terms and describe some basic concepts that you need to know to get started. If you've done some programming, feel free to skim or skip ahead to a later section that interests you.

What is a programming language?

A computer *programming language* is a means of communicating to the computer what you want it to do. Computer programming languages are a lot like human languages. Like human languages, each computer language has a vocabulary of words. Likewise, each language has syntax rules for putting the words together in meaningful ways.

However, unlike human languages, computer languages are very precise. Human languages might have five different words that mean the same thing, whereas a computer language has only one. And, in a human language, you can change the word order in a sentence or even bend the syntax rules now and then and still make sense. Computers require that you follow their syntax to the letter. If you don't, the computer doesn't understand and generates an error.

Also, human language is designed for two-way communication, whereas programming is a one-way street: You tell the computer exactly what it's supposed to do and how it should respond to every situation. Instead of a conversation, it's more like a recipe or a to-do list. The computer then simply follows your instructions. The computer can't argue with you. (However, when it throws error messages your way, you might feel like it's being argumentative!)

That's why the words in a computer language's vocabulary are often called *commands* or *statements*. When you put a series of commands together, the result is referred to as *source code,* or simply *code*. When you bring all the source code together, you have a computer *program* or *application*.

Compiling and running a program

After you create an application, you still have one problem: The computer can't read the source code directly. The computer really only understands binary numbers — 1s and 0s. A series of commands given to the computer in binary form is called *machine code*. After you finish writing and debugging your source code, you run a piece of software called a *compiler,* which translates your source code into machine code.

You need to compile your program only once. After that, you *run* or *execute* the program, causing the computer to carry out your commands. You can run the compiled code again and again. You don't need to compile it again unless you change the source code.

The machine code usually takes the form of an `.exe` file, or *executable* file. This file is distributed to those who need to use the application, people who are fondly referred to as *users* or, in the case of Web sites, *visitors*.

Looking at the ASP.NET Process

For an ASP.NET Web page, the programming process is just a bit more interesting than the one I describe in the preceding sections of this chapter.

You create an ASP.NET page by typing in HTML and Visual Basic 2005 source code. When you finish the page, you copy it to the Web server where users can access it.

The first time a user requests the ASP.NET page, the Web server notices that the page has not been compiled. The Web server automatically compiles it and then executes it. From then on, the compiled version is executed whenever the page is requested by that user or any other. If you change the page, the Web server notices when the next request for that page comes and automatically recompiles and executes it.

The upshot of all this is that the Web server takes care of compiling your ASP.NET pages for you when necessary. You should know that it is happening, but you don't have to worry about doing it yourself!

Understanding Web Applications

You know what a software application is, but what's a *Web application?* Is it like a Web page or a Web site?

A Web application is a set of Web pages that work together to do something more useful and interactive than just displaying static information.

You've probably used many Web applications on the Internet yourself already, but hadn't thought of them that way. A Web auction, such as eBay, is a Web application. A Web-based chat room is a Web application. And when you go shopping on the Internet, the catalog and shopping cart you use are Web applications.

These examples work like a traditional Windows application might — the only difference is that they use Web pages to communicate with their users rather than windows.

Keeping Your Tags and Code Apart with Delimiters

Because your Visual Basic 2005 code is a part of your HTML page and coexists right alongside the HTML tags, you need some way to separate the HTML from the Visual Basic 2005 code. That's what *delimiters* do. Delimiters are the <% and %> signs that surround these lines of Visual Basic 2005 code. Here's the example from Chapter 1:

```
<%@ Page Language="VB" Debug="True" %>
<html>
<head>
<title>Hello and Welcome Page</title>
</head>
<body>
<center>
<% Dim TextSize As Integer %>
<% For TextSize = 1 To 7 %>
<font size = <%=TextSize%>>
Hello and Welcome!<br>
</font>
<% Next %>
</center>
</body>
</html>
```

The tags appear and work in the document just as they would in a normal HTML page. The only difference between this ASP.NET page and an HTML page are the lines of Visual Basic 2005 code and the necessary delimiters that are used throughout the page.

Delimiters can contain more than one line. For example, I could have written the first two lines of Visual Basic 2005 code in the body of the page like this:

```
<% Dim TextSize As Integer
For TextSize = 1 To 7 %>
```

Or like this:

```
<%
Dim TextSize As Integer
For TextSize = 1 To 7
%>
```

You decide how you organize your delimiters and your code. The code works as long as you keep all Visual Basic 2005 code *inside* the delimiters and all HTML tags *outside* the delimiters.

Using the ASP.NET Page Directive

The page directive often appears at the top of an ASP.NET page. Although not required, including it is always a good idea. Make sure it's on the very first line:

```
<%@ Page Language="VB" Debug="True" %>
```

The syntax for the directive requires that the entire line appear inside the `<%` and `%>` delimiters (which I discuss in the preceding section) and that it begins with `@ Page`. Following that, you can specify various things about the page. For example, you can specify which computer language you use in this page. VB is the abbreviation for Visual Basic 2005.

My sample directive also assigns the value `True` to `Debug`. Include this setting when you create and debug your pages. It ensures that you get detailed error messages if you make a mistake. After your pages are complete and ready to use on a real Web server, you can remove `Debug="True"` from the page directive to make your page run faster.

When you type in Visual Basic 2005 page directives, commands, variable names, and so on, you can use upper- and lowercase characters however you like. However, even though case doesn't affect how the code works, you should pick a standard and stick to it. Throughout this book, I capitalize the first letter of each Visual Basic 2005 command.

Creating and Using Variables

A variable is a place to store information in your pages. Think of variables as named boxes that you use to temporarily hold information so you can use it later. After you create a variable, you can put information inside it and then use the variable anywhere you'd normally use that information. Variables are very handy in all kinds of situations. For example, you can use one to store the result of a calculation until you have a chance to show it to the user.

Creating variables

In VB 2005, you *create* (or *declare*) a new variable by using the `Dim` statement.

Create a page, carefully type in the code in Listing 5-1, and then test it with the process I describe in Chapter 1. (By the way, don't expect to actually *see* anything in the browser when you try this one — I tell you why later in this section.)

Listing 5-1:   Calculating the Total Cost

```
<%@ Page Language="VB" Debug="True" %>
<html>
<body>
<%
Dim Cost, Tax, Total As Integer
Cost = 40
Tax = 2
Total = Cost + Tax
%>
</body>
</html>
```

After the page directive and the opening tags, the `<%` delimiter separates the VB 2005 code from the rest of the page. After the delimiter, the first line of code begins with `Dim` and creates three variables named `Cost`, `Tax`, and `Total`. You can give the variables any name you want, but choose names that remind you of what they hold.

All three variables are identified as integers with the `As Integer` statement, which means they can hold whole numbers. (For more information on this topic, see "She's not my data type," later in this chapter.)

After they are created, the `Cost` and `Tax` variables are immediately assigned values of 40 and 2, respectively. Then, the values held by `Cost` and `Tax` are added, and the sum is placed in the `Total` variable. Simple enough.

What not to name your variables

VB 2005 keeps several keywords for its own use. These are called *reserved words*. VB 2005 doesn't allow you to use these words as variable names because it already uses them for something else. For example, `Dim` is a reserved word. You'd be pretty confused if you saw a variable declaration like this:

```
Dim Dim As Integer
```

I don't have room to list all the reserved words here, but be aware that any keyword that has a special use in VB 2005 is off limits as a variable name. Examples include `Dim`, `For`, `Next`, `Do`, `Loop`, `While`, `Until`, and so on.

You can do this kind of math with any combination of numbers and variables. You use the normal + and – signs for addition and subtraction, respectively. Multiplication uses the * symbol, and division uses the / symbol. You create exponents by using the ^ symbol.

So, what does the code from Listing 5-1 do when you run it? Absolutely nothing. Or at least that's the way it seems. Actually, the page does exactly what it's told to do. The page creates three variables, assigns values to two of them, and then adds them and puts the sum in the third variable. The code never told the page to display any values, though. I show you how to do that in the next section!

Dim? What the heck is Dim? Wouldn't something like Variable or Var be a better command for creating new variables? Yes, it would! Dim stands for dimension. Why? It's a long and boring story, but suffice it to say that it's a holdover from way back, when people were carving Basic programs on cave walls. And now you're stuck with it. Sorry.

Displaying variable values

In the preceding section, I show you a page that does some math but doesn't display its result. To display the result, you need to add only one line. Change that code (or create a new page) to look like this:

```
<%@ Page Language="VB" Debug="True" %>
<html>
<body>
<%
Dim Cost, Tax, Total As Integer
Cost = 40
Tax = 2
Total = Cost + Tax
%>
<%=Total%>
</body>
</html>
```

What happens when you run it now? The number 42 appears in the upper-left corner of an otherwise blank page. But how did you do that? What kind of funky syntax does the added line (shown in bold) contain? That line has the normal delimiters <% and %> surrounding a variable name with an equal sign in front of it (=Total).

This little shortcut enables you to indicate that ASP.NET should replace that short section of code with the value in the variable. So if you choose View⇨ Source in the browser, you see this:

```
<html>
<body>
42
</body>
</html>
```

Using this syntax is a very handy technique. Not only can you use it to print the value in a variable, but you can also use it within HTML tags themselves:

```
<%@ Page Language="VB" Debug="True" %>
<html>
<body>
<%
Dim TextSize As Integer
TextSize = 5
%>
<font size = <%=TextSize%>>
All creatures, big and small . . .<br>
</font>
</body>
</html>
```

When you try out this page, you see the phrase All creatures, big and small . . . on the page in the font size specified in the TextSize variable.

Using View⇨Source in your browser, you can see the HTML that your page generated:

```
<html>
<body>
<font size=5>
All creatures, big and small . . .<br>
</font>
</body>
</html>
```

The <%=TextSize%> was replaced by the *value* in the TextSize variable: 5.

Change the number, save the page, and then refresh the browser to see the result.

Can you use a variable you didn't declare?

Do you always have to create a variable by using the Dim statement before you can use it in your code? Actually, no, you don't. If you just start using a variable name that you've never declared in the code, VB 2005 automatically creates it for you. Is this a good idea? Absolutely *not!*

With these simple pages, using a variable that you haven't created probably isn't a big deal. But when pages start to get complicated, figuring out what all the variables are and what they do can be a real pain. If you start using variables that you haven't even created, the code gets even more complicated. As a general rule, always declare your variables with Dim before you use them.

Vee have VAYS of making you declare . . .

You can use a setting in the page directive to force yourself to always create your variables before you use them. Just set an option called Explicit. Modify your directive so that it looks like this:

```
<%@ Page Explicit="True" Language="VB" Debug="True" %>
```

After you make this change, you get an error if you try to use a variable that you haven't created.

Always use the Explicit option in your page directive.

Why would you want to do this? Well, if you set the Explicit option on and then you accidentally misspell a variable name in your code, VB 2005 flags the misspelled variable as an error. If you don't have the Explicit option on, VB 2005 just assumes that you're trying to make a new variable and goes on.

By default, Visual Web Developer Express automatically gives you an error message if you try to use a variable without declaring it, regardless of whether you have Explicit defined in the page directive.

She's not my data type

Here's a snippet of code from an earlier section in the chapter (see Listing 5-1):

```
<%
Dim Cost, Tax, Total As Integer
. . .
%>
```

As I explain in that section, you use Dim to create variables, and this line identifies three new variables as integers. So, these variables have an integer *data type*.

If you think of a variable as a box for holding data, you can imagine that different boxes have different sizes and shapes. A box's size and shape determine what the box can hold. This "size and shape" is analogous to a variable's *data type* — that is, the type of data the variable can contain. Just as you can't put a pair of shoes in a matchbox, you shouldn't try to store someone's last name in a variable that's supposed to store a number.

A variable declared as an integer, as these three are, can contain whole numbers (that is, numbers *without* a decimal point). You can also create variables to hold other types of numbers — for example:

```
<%
Dim Pi As Single
Pi=3.14159
%>
```

Variables with the data type `Single` can hold what are called *single-precision* values. That's a confusing way of saying that a variable with the `Single` data type can hold a number that *has* a decimal point and digits after the decimal.

Where does the term *single-precision* come from? Well, it refers to the fact that variables of this type can hold numbers with a decimal point, but some numbers are too small for it to keep track of accurately. As you might expect, you also can declare *double-precision* variables, which use the `Double` data type. Variables with the `Double` data type can hold very, very small numbers accurately. But, really, unless you're doing seriously complex scientific calculations, you probably can get by with the `Single` data type.

So, now you know what data type to use for a variable to hold almost any number you want. If it's a whole number, use `Integer`. If it includes a decimal point, use `Single`.

For information on more data types designed to hold numbers, see Chapter 16.

Why not use Single for every number?

Perhaps you're thinking, "Hmm . . . a `Single` variable can hold numbers with decimal places. Even numbers like 3.0, right? So, why not use `Single` as the data type for *all* number variables, just to keep it simple?"

Well, that might be simple for you, but it isn't simple for Mr. Computer. When the computer does math calculations, they're much more complex with a `Single` data type variable than with an `Integer` data type variable and thus take more time.

So if you're working with whole numbers but you put them in `Single` data type variables, the computer works with them as though they were decimal numbers, whether they are or not. To save your computer headaches and to make your programs run faster, always use variable types that match your data as closely as possible.

Don't string me along . . .

In addition to holding numbers, variables can hold *strings*. A string is a bunch of letters, symbols, and/or numbers put together to form words, sentences, or maybe just nonsense. In the following code, you see the strings in bold:

```
<%@ Page Explicit="True" Language="VB" Debug="True" %>
<html>
<body>
<%
Dim FirstName, LastName, WholeName As String
FirstName = "Bill"
LastName = "Gates"
WholeName = FirstName & LastName
%>
<%=WholeName %>
</body>
</html>
```

Strings are always enclosed by quotation marks so you know exactly where they begin and end, even though the quotes aren't actually a part of the string. In this example, the variable FirstName is assigned the string Bill, and LastName is assigned Gates. The WholeName variable is assigned to be equal to both FirstName and LastName. Notice the & separating the FirstName and LastName variables on the right side. In VB 2005, & sticks two strings together, or *concatenates* them.

Always put spaces on either side of the & in your code when you use it. You get an unusual error if you don't.

The page displays the following:

```
BillGates
```

What's wrong with this page? Well, there's no space between the first and last names. You have to add the space when you stick them together.

In the code, change the line that assigns a value to the WholeName variable to look like this:

```
WholeName = FirstName & " " & LastName
```

This time, *three* strings are concatenated: the one in FirstName, a space, and the one in LastName. You can see the result:

```
Bill Gates
```

Giving a variable a value when you create it

TIP

Here's a shortcut for you. Instead of declaring all your variables and then assigning values to them as a separate step, you can do it all at once!

```
<%@ Page Explicit="True" Language="VB" Debug="True" %>
<html>
<body>
<%
Dim FirstName As String = "Bill"
Dim LastName As String = "Gates"
Dim WholeName As String = FirstName & " " & LastName
%>
<%=WholeName %>
</body>
</html>
```

This handy technique can save you a few keystrokes.

Controlling Cantankerous Constants

A *constant* is a lot like a variable, with one important difference: You always give a constant a value when you create it, and from then on, you aren't allowed to change its value.

If you have a common number that you'll be using in several places throughout your page, you can assign that number to a constant at the top of your page and then use the constant name everywhere you'd normally use the number. This has two advantages:

- ✔ Because you're giving the number a meaningful *name,* the code is more readable.
- ✔ If that number ever changes in the future, you won't have to hunt it down everywhere you use it on the page. You can simply change the constant declaration, and you're ready to go!

You declare a constant in much the same way you declare a variable, replacing Dim with Const:

```
Const Temperature As Single = 98.6
Const CompanyName As String = "Colonial Systems, Inc."
```

You might want to create a naming standard to differentiate between constants and variables so that you can keep them straight. For example, you might put constants in all uppercase letters, and use mixed case for variables. Or, you might want to put a prefix (like con) before all constant names.

Keeping Your Comments to Yourself

Comments, also called *remarks,* are notes to yourself or others inside your page without changing the way the page works.

In HTML, you use `<!--` and `-->` to enclose comments that you want to include in the page, but don't want to display in the browser.

With ASP.NET 2.0, you can still use the HTML comment symbols in your pages. But if you want to add comments to VB 2005 code as you create it, you can also use the VB 2005–style comment, as on the bold lines in the following example:

```
<%@ Page Explicit="True" Language="VB" Debug="True" %>
<%
' This page calculates
' the total cost by adding
' the price and tax.
. . .
Total = Cost + Tax
%>
. . .
```

The VB 2005 comment always begins with an apostrophe (or single quote) and ends automatically at the end of the line. So, you need a new apostrophe at the beginning of each new comment line.

You can also put a comment on the same line as code:

```
<% TextSize = 1 ' Sets TextSize to 1 %>
```

Although this works fine for normal lines of VB 2005 code, you can't use comments inside the special syntax that's used to display variables:

```
<%=Total    ' This comment causes an error %>
```

You get the following error:

```
Expected ')'
```

Because that error message doesn't make much sense in this context, it can be very confusing!

ASP.NET removes the VB 2005 comments, along with all the rest of the ASP.NET code, before the server sends the page to the user's browser. So, unlike the HTML comments, these comments can't be seen when the person browsing your page chooses View➪Source from the Internet Explorer menus.

During testing of a new page, you can temporarily disable some lines, but still easily get them back later if you need to. Rather than delete a line of code, simply put an apostrophe in front it. The apostrophe turns the line into a comment. The line of code no longer affects the way the page works, but it's there if you want to bring it back. To put that line of code back into service, simply remove the apostrophe. Adding an apostrophe is called *commenting out* a line of code. Removing the apostrophe is referred to as *uncommenting* the code.

If you want to comment out a bunch of lines at once, you can simply select the lines and click the Comment Out the Selected Lines button on the toolbar. There's also a corresponding Uncomment the Selected Lines button.

Understanding How Functions Function

Commands in VB 2005 come in two flavors: statements and functions. A *statement* is a command that stands on its own and simply does something. Dim, which declares variables, is a statement:

```
Dim Artist, CD As String
```

A *function,* on the other hand, does some processing and then returns a value — typically the result of its processing — for you to use in your code. VB 2005 has many functions you can use and, in the next chapter, I show you how to create your own. In this section, I describe how functions work and introduce you to some functions that are handy when dealing with dates.

Getting a date

The code in Listing 5-2 shows how you can use the Today function:

Listing 5-2:   Displaying the Date

```
<%@ Page Explicit="True" Language="VB" Debug="True" %>
<html>
<body>
<%
Dim CurrentDate As String
CurrentDate = Today
%>
```

```
The current date is <%=CurrentDate %>.<br>
</body>
</html>
```

This code creates the variable CurrentDate and then assigns the value that is returned from the Today function to the CurrentDate variable. Then, the value of CurrentDate is used within a sentence to inform the user of the current date.

You might think that Today looks like a variable that simply isn't declared. And you're right — it does look like that. However, you know it isn't a variable because it isn't declared and because you happen to know that Today is a built-in function with a special meaning in VB 2005. (Okay, you might not have known that before, but you do now!) You can discover more built-in functions by exploring VB 2005 in later chapters.

Let the arguments commence!

A function can have *arguments* (sometimes referred to as *parameters*). An argument is a value that you can send to the function when you call it. By passing an argument to a function, you give the function information to work on. For example, take a look at the Weekday function, and notice the argument in bold:

```
<%@ Page Explicit="True" Language="VB" Debug="True" %>
<html>
<body>
<%
Dim ThisDay, ThisDate As String
ThisDate = Today
ThisDay = Weekday(ThisDate)
%>
It is day number <%=ThisDay %>.<br>
</body>
</html>
```

First, ThisDay and ThisDate are declared as strings.

The next line calls the Today function. The Today function gets the system date and returns it. The value returned is assigned to ThisDate.

The next line calls the Weekday function and passes the value of ThisDate as an argument. Weekday uses this date to determine the weekday on which the date falls. Notice that you pass arguments by placing them after the function name and putting them in parentheses. If this function had taken two arguments, you would put them both inside parentheses and separate them with a comma.

What do you mean it "returns a value"?

If you haven't used a computer language with functions before, the concept of a function returning a value can be confusing. When I say a *value is returned,* what do I mean?

You *call* the built-in VB 2005 function `Today` when you use its name in the code. When it's called, the function goes out to the system clock and finds out the current date. Then, the function sends that current date back to *this* code and places the value in the code *right where the*

`Today` *function appears.* In Listing 5-2, the date returned by the function is then assigned to the `CurrentDate` variable:

```
CurrentDate = Today
```
So this line does *two* things:

- ✔ It calls the `Today` function.

- ✔ It assigns the date returned from the `Today` function to the `CurrentDate` variable.

The value returned is a number from 1 to 7, indicating Sunday through Saturday.

If you want to make this code more concise, you could do it this way:

```
<%@ Page Explicit="True" Language="VB" Debug="True" %>
<html>
<body>
<%
Dim ThisDay As String
ThisDay = Weekday(Today)
%>
It is day number <%=ThisDay %>.<br>
</body>
</html>
```

The `Today` function is called first and then the value it returns is immediately sent to the `Weekday` function as an argument.

Chapter 6

Asking Questions and Jumping Through Loops

In This Chapter

▶ Asking questions with simple and compound `If...Then` statements

▶ Using `ElseIf` to ask several questions at once

▶ Cleaning up your code with `Select Case`

▶ Counting with `For...Next` loops

▶ Doing a loop `While` a condition is true

▶ Repeating a loop `Until` something happens

▶ Nesting loops inside other loops

▶ Repeating a set of tasks `For Each` element in an array

*I*n this chapter, you discover *conditionals,* which enable you to ask questions and do different things based on the answer. You also discover *loops,* which you use to repeat certain parts of your code again and again.

Decisions, Decisions, Decisions: Using If...Then

Your Web pages can make decisions on their own based on information they gather from the visitor, from databases or any other source. But first you have to tell your Web pages which decisions to make and how to make them. The keywords you use to do that, naturally enough, are `If` and `Then`:

```
If condition Then
    statement
End If
```

This `If...Then` structure is often called a *conditional*. A conditional has two parts:

- ✔ The **condition,** or the question part. The condition portion falls between `If` and `Then`.

- ✔ The **statement,** or the thing-to-do part. Everything between the `Then` and the `End If` is part of the statement portion, whether it is additional VB 2005 commands or HTML.

The `End If` just tells VB 2005 when the statement part is over.

IF you want cool Web pages, THEN use conditionals

So, how do you use conditionals in your Web pages? Good question. Listing 6-1 shows a simple example. The code in this page presents a game where the computer spins a wheel that has five sections numbered 1 through 5. Section 3 is the only winning section on that wheel, so an If...Then statement is used to determine if the spin was a winner.

Listing 6-1:   Spinning for Threes

```
<%@ Page Explicit="True" Language="VB" Debug="True" %>
<html>
<body>
<%
Dim Wheel, Won As Integer
Randomize
%>
<p>My favorite number is 3. I'm spinning the wheel!</p>
<% Wheel = Int(Rnd * 5) + 1 ' Random number: 1-5 %>
<p>The Wheel landed on <%=Wheel%>.</p>
<%
If Wheel = 3 Then
    Won = 50
%>
<p>It landed on my number!</p>
<p>I win $<%=Won%></p>
<% End If %>
<p>All done.</p>
</body>
</html>
```

First, the page displays a little text to explain the premise of the game. Next, the wheel is spun by generating a random number between 1 and 5. Then, the page displays the value that the wheel landed on. (For more information on Randomize, Rnd, and this formula used to generate random numbers, see the .NET Framework online help — search for the Randomize statement and Rnd function.)

Next up is the If...Then statement. The condition part of the If...Then asks the question, "Does the Wheel variable hold a value that equals 3?"

If there is HTML within an If...Then statement, it may not be displayed on the page (if the condition fails). This means that when you create an ASP.NET page, you aren't creating the Web page itself. You're creating a set of instructions that tells the server *how to create* the Web page. The HTML that ends up getting sent out depends on what happens when the code runs.

Now, if you haven't already, try out this example. After you bring it up in your browser, click Refresh several times. Depending on what number is generated, you see one of the possibilities that I describe in the next two sections.

If a condition is true

If a condition is true, the statement portion is performed. So, if Wheel equals 3, two things happen:

- ✔ The Won variable is set to 50.

- ✔ This HTML becomes part of the Web page that is sent back (after evaluating the value of Won):

```
<p>It landed on my number!</p>
<p>I win $50</p>
```

If the random number generated is 3, the final Web page sent to the browser looks like this (which you can see by choosing View➪Source):

```
<html>
<body>
<p>My favorite number is 3. I'm spinning the wheel!</p>
<p>The Wheel landed on 3.</p>
<p>It landed on my number!</p>
<p>I win $50</p>
<p>All done.</p>
</body>
</html>
```

Note: If you keep clicking Refresh, the Won variable doesn't accumulate an additional $50 every time you win. That's because the page (and therefore the variable) is reset every time you click Refresh. I explain how to create variables that last from one refresh to another in Chapter 9.

If a condition is false

If a condition is false, the statement portion is ignored. In Listing 6-1, if the random number generated is not 3, the page sent from the server looks something like this:

```
<html>
<body>
<p>My favorite number is 3. I'm spinning the wheel!</p>
<p>The Wheel landed on 1.</p>
<p>All done.</p>
</body>
</html>
```

Using Boolean variables with conditions

In Chapter 5, you discover three different data types for variables: `Integer` and `Single` to hold whole numbers and decimal numbers, and `String` to hold letters, words, and sentences.

Another data type you might use from time to time is called `Boolean` (named after George Boole, a famous mathematician who brought together math and logic). A variable with a `Boolean` data type can have only one of two possible values: `True` or `False`.

You can use these variables in an `If...Then` statement, too:

```
<%
Dim AccountBalanced As Boolean
. . .
AccountBalanced = True
. . .
If AccountBalanced = True Then
%>
. . .
```

In fact, when you're working with `Boolean` variables like this, you don't even need the `= True` part in the `If...Then` statement!

```
<%
Dim AccountBalanced As Boolean
. . .
AccountBalanced = True
. . .
If AccountBalanced Then
%>
. . .
```

Why does this work? The condition part of the `If...Then` statement is looking for a `True` or `False` anyway. You can just use the variable by itself. If the variable holds the value `True`, the statement part is executed. If the variable holds the value `False`, it is not.

Accepting inequalities as a fact of life

`If...Then` statements can use what math professors call *inequalities*. Inequalities are ways of comparing numbers to see whether they are greater than or less than each other. And, to keep it simple, VB 2005 uses the same symbols that you used in your sixth-grade math class.

The example in Listing 6-2 shows how inequalities work in an `If...Then` statement.

Listing 6-2:   Checking for an A

```
<%@ Page Explicit="True" Language="VB" Debug="True" %>
<html>
<body>
<%
Dim Grade As Integer
Grade = 95
If Grade > 90 Then
%>
<p>You get an A!</p>
<% End If %>
</body>
</html>
```

The happy result:

```
You get an A!
```

Because the variable `Grade` holds a value greater than 90, the message `You get an A!` appears. However, suppose you get a score of 90 right on the nose. Shouldn't that be an A, too?

Try changing the preceding code so that `Grade = 90`. Save the file and Refresh the browser. The page is blank. According to the code, a 90 doesn't receive an A.

How do you fix the code so that a 90 receives an A? Well one way is to change the `If...Then` line to look like this:

```
If Grade > 89 Then
```

But sticking with round numbers makes more sense. A better way is to use another symbol, >=. Change the If...Then line so that it looks like this:

```
If Grade >= 90 Then
```

That's better. A grade of 90 now receives the You get an A! message.

As you may expect, you also can use a <= symbol, which means less than or equal to. These symbols are a little different from the ones you learned in sixth-grade math, but these are easier to remember anyway.

You can use one more symbol to compare variables: <>, which means does not equal. Here's an example of the <> operator at work:

```
<% If Grade <> 100 Then %>
<p>You did not get a perfect score.</p>
<% End If %>
```

Creating a compound If...Then

You can use what programmer-types like to call a *logical expression* in an If...Then condition. This simply means that you can put more than one question together inside the same condition by using an And or an Or keyword to separate them. This creates a *compound* If...Then statement.

A compound If...Then statement works just like you might expect:

- ✔ **If an And separates the two conditions,** the statement succeeds only if both conditions are true. If either condition is false or both are false, the statement portion is ignored.

- ✔ **If an Or separates the two conditions,** the statement succeeds if either condition is true or if both are true. If both conditions are false, the statement portion is ignored.

You can connect as many conditions as you like as long as an And or an Or separates each condition:

```
<% If Temperature <= 32 And Liquid = "Water" Then %>
<p>Looks like ice...</p>
<% End If %>
```

Of course, too many conditions can make your statement very confusing. When you're creating Web pages, one rule always applies: As much as possible, keep it simple.

As I was saying: line continuation

In some cases, a line of code gets really long and a little difficult to deal with, especially when you're using a compound `If...Then`. Fortunately, you can break your line in two without confusing VB 2005 into thinking it's supposed to treat that code as two separate lines. Here's an example:

```
<%
If Weekday(Today) > 3 And _
    Weekday(Today) < 6 Then
%>
```

Lies! All lies! Or, what to do if the condition isn't true

In the preceding sections of this chapter, all the `If....Then` statements tell the computer what to do only if a condition is true. What if you want the computer to do something else when the condition is false? That's where `Else` comes in. Take a look at Listing 6-3.

Listing 6-3: The Pass/Fail Test

```
<%@ Page Explicit="True" Language="VB" Debug="True" %>
<html>
<body>
<%
Dim Grade As Integer
Randomize
Grade = Int(Rnd * 100) + 1 ' Random number between 1 and
          100
%>
<p>Your grade is <%=Grade%>.</p>
<% If Grade >= 60 Then %>
<p>You passed!</p>
<% Else %>
<p>You failed...</p>
<% End If %>
</body>
</html>
```

After you try this page, click Refresh in your browser several times. You should see both the passing and failing results.

So, with `If...Then`, you can choose whether to include some HTML based on a condition. By adding `Else` to the mix, you can go one step further, choosing to include one bit of HTML if the condition is true and a different chunk of HTML if it isn't.

Handling multiple conditions

If you can ask one question, why not more? Of course, you can always just write one `If...Then` statement after another. For example, if you want to translate a percentage grade to a letter grade, your code might look like the code in Listing 6-4.

Listing 6-4: Multiple If...Thens to Determine a Letter Grade

```
...
<% If Grade >= 90 Then %>
<% LetterGrade = "A" %>
<p>You got an A! Congratulations.</p>
<% End If %>
<% If Grade >= 80 And Grade < 90 Then %>
<% LetterGrade = "B" %>
<p>You got a B. Good job.</p>
<% End If %>
...
```

The preceding code has two major problems: It's wordy, and you end up repeating yourself a lot. To make the process easier, VB 2005 includes another statement to help you in situations like this: `ElseIf`.

If you use `ElseIf`, your page begins to look simpler and is easier to understand, as in Listing 6-5.

Listing 6-5: Letter Grades with ElseIf

```
<%@ Page Explicit="True" Language="VB" Debug="True" %>
<html>
<body>
<%
Dim Grade As Integer
Dim LetterGrade As String
Randomize
Grade = Int(Rnd * 100) + 1 ' Random number between 1 and
          100
```

```
%>
<p>Your grade is <%=Grade%>.</p>
<% If Grade >= 90 Then %>
<% LetterGrade = "A" %>
<p>You got an A! Congratulations.</p>
<% ElseIf Grade >= 80 Then %>
<% LetterGrade = "B" %>
<p>You got a B. Good job.</p>
<% ElseIf Grade >= 70 Then %>
<% LetterGrade = "C" %>
<p>You got a C. Not bad.</p>
<% ElseIf Grade >= 60 Then %>
<% LetterGrade = "D" %>
<p>You got a D. Try harder next time.</p>
<% Else %>
<% LetterGrade = "F" %>
<p>You failed. I'm sorry.</p>
<% End If %>
</body>
</html>
```

Now I've written one big, long If...Then, instead of multiple separate If...Thens. You know that because the code has only one End If — all the way at the end.

Here's the way the If...Then...ElseIf statement works:

1. If the Grade is greater than or equal to 90, the LetterGrade variable is set to A, the first HTML statement is displayed, and then the statement ends. The rest of the conditions are ignored after a condition is met.

2. If the first condition is false, the computer checks the second condition. Here the computer has only to check whether the Grade is 80 or better. The computer doesn't have to specify that the grade is less than 90 because if it had been 90 or greater, the computer wouldn't be executing this condition. Right?

3. If needed, the computer checks the third and fourth conditions the same way it checked the second.

4. If the computer gets through all the conditions and still doesn't have a match, the Else statement catches everything else — which, in this case, is bad news.

Notice that ElseIf is one word, but End If is two words. Why? Don't ask me!

Developing your nesting instincts

You can put an `If...Then` statement inside another `If...Then`.
Programmers call this *nesting*. Listing 6-6 shows an example.

Listing 6-6:   Calculating Cards in 21

```
<%@ Page Explicit="True" Language="VB" Debug="True" %>
<html>
<body>
<%
Dim Card, Total As Integer
Total = 15 ' Total value of cards so far
Card = 1 ' Your next card
If Card = 1 Then ' If it's an ace
    If Total + 11 <= 21 Then ' Will 11 make you bust?
        Total = Total + 11 ' If not count ace as 11
    Else
        Total = Total + 1  ' Else count ace as 1
    End If
End If
%>
<p>The card you drew was <%=Card%></p>
<p>That makes your total <%=Total%></p>
</body>
</html>
```

In the card game 21 (or Blackjack), the goal is to draw enough cards to get as
close as you can to 21 without going over (or *busting*). Face cards count as 10,
and aces can count as either 1 or 11 — your choice. You normally count an
ace as 11 unless it would make you bust; then, you count it as 1.

In the code in Listing 6-6, the `Total` variable holds the value of your hand so
far. `Card` is the next card you are dealt. In this case, you are dealt an ace.

The `If...Then` statement evaluates what card you just got and, if it's an ace,
checks whether it should be counted as 11 or 1. If you can add 11 to your
total without busting, it adds 11. Otherwise, it adds 1.

The `If...Then` that checks the `Card` variable gets executed first. Only if
that condition is true does the second `If...Then` get executed.

Try changing the starting `Total` from 15 to 8. Save and click Refresh in your
browser.

You can nest `If...Then` statements inside the `Then`, `ElseIf`, or `Else` portions of other `If...Then` statements. And they can also have additional
`If...Then` statements nested within them! You can go as deep as you like
with this nesting.

Listing 6-7 extends the previous example so that the next card you draw is random.

Listing 6-7:   Calculating Cards in 21, Version 2.0

```
<%@ Page Explicit="True" Language="VB" Debug="True" %>
<html>
<body>
<%
Dim Card, Total As Integer
Randomize
Total = 15 ' Total value of cards so far
Card = Int(Rnd * 13) + 1 ' Your next card
If Card = 11 Or Card = 12 Or Card = 13 Then ' If it's a
          face
   Total = Total + 10
ElseIf Card = 1 Then ' If it's an ace
   If Total + 11 <= 21 Then
      Total = Total + 11
   Else
      Total = Total + 1
   End If
Else
   Total = Total + Card  ' It's a numbered card (2-10)
End If
%>
<p>The card you drew was <%=Card%></p>
<p>That makes your total <%=Total%></p>
</body>
</html>
```

The If...Then structure calculates the updated Total variable for whatever card you draw. When you try this page, click Refresh several times and note the result of the different cards on the total.

The first condition checks to see whether the card is one of the face cards. If so, the Total variable is increased by 10. However, if this condition fails, an ElseIf clause checks another condition. If the card is not a face card, but it is an ace, the computer checks the total, as before, to see how the ace should be calculated. Finally, if the card is neither a face card nor an ace, it must be a numbered card, in which case, the computer simply adds the number to Total.

Get off My Case!

Like the If...Then statement, you use the Select Case statement for decision-making. Select Case enables you to do various comparisons against one variable that you use throughout the whole statement.

Counselor, present your case . . .

Listing 6-8 shows a simple Select Case statement that checks an employee's status and displays the result to the user.

Listing 6-8:   Displaying Employee Status

```
<%@ Page Explicit="True" Language="VB" Debug="True" %>
<html>
<body>
<%
Dim EmployeeStatus As String

EmployeeStatus = "L"

Select Case EmployeeStatus %>
<% Case "G" %>
<p>Employee is employed in good standing.</p>
<% Case "L" %>
<p>Employee is on leave.</p>
<% Case "F" %>
<p>Employee no longer works here.</p>
<% End Select %>
</body>
</html>
```

Here's how this Select Case statement works:

1. Always begin your Select Case statements with the words Select Case. (Easy enough?)

2. After that comes a variable name. Here, the variable is EmployeeStatus. This variable is used throughout the rest of the Select Case statement.

3. Next comes a series of lines that each contain the word Case followed by a value. The Select Case statement automatically compares the first value ("G") to the variable at the beginning of the Select Case statement (EmployeeStatus) to see whether they're equal.

4. If the first value is equal to the variable at the beginning, the line after Case "G" and before Case "L" is executed. After that line is finished, the statement is done, and any other Case lines are ignored. Anything after the End Select gets processed next.

5. If the first value isn't equal to the variable at the top, the next Case statement is checked (Case "L") and that value is compared with the variable at the beginning (EmployeeStatus). If a match exists, the lines under Case "L" are executed. If not, VB 2005 proceeds to the next Case statement.

If none of the `Case` statements match, none of the lines within the `Select Case` get executed, and execution continues after the `End Select`. This situation would happen in the code in Listing 6-8 if the `EmployeeStatus` was something other than `"G"`, `"L"`, or `"F"`.

Notice that you don't need to repeat the variable name or even the equal sign again and again as you would in an `If...Then...ElseIf`. Both are automatically assumed. This strategy makes the `Select Case` much cleaner and easier to understand if you're continually comparing against one variable.

Cracking a tougher case

The `Select Case` statement is very flexible. It can do more than simple checks for equality. Like `If...Then` statements, it can do inequalities (with the <, >, <=, >=, and <> operators, which I discuss in the section "Accepting inequalities as a fact of life," earlier in this chapter).

Listing 6-9 displays the letter grade calculator I demonstrate in the section "Handling multiple conditions," earlier in this chapter. However, instead of using the `If...Then...ElseIf` statement, I convert the code to use `Select Case`.

Listing 6-9:   Letter Grades with Select Case

```
<%@ Page Explicit="True" Language="VB" Debug="True" %>
<html>
<body>
<%
Dim Grade As Integer
Dim LetterGrade As String
Randomize
Grade = Int(Rnd * 100) + 1 ' Random number between 1 and
         100
%>
<p>Your grade is <%=Grade%>.</p>
<% Select Case Grade
Case Is >= 90
   LetterGrade = "A" %>
<p>You got an A! Congratulations.</p>
<% Case Is >= 80
   LetterGrade = "B" %>
<p>You got a B. Good job.</p>
<% Case Is >= 70
   LetterGrade = "C" %>
<p>You got a C. Not bad.</p>
<% Case Is >= 60
   LetterGrade = "D" %>
```

(continued)

Listing 6-9 *(continued)*

```
<p>You got a D. Try harder next time.</p>
<% Case Else
    LetterGrade = "F" %>
<p>You failed. I'm sorry.</p>
<% End Select %>
</body>
</html>
```

Notice that when comparing to see whether something is equal in a `Select Case`, you only have to put the value on the `Case` line, as I did in Listing 6-8: However, when you check for inequality, you have to use the keyword `Is` and you have to include the inequality operator you want to use, as I did in Listing 6-9: `Case Is >= 90`. Using the keyword `Is` here might seem odd, but that's how it works!

You can also do some other fancy comparisons on the `Case` line. For example, if you were checking a value to see if it's between 80 and 89. You might have a case line that looks like this:

```
Case 80 To 89
```

This matches if the variable is between 80 and 89 (including 80 and 89). If you want to specify several nonconsecutive values, use commas:

```
Case 80, 90, 100
```

You can even combine the two techniques:

```
Case 80, 90, 95 To 100
```

This would match on 80, 90, 95, 96, 97, 98, 99 or 100.

Loop the Loop

Loops enable you to execute the same commands (or HTML) again and again. VB 2005 has two types of loops. The `For...Next` loop counts off a certain number of times and then quits. The `Do...Loop` uses a condition similar to an `If...Then` statement to determine whether it should continue looping each time.

Counting with For...Next

With the `For...Next` loop, you can easily execute some commands a set number of times while keeping track of how many times you've gone through the loop. Listing 6-10 contains a page like the one in Chapter 1.

Listing 6-10:   Hello and Welcome!

```
<%@ Page Explicit="True" Language="VB" Debug="True" %>
<html>
<head><title>Hello and Welcome Page</title>
</head>
<body>
<center>
<% Dim TextSize As Integer %>
<% For TextSize = 1 To 7 %>
<font size=<%=TextSize%>>
Hello and Welcome<br>
</font>
<% Next %>
</center>
</body>
</html>
```

This code displays the same line seven times at seven different font sizes. The result looks something like Figure 6-1.

Figure 6-1:
Hello and
Welcome.

The `For` line marks the beginning of the loop. `For` also identifies the *index variable* (in this case, `TextSize`), the number of the first loop (1), and the number of the last loop (7). The index variable holds the number of the current loop.

The line that contains `Next` marks the end of the loop. Everything between the `For` line and the `Next` line is a part of the loop's *body* — that is, the stuff that gets executed again and again.

The first time through the loop, `TextSize` is set to 1. The second time, it's set to 2, and so on, up through 7.

You can use any `Integer` variable as an index variable in a `For...Next` loop. The index variable is simply assigned the loop value each time the `For` line is executed. You can use the index variable as I do in the example. You can even display it in your page, if you like. But remember that *changing* the index variable's value is never a good idea. The `For` loop really gets confused when you do that.

Most loops start with 1. But they don't have to. You can create a loop like this:

```
For Items = 10 To 100
```

This loop sets the variable `Items` to 10 the first time through, to 11 the second time through, and so on, up to 100. This loop executes 91 times.

Here's another example:

```
For Counter = 0 To 5
```

Again, the first time through, `Counter` is set to 0, then to 1, and so on, up to 5. This loop executes 6 times.

You can even do this:

```
For Coordinate = -5 To 5
```

The first time through, the loop is set to –5, then to –4, then on up through 0, ending with 5. This loop executes 11 times (counting 0).

Watching where you Step

By using the keyword `Step` with your `For...Next` loops, you can tell VB 2005 what number the `For` loop counts by. Here's an example:

```
For Num = 2 To 10 Step 2
```

In this loop, the first time through, Num is assigned 2, then 4, then 6, then 8, and finally 10. Here's another example:

```
For Weeks = 0 To 35 Step 7
```

Weeks is assigned 0 the first time, then 7, then 14, 21, 28, and 35.

You can even step backward! (But don't fall down.) In Listing 6-11, you see an extended version of the "Hello and Welcome" example to demonstrate.

Listing 6-11: Hello and Welcome, Version 2.0

```
<%@ Page Explicit="True" Language="VB" Debug="True" %>
<html>
<head><title>Hello and Welcome Page</title>
</head>
<body>
<center>
<% Dim TextSize As Integer %>
<% For TextSize = 1 To 7 %>
<font size=<%=TextSize%>>
Hello and Welcome<br>
</font>
<% Next %>
<% For TextSize = 6 To 1 Step -1 %>
<font size=<%=TextSize%>>
Hello and Welcome<br>
</font>
<% Next %>
</center>
</body>
</html>
```

The result looks something like Figure 6-2.

In this example, I've added another loop after the first one to count down from 6 to 1, counting by –1. It's okay to re-use an index variable in another loop after you're completely done with the first loop.

Nesting loops

Just as you can nest an If...Then statement inside another If...Then statement, you can nest a loop inside another loop, as in Listing 6-12.

Figure 6-2:
Hello and
Welcome —
small to big
and back
again.

Listing 6-12: Nested Loop Example

```
<%@ Page Explicit="True" Language="VB" Debug="True" %>
<html>
<body>
<%
Dim OuterLoop, InnerLoop
For OuterLoop = 1 To 5
    For InnerLoop = 1 To 3
%>
OuterLoop = <% =OuterLoop %>, InnerLoop = <% =InnerLoop %>
<br>
<%
    Next
Next
%>
</body>
</html>
```

The HTML for the page in Listing 6-12 looks like this:

```
<html>
<body>
OuterLoop = 1, InnerLoop = 1
<br>
OuterLoop = 1, InnerLoop = 2
<br>
```

```
OuterLoop = 1, InnerLoop = 3
<br>
OuterLoop = 2, InnerLoop = 1
<br>
OuterLoop = 2, InnerLoop = 2
<br>
OuterLoop = 2, InnerLoop = 3
<br>
OuterLoop = 3, InnerLoop = 1
<br>
OuterLoop = 3, InnerLoop = 2
<br>
. . .
```

OuterLoop begins at 1, as does InnerLoop. The page displays the information and then the computer runs into Next. The first Next goes with the *inner* loop. That's why I indented it to line up with the inner loop's For line. The Next causes control to jump back up to the inner loop's For line and execute again. The inner loop executes all three times before the outer loop can continue. Then the outer loop is incremented by one and the inner loop executes three more times.

So, when you have a loop within a loop, the innermost loop executes all its times and ends before the outer loop has a chance to loop a second time.

Also notice that the HTML shows no indication of a loop at all — the loop is done on the server in VB 2005. Only the results get sent to the browser.

Doobee-Doobee-Do...Loop

The VB 2005 Do...Loop is a very different kind of looping structure from the For...Next loop. Do...Loop enables you to loop while a condition is true or while a condition is false (until it *becomes* true).

Do While and Do Until

A Do...Loop begins with the Do keyword and ends with the Loop keyword. Everything in between is the body of the loop.

In the example in Listing 6-13, Loop is immediately followed by the keyword While. This keyword indicates that a condition will follow and that the loop will continue executing as long as the condition remains true. When the condition is tested and is false, the loop stops repeating.

Listing 6-13:   How Many Quarters

```
<%@ Page Explicit="True" Language="VB" Debug="True" %>
<html>
<body>
<%
Dim Amount As Single
Dim Quarters As Integer
Amount = 3.85
Quarters = 0
Do
    Quarters = Quarters + 1
    Amount = Amount - .25
Loop While Amount >= .25
%>
<p>You can buy <%=Quarters%> $.25 gumballs</p>
</body>
</html>
```

The result?

```
You can buy 15 $.25 gumballs
```

You can change the `Loop` line to use `Until`, instead:

```
Loop Until Amount < .25
```

`Until` is the logical opposite of `While`. If you use `Until`, the loop continues as long as the condition remains *false*. When the condition is tested and is true, the loop stops repeating.

So, to change this program to use `Until`, I have to change the condition so that the program still works the same way, as I've done in the line above.

Testing loops at the top

The gumball counting program in Listing 6-13 has just one problem. The problem is . . . well, you'd better see for yourself. Set `Amount` to .17. Now try running the program again. You get the following result:

```
You can buy 1 $.25 gumballs
```

Hmm. It says you have enough to buy one gumball. And that isn't true. You don't have $.25, so the result should be 0. Why did this happen?

Well, when the `While` or `Until` keyword appears on the `Loop` line at the bottom of the loop, you can always be sure that the body of the loop will be executed once. That's because the condition after the `While` or `Until` keyword isn't checked until the computer gets to the `Loop` line — after it has gone through all the lines in the body. This is called a *bottom-tested loop*.

In this case, it counts off .25 and subtracts the .25 from the `Amount` variable. Of course, `Amount` has a negative number at that point, but 1 has already been added to the `Quarters` variable, which means you get a gumball.

To fix this, you can switch to a *top-tested loop*. It's easy. Just move the `While` or `Until` keyword and the condition to the top of the loop, after the `Do` keyword. Listing 6-14 shows you what I mean.

Listing 6-14:   How Many Quarters, Version 2.0

```
...
Do Until Amount < .25
   Quarters = Quarters + 1
   Amount = Amount - .25
Loop
...
```

This time, the condition is checked first thing, before the body of the loop ever executes. This loop is to execute until the `Amount` variable is less than .25. In other words, after the value goes below .25, the loop stops. And because `Amount` starts at .17, the loop stops before it ever starts, and none of the lines in the loop get executed. The computer simply jumps over the entire loop and begins with whatever follows `Loop`:

```
You can buy 0 $.25 gumballs
```

So a top-tested loop is better than a bottom tested loop, right? Not necessarily. The best method depends on what you're doing and how you want to set it up. In some cases, you want the loop to execute at least once. Use whatever works best for your situation.

Exit, stage left

You might discover, right in the middle of a loop, that you want the computer to get out of the loop entirely — no matter what else is happening. VB 2005 makes this possible with the `Exit` command:

```
For Count = 1 To 100
   . . .
   If Temp > Threshold Then
      Exit For
   End If
   . . .
Next
```

Usually, you find the `Exit For` command within an `If...Then` statement that checks for some special case why the loop needs to end. You can use the `Exit Do` command in exactly the same way to exit a `Do...Loop`.

If the computer is inside a nested loop, an `Exit` pops the computer out of only the inner loop. It doesn't pop the computer out of the outer loop, too.

Before you Continue . . .

`Continue` is another command you can use inside a loop. But instead of jumping out of the loop entirely, `Continue` causes the computer to just skip over the rest of the loop body and go on to the next execution of the loop.

```
For Count = 1 To 100
    . . .
    If ValidRecord = False Then
        Continue
    End If
    . . .
Next
```

Like `Exit For`, `Continue` is usually inside an `If...Then` statement that checks some condition to see whether the rest of the loop body should be skipped. In this case, if the `ValidRecord` variable contains `False`, everything after the `End If` and before the `Next` is skipped, `Count` is increased, and execution starts again at the top of the loop.

Juggling Information with Arrays

An *array* is a way of declaring a whole group of variables at once. (For information about creating and using variables, see Chapter 5.) In this section, I show you how arrays can be used to store collections of data and how that data can be filled in and searched.

Creating and using arrays

An array declaration looks like this:

```
Dim Friends(5) As String
```

This single line creates six different variables. Why six? Because arrays always begin counting with zero. Each of these six variables, or *elements* as they're sometimes called, has the same name: `Friends`. You refer to each variable individually by using its name *and* its number. For example, you can assign a value to `Friends`, element number 3, by using this syntax:

```
Friends(3) = "Brad Jones"
```

But why would you want to do this at all? Why not create six different variables the normal way?

```
Dim Friends0, Friends1, Friends2 As String
Dim Friends3, Friends4, Friends5 As String
```

Well, being able to refer to variables by their array numbers has one significant advantage: you can search through them one-by-one with a loop. Try the code in Listing 6-15.

Listing 6-15:   Searching the Friends Array

```
<html>
<body>
<%
Dim Friends(5) As String
Dim CurrentFriend As Integer
Dim Found As Boolean

Friends(0) = "Mike LaFavers"
Friends(1) = "Curtis Dicken"
Friends(2) = "Dee Townsend"
Friends(3) = "Brad Jones"
Friends(4) = "Wayne Smith"
Friends(5) = "TaKiesha Fuller"

Found = False
For CurrentFriend = 0 To 5
   If Friends(CurrentFriend) = "Wayne Smith" Then
      Found = True
      Exit For
   End If
Next
If Found = True Then
%>
<p>I found Wayne Smith!</p>
<% Else %>
<p>I didn't find Wayne Smith.</p>
<% End If %>
</body>
</html>
```

This code creates a couple of variables. Then, the values for all five array elements are set. A little later on in the page, the code searches through the entire array by using a For...Next loop to find the element that matches a particular name. The first time through the loop, CurrentFriend is 0 and so when the code refers to Friends(CurrentFriend), it is looking at the element zero of the array. The next time through the loop, the code is looking at element one, and so on.

In fact, using a `For...Next` loop with an array is so common that VB 2005 has a special version of the `For...Next` loop designed for arrays: the `For Each...Next` loop.

Using For Each...Next with arrays

The `For Each...Next` statement works just like a `For...Next` loop, except for one thing. Instead of specifying the numbers, you simply specify the array's name, and it knows to go through all the elements — no matter how many there are.

Try changing the example in Listing 6-15 to use a `For Each...Next` loop by modifying the lines to look like this:

```
Dim CurrentFriend As String
. . .
For Each CurrentFriend In Friends
    If CurrentFriend = "Wayne Smith" Then
        Found = True
        Exit For
    End If
Next
. . .
```

Three parts change as follows:

✔ The `CurrentFriend` variable is declared as a string instead of an integer. I explain why in the next bullet.

✔ The `For` line changes to `For Each`. This works a little differently from a normal `For...Next` loop. The `For Each` statement assumes that you're going to work your way through an array. So you don't need to tell `For Each` where to start and end. You just need to give it the array to work with (after the `In` keyword) and a variable to assign the value of the current element in the array. Notice that the `CurrentFriend` variable won't hold the *number* of the loop this time. Instead, it holds the *value* of the current array element (like `"Curtis Dicken"` or `"Dee Townsend"`).

✔ Because `CurrentFriend` actually contains the value of the current array element, the `If` statement inside the loop simply checks `CurrentFriend` to see whether it equals what the code is looking for.

The `For Each` statement is handy to use and is safer than `For...Next` in the long run. If, in the future, the number of elements in `Friends` changes, you won't have to change this loop. `For Each` automatically goes through all of them, no matter how many there are.

Chapter 7

Divide and Conquer: Structured Programming

*A*fter you get the hang of it, writing small programs is easy. But big programs get complex fast! Even the most experienced programmers get confused. So, developers have spent lots of time and effort trying to find ways to simplify and organize the way people write programs.

The first major effort to really address the issue of programming complexity was called *structured programming*. Structured programming breaks down programs into smaller pieces. That makes each piece easier to understand. It has another benefit, too: If you write a program that breaks down into lots of pieces, and then I write a program, I might be able to use some of the pieces you've already written! That's called *code reuse,* and it's one of the more important ways of reducing software development time and increasing the quality of the final application.

In this chapter, you see how structured programming affects VB 2005 and how you can apply its principles to your pages. This is important not only for helping organize your own pages, but also in helping you understand how the .NET Framework is organized and how you make use of it.

Simplifying Your Life: Structured Programming and Functions

The core idea of structured programming is to break big problems into a bunch of smaller ones and then solve each of them. Its practical result was the introduction of a new concept in programming languages — the *function*. In Chapter 6, I introduce the concept of a function and demonstrate a couple of VB 2005 built-in functions — Weekday and Today. But you can create your own functions, too.

A function is simply a group of commands that has a name. Whenever the program needs to have those lines executed, it can simply call that function by name, and the commands are performed. When the function completes its work, the computer returns back to its original location within the main program.

Giving Your Functions a Place to Live: The Script Tag

ASP.NET 2.0 offers a special place for you to put your functions: inside a `<script>` tag. This snippet shows how you use the `<script>` tag:

```
<%@ Page Explicit="True" Language="VB" Debug="True" %>
<html>
<script runat="server">
' My functions here
. . .
</script>
<body>
. . .
</body>
</html>
```

The `<script>` tag must appear before the `<body>` tag in your page. It can even appear above the `<html>` tag, but you should always be sure it's below the @ Page directive — the VB 2005 compiler requires it. Otherwise, you'll get an error.

The `<script>` tag has an attribute called runat, which you set to the value "server". This attribute indicates that this tag contains ASP.NET code that runs on the server (as opposed to JavaScript code that runs in the browser).

Only ASP.NET code is allowed inside the <script> tag. Because you can't put HTML tags in there, you don't need to use the delimiters (<% and %>). In fact, you get an error if you try to.

Also, the <script> tag is specifically designed for you to write your own functions. Inside the tag, don't write code that isn't part of a function.

Visual Studio Web Developer 2005 Express provides an option in the Add New Item dialog when you add a page to your project — a check box labeled Place Code in Separate File. If this check box is *not* selected, your code is placed in a <script> tag at the top of the page (below the @ Page directive and before the <html> tag). This is the approach that works best with the examples in this book. If you select this check box, VSWDE creates a separate file and puts your code there. This approach is called *code behind.* The approach you choose has no effect on the way the code executes. Which you decide to use in your own development is up to you. For more information on this topic, see Chapter 4.

Creating Functions

In VB 2005, you can use a formula to generate random numbers between 1 and any number you like. For example, this line generates a number between 1 and 6:

```
RandNum = Int(Rnd * 6) + 1
```

That's handy if you want to simulate rolling a die. But wouldn't it be nice if you had a RollDie function that simply returned the random number so you didn't have to remember to write out that formula every time? VB 2005 doesn't have a built-in RollDie function, but you can make your own, as you see in Listing 7-1.

Listing 7-1:   Creating and Using a Function

```
<%@ Page Explicit="True" Language="VB" Debug="True" %>
<html>
<script runat="server">

Function RollDie As Integer
   Dim Roll As Integer
   Randomize
   Roll = Int(Rnd * 6) + 1
   Return Roll
End Function
```

(continued)

Listing 7-1 *(continued)*

```
</script>

<body>
<p>I'll roll two dice; let's see what
we get!</p>
<%
Dim FirstRoll, SecondRoll As Integer
FirstRoll = RollDie
SecondRoll = RollDie
%>
First roll: <%=FirstRoll%><br>
Second roll: <%=SecondRoll%><br>
</body>
</html>
```

I put the <script> tag at the top of the page before the <body> tag. Inside the <script> tag, you see a line that begins with the Function keyword and one a little later that says End Function. All the code between those lines is referred to as the *body* of the function. These commands are executed when the function is called. (In this listing, I indent these lines to show clearly that they are the body of the function. Although not required, this indentation makes the code more readable.)

After the keyword Function, the first line has the name you want to give your function — in this case, RollDie. Like variables, you can give functions any name you like. But, also like variables, the name you give each function should somehow indicate what that function does.

The name of the function is followed by the As Integer clause. It's almost as if you were declaring a variable! But you aren't. Instead, you're specifying what kind of value this function will *return*. I describe how functions return values in the next section.

Because the commands in the function appear first in the page, you might think they're executed right away. But that isn't so! A function's body isn't executed until the function is specifically called.

Calling Functions

How do you call a function? The same way you call your dog! Just say its name:

```
. . .
<body>
<p>I'll roll two dice; let's see what
we get!</p>
<%
Dim FirstRoll, SecondRoll As Integer
FirstRoll = RollDie
SecondRoll = RollDie
%>
First roll: <%=FirstRoll%>
Second roll: <%=SecondRoll%>
</body>
</html>
```

This code creates two integer variables: `FirstRoll` and `SecondRoll`. Then, the function is called by invoking its name: `RollDie`. The function's body is executed:

```
Function RollDie As Integer
    Dim Roll As Integer
    Randomize
    Roll = Int(Rnd * 6) + 1
    Return Roll
End Function
```

The function creates a variable called `Roll` and assigns it the value from the random number formula. Now `Roll` has a value between 1 and 6.

The last line of the function body indicates what value the function will return. In this case, the function returns the number that's in the `Roll` variable. The value returned must match the type at the end of the `Function` line — in this case, `As Integer`. If the value doesn't match the type, you'll receive an error.

When the function is done, execution returns to the place where the function was called. The value returned from the `RollDie` function is assigned to the variable `FirstRoll`:

```
FirstRoll = RollDie
```

To clarify, the preceding line does two things:

- It calls the `RollDie` function created in the `<script>` section at the top of the page. All the lines in the body of the function are executed.
- After the function is called, the value returned effectively replaces the name of the function in the code. So in this case, the function generates a random number between 1 and 6, and that number comes back and gets assigned to the `FirstRoll` variable.

The `RollDie` function is called again on the next line to put another random number in the `SecondRoll` variable:

```
SecondRoll = RollDie
```

Finally, the page displays both values:

```
First roll: <%=FirstRoll%>
Second roll: <%=SecondRoll%>
```

As you try this example, click the Refresh button several times. You get a different roll each time. The results look something like this:

```
I'll roll two dice; let's see what we get!

First roll: 2
Second roll: 4
```

You can create as many functions as you like. Each can contain any number of commands, and you can call these functions from anywhere in your program as many times as you like. You can even call functions from within other functions.

Opening Arguments

In some cases, you need to give a function some information so that it can do its job. You pass information to a function by using *arguments*.

To demonstrate this concept, I go back to the drawing board for generating random numbers. The example in the preceding section uses a `RollDie` function. You could create a `FlipCoin` function and a `DrawCard` function, each returning random numbers within different ranges. Or you could create a more generalized random number function as shown in Listing 7-2:

Listing 7-2: Generalizing the Function

```
<%@ Page Explicit="True" Language="VB" Debug="True" %>
<html>
<script runat="server">

Function RandNum(Limit As Integer) As Integer
   Dim Num As Integer
   Randomize
   Num = Int(Rnd * Limit) + 1
   Return(Num)
End Function
```

```
</script>
<body>
<p>And now, the multi-talented RandNum function!</p>
A Die Roll: <%=RandNum(6)%><br>
A Card Draw: <%=RandNum(13)%><br>
A Coin Flip: <%=RandNum(2)%><br>
</body>
</html>
```

Again, the Function and End Function lines surround the indented body of the function. The name of the function is RandNum. But this time, parentheses follow the function name and something that looks like a variable declaration (without the Dim) appears inside. What's going on there?

Inside the parentheses you create a variable declaration of sorts so that you can identify the information sent as an argument to the function with a name and a data type. It looks like a normal variable declaration without the Dim. You only use Dim when you create stand-alone variables. With arguments when you call this RandNum function, you use the integer variable Limit to refer to the information that you pass into this function as an argument.

The As Integer clause that *follows* the parentheses looks a little out of place now, but it's the same As Integer clause that appears immediately after a function name when there are no parentheses (like the RollDie function created in the preceding section). It indicates that this function will return an integer value.

All the rest of the function looks the same as the earlier example (in Listing 7-1) except for one thing. I use the Limit variable in the random number formula to indicate the highest random number generated. So, if the programmer passes in a 5, the function generates a random number between 1 and 5. If the programmer passes in 500, the function returns a random number between 1 and 500.

The body of the function isn't executed until the function is called. That happens in the body of the page. In this example, I don't bother with creating variables, calling the function, assigning the returned value to the variable, and then displaying the variable, as I do in Listing 7-1. Instead, I just call the function and immediately display whatever it sends back:

```
. . .
A Die Roll: <%=RandNum(6)%><br>
A Card Draw: <%=RandNum(13)%><br>
A Coin Flip: <%=RandNum(2)%><br>
. . .
```

You see results like this:

```
And now, the multi-talented RandNum function!
A Die Roll: 3
A Card Draw: 8
A Coin Flip: 2
```

Click Refresh in your browser several times to make sure that each number returned by the function falls within the appropriate range.

Functions in All Shapes and Sizes

You can create as many functions as you like inside the `<script>` tag at the beginning of your page:

```
<%@ Page Explicit="True" Language="VB" Debug="True" %>
<html>
<script runat="server">
Function RollDie As Integer
    . . .
End Function

Function FlipCoin As Integer
    . . .
End Function

Function RandNum(Limit As Integer) As Integer
    . . .
End Function
</script>
<body>
. . .
</body>
</html>
```

If a function has an argument, you simply put a variable declaration (minus the `Dim`) inside parentheses on the `Function` line, after the name, as in the `RandNum` function that you see in Listing 7-2. Don't forget the `As` keyword after the parentheses to indicate the type of value the function returns!

If a function has more than one argument, just put each declaration inside the parentheses, separated by commas:

```
Function AddNums(A As Integer, B As Integer) As Integer
    Return A + B
End Function
```

Then, when you *call* the function, you include the arguments in parentheses. The variable names passed when you call the function don't have to match the variable names used in the function. In fact, you can send values directly, without using a variable. This example passes MyNum for the first argument (which is called A in the function) and 5 for the second argument (which is called B in the function).

```
Sum = AddNums(MyNum, 5)
```

The values passed should be of the same type as the arguments you specified when you created the function. For example, the AddNums function expects you to pass two integers. If you pass numbers with a decimal value, they get rounded to integers and then added.

For arguments, you can send any type of data you want. And you can also return any type. Here's a function that accepts a string and an integer and returns a string:

```
Function Greet(Name As String, Age As Integer) As String
    Return("Hi, I'm " & Name & " and I am " & Age & "!")
End Function
```

Creating and Using Subroutines

In addition to functions, VB 2005 supports another feature for chopping up your code: subroutines. But don't worry; subroutines aren't complicated. In fact, they're identical to functions except for one thing: A subroutine doesn't return a value.

You specify a subroutine by using the Sub and End Sub keywords:

```
Sub DisplayIngredient (Amount As Single, Units As String)
. . .
End Sub
```

You specify your arguments inside parentheses after the subroutine's name just as you do with a function.

Unlike a function, a subroutine has no As clause after the parentheses on the first line because no return value exists. That also means, of course, that you won't see Return in the body of the subroutine.

When you call the subroutine, you simply use the name of the subroutine and include the arguments you want to pass inside parentheses, just as you do for a function:

```
DisplayIngredient(3,"cups")
```

Making a Quick Exit

Sometimes, you're in the middle of a function or subroutine and you realize that you need to get out — now. VB 2005 makes that possible with the `Exit`, `Function`, and `Exit Sub` keywords:

```
Function CalculateValue(Age As Integer)
If Age < 1 Then
    Exit Function
End If
. . .
```

This function accepts an argument — a person's age. First, the function checks to see if the age is less than 1. If not, the function continues executing. If it is, `Exit Function` is called. This causes the function to end right away and return to the code that called the function. The `Exit Sub` command works exactly the same way for subroutines.

Oh, the Places Your Variables Will Go!

Once you understand functions and subroutines, the options you have for creating and using variables become more interesting and a little more complicated. *Where* you create your variables can make a big difference in how you can use them. In this section I'll describe three different places where you can declare your variables and how this decision impacts how you access and use them.

Three kinds of variables

There are three kinds of variables. What kind of variable you create depends on where you declare it. This characteristic of variables is often referred to as the variable's *scope*. A variable's scope determines where you can *use* that variable. The three kinds of variables and the locations where they are declared are:

- **Body variables:** Declared in the body of the HTML page, between the `<body>` tags
- **Local variables:** Declared in a function or subroutine
- **Global variables:** Declared within the `<script>` tag

The example in Listing 7-3 creates variables in the three different places where they can be created and then uses the variables wherever they can be used. It does not, however, produce any output in your browser. (However, if you try to use a variable somewhere you shouldn't, you see an error message in the browser!)

Listing 7-3:   Testing Out Variable Scope

```
<%@ Page Explicit="True" Language="VB" Debug="True" %>
<html>
<head></head>
<script runat="server">
Dim GlobalVar As Integer = 1

Sub SomeSubroutine
   Dim LocalVar As Integer = 1

   LocalVar = 99
   GlobalVar = 99
End Sub

</script>
<body>
<%
Dim BodyVar As Integer = 1

SomeSubroutine

BodyVar = 55
GlobalVar = 55
%>
</body>
</html>
```

The preceding listing includes three Dim statements in the three different possible locations:

- ✔ BodyVar is a *body variable,* created in a Dim statement in the body of the HTML page — that's where I've typically created variables in the examples I've used in previous chapters.

- ✔ LocalVar is a *local variable,* created in a subroutine. Earlier examples in this chapter show you variables created in functions and subroutines.

- ✔ GlobalVar is a *global variable,* created *between* the <script> tags at the top of the page (where the functions and subroutines go), but *outside* any individual function or subroutine. This might be the first time you've seen a Dim statement here.

Two places you can use variables

A page has two places where you can write code and use a variable: in the body of the page and in a function or subroutine.

In the *body* of a page, you can use a

- **Body variable:** A variables that was created in the body of the page. In Listing 7-3, `BodyVar` is a body variable.

- **Global variable:** A variable created inside the `<script>` tag but outside of any function or subroutine. In Listing 7-3, `GlobalVar` is a global variable.

In the body of a page, you *cannot* use variables that were created inside a function or subroutine (like `LocalVar` in Listing 7-3), even after you call the function or subroutine. Local variables are just that — local. You can only use them in the function or subroutine where they are created.

That leads me to the next place where you can write code and use variables. Inside *functions* or *subroutines,* you can use a

- **Local variable:** A variable declared inside a function or subroutine.

- **Global variable:** A variable created inside the `<script>` tag but outside any function or subroutine.

In functions and subroutines, you *cannot* use variables that were declared in the body of the page. So, in Listing 7-3, inside `SomeSubroutine,` you can change the value of `LocalVar` and `GlobalVar`, but not `BodyVar`.

Finally, if you have two subroutines, you can't use the local variables from one subroutine in the other subroutine. You can use local variables only in the function or subroutine where they were created. Further, a local variable lives only as long as the subroutine or function is being executed. After the subroutine or function is done, the local variable goes away. If you call that same subroutine or function again, the local variable is created anew and is reinitialized. That is, it doesn't have the same value it did when the subroutine or function was called last.

Understanding how scope impacts your ASP.NET pages

So where should you put your `Dim` statements? You might be tempted to say in the `<script>` tag — after all, global variables can be accessed anywhere!

However, that's a bad idea. For simple pages, it doesn't make much difference, but when you start creating more complex pages, you end up with lots of variables floating around. And if they're all global, you could accidentally change the value of a variable in one part of your page and have it affect something totally different somewhere else. This can be a big debugging headache.

So, here's the best guideline to use: Create your variables where you're going to use them. If you use a variable in the body of your page, declare it there. If you're going to use it only in a function or subroutine, declare it there.

If you really, really need to access a variable everywhere, you can consider a global variable. If you find yourself passing the same variable in and out of several different functions, it might be a good candidate to become a global variable.

Before you create a global variable, always ask yourself, "Do I have another option?" If you need access to a variable both in the body and in a function, for example, you can always pass the variable to your function by using arguments. And, of course, a function can send information back, too. That should be your usual way of sharing information.

I'm not saying that you shouldn't use global variables. I'm just saying, "Don't make them your first choice!"

Part IV
Classy Objects and Methodical Properties

The 5th Wave   By Rich Tennant

THE GREAT THING ABOUT OBJECT-ORIENTED PROGRAMMING IS, IT'S MADE SOFTWARE DEVELOPMENT AS EASY AS PUTTING ONE FOOT IN FRONT OF THE OTHER.

In this part . . .

To make your pages cool, you need objects. Objects are a way of organizing code so that it's more intuitive and easier to understand. In this part, I show you how object-oriented programming (OOP) makes your pages simpler and more powerful.

After you know what objects are, you can put them to use! You uncover a variety of objects that ASP.NET 2.0 makes available to enable you to communicate with both the Web server and the user's browser.

Chapter 8

OOPs — No Mistake Here!

• •

• •

As I explain in Chapter 7, structured programming helps developers make their code much more readable and maintainable. But, as you might expect, programmers continue to write longer and more complex programs.

To handle this complexity, many programmers have turned to a new way of organizing their code: object-oriented programming (OOP). However, OOP doesn't replace structured programming. Instead, this new technique was built on top of structured programming.

What is OOP? Well, if you ask most programmers, they usually start waving their arms and throwing around even bigger buzzwords like *encapsulation* and *polymorphism*. (Say that three times fast!) It's just one of those topics that some people like to make more complex than it really is.

In reality, the fundamental concepts of OOP are simple. That's the very reason why it works so well. And because it works so well, Microsoft has made OOP the very foundation on which ASP.NET 2.0 and the whole .NET Framework are built.

This chapter helps you understand OOP's basic concepts. Chapter 9 provides many examples of how you can use those concepts to do very cool programming techniques in your ASP.NET 2.0 pages.

Looking at a Real-World Example: My Car

Objects are everywhere! Your chair is an object, your computer is an object, and even your mother-in-law is an object. An object is just a thing that you give a name. Most objects have characteristics or properties that describe them, and most objects can do things and even interact with other objects. You deal with these kinds of real-world objects every day.

To help you understand software objects, indulge me for a moment while I provide a more detailed, real-world object example.

My car is parked in my driveway. (It's exactly the kind of car you'd expect a famous, big-shot computer book author would drive, too: a Toyota Camry.) Now, that car didn't appear out of nowhere. Far from it! A few years ago, several men and women in long white lab coats stood around a table. On that table lay the plans for what would, one day, be my car. If I'd shown up that day, sat on the table, and tried to drive those plans out of the room, they would've called security and had me hauled out with no questions asked. You can't drive the plans. They're just a detailed description of what the car will be. They aren't the car itself.

To turn that plan into a real car, it had to go through a process. In this case, the process is called manufacturing. Now that my car has been manufactured, I can appreciate many things about it, such as its fetching burgundy color, its fake leather interior, and its roomy trunk. The following minitable lists these *properties* of the car.

Property	Value
Color	Burgundy
Interior	Fake Leather
Trunk	Roomy

Another fact about my car is that it can *do* certain things — if I ask it to. For example, if I ask it to Go (by pressing the gas pedal), it moves forward. If I ask it to Stop (by pressing the brake pedal), it stops.

All right, enough speaking in riddles. What's this all about? Well, this real-world object example actually goes a long way toward explaining the key concepts of software objects used in OOP.

First, the plans used to create the car are referred to in OOP terms as a *class*. A class is a detailed description of an object. The car itself is an object. Just as the plans are a detailed description of a car, so a class is a detailed description of an object. But what's inside an object?

An object contains two things:

- **Properties** hold information about the object. Think of them as a description of different aspects of the object. Color, Interior, and Trunk are the names of three properties of the Car object. The values those properties hold are Burgundy, Fake Leather, and Roomy, respectively.

- **Methods** are actions that the object can do. Go and Stop are the two methods of the car. (You might be thinking, "Perhaps I'm missing something, but *method* seems like a really strange term to use for that." You aren't missing anything. It is a strange term.)

Programming Objects

How do objects apply to programming and organizing your code? Well, you already know what a variable is. And you know what functions and subroutines are. (If you don't, see Chapter 7.) So, imagine taking a bunch of variables, functions, and subroutines that all work together and putting them in an object, as shown in Figure 8-1.

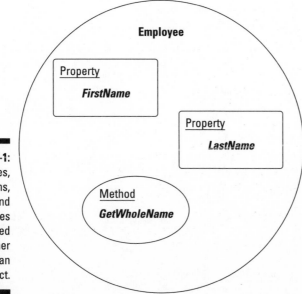

Figure 8-1:
Variables, functions, and subroutines all pulled together make up an object.

The variables in the object are properties, and the functions and subroutines in the object are methods. Properties and methods are just variables, functions, and subroutines that are *associated with* or *inside* a particular object.

By packaging up the data and code in your application, you create a new way of dividing up your application. You still use functions, but you then put them together with other functions and the variables they use. Putting them together creates a higher-level division: an object.

Creating a Class

The code in Listing 8-1 demonstrates how to create a class, how to use a class to make an object, and how to work with the properties and methods of an object.

Listing 8-1: Creating a Class

```
<%@ Page Explicit="True" Language="VB" Debug="True" %>
<html>
<script runat="server">

Class Employee
    Public FirstName As String
    Public LastName As String

    Function GetWholeName As String
        Dim Whole As String
        Whole = FirstName & " " & LastName
        Return(Whole)
    End Function
End Class

</script>
<body>
<%
Dim Emp1 As Employee
Emp1 = New Employee
Emp1.FirstName = "Bob"
Emp1.LastName = "Smith"
%>
Whole Name: <%=Emp1.GetWholeName%><br>
</body>
</html>
```

And here's the result:

```
Whole Name: Bob Smith
```

Objects are a great way to help you organize your functions and variables. So, how do you create an object? The first step to creating an object is to create a class that describes it.

Like functions, you put classes between the <script> tags at the top of the page. The words Class and End Class surround the class's body. Following the word Class, you see the class's name: Employee.

In the body of the class, this example declares two string variables: FirstName and LastName. Instead of the Dim keyword, this declaration uses the keyword Public.

Public indicates that you can use variables outside the class (as I show you later in Listing 8-2).

In addition to the variables, the class contains a function named GetWholeName. This function doesn't accept any arguments, but it does return a string. Basically, it just sticks the first and last names together with a space in the middle and returns that.

Using the Class to Make an Object

Like a function, a class doesn't actually do anything until you use it in the body of your page. So, that's the next step:

```
<body>
<%
Dim Emp1 As Employee
Emp1 = New Employee
```

This code creates a new variable: Emp1. It isn't an Integer or a String. It's an Employee. What's that? That's the class you just created. So, Emp1 is a variable that's designed to hold an Employee object.

So, the next step is to put an Employee object in the Emp1 variable! But how do you create an object by using the Employee class? You use the New keyword.

The last line of the preceding code assigns a value to the Emp1 variable. The value is New Employee. New is a special keyword that takes a class and makes an object out of it. In this case, it takes the Employee class and creates an Employee object and then puts that object in the Emp1 variable. From that point on, the page can refer to the new object by the name Emp1.

You can even combine the two lines into one:

```
Dim Emp1 As Employee = New Employee
```

You can shorten it even further like this:

```
Dim Emp1 As New Employee
```

All three approaches do exactly the same thing. They create a variable called `Emp1`, create a new object from the `Employee` class, and assign the object to `Emp1`.

Using the Properties and Methods in an Object

After you create an object, you can work with its properties and methods:

```
Emp1.FirstName = "Bob"
Emp1.LastName = "Smith"
%>

Whole Name: <%=Emp1.GetWholeName%>
</body>
</html>
```

The variables inside the `Emp1` object are `FirstName` and `LastName`. You know that because you created the `Emp1` object from an `Employee` class, and all `Employee` class objects have those variables in them.

The syntax you use to access properties and methods is called *dot notation*. Because the variables are inside an object, you must use the object's name first, then a dot (period), and then the name of the variable — for example, `Emp1.FirstName`.

The same goes for calling a function that's inside an object. In this case, `Emp1` is the object name, followed by the dot, and then the function `GetWholeName`. This calls the function and returns the whole name, which appears in the browser.

Creating Multiple Instances

You might wonder why you have to create a class separately and then create an object from that class before you use the object. Why the extra step? There's a good reason: You might want more than one `Employee` object.

Jargon watch

OOP is full of jargon. I try to avoid jargon when I can, but you just have to put up with some of it because that's how programmers talk. Here are some OOP-related words and phrases that you'll encounter in other books and magazines.

In Listing 8-2, the Emp1 and Emp2 variables, which hold objects, are called *reference variables*. That's because each one holds a reference to the object. This jargon differentiates them from normal variables that just hold numbers and strings.

The term *instantiation* refers to the process of creating a new object by using the New keyword. This fancy term simply means *making an instance of* — that is, you make an instance of the class. In the code in Listing 8-2, you actually make two instances of the same class. The words *instance* and *object* are more or less interchangeable here.

Finally, the word *members* is commonly used to refer collectively to all the stuff in a particular object — all its properties and methods.

Replace the body of the code in Listing 8-1 (everything between and including the <body> tags), with this code:

Listing 8-2:   Creating Two Employees

```
<body>
<%
Dim Emp1, Emp2 As Employee
Emp1 = New Employee
Emp2 = New Employee
Emp1.FirstName = "Bob"
Emp1.LastName = "Smith"
Emp2.FirstName = "Abbey"
Emp2.LastName = "Hatfield"
%>
Emp1 Name: <%=Emp1.GetWholeName%><br>
Emp2 Name: <%=Emp2.GetWholeName%><br>
</body>
```

The new page looks like this:

```
Emp1 Name: Bob Smith
Emp2 Name: Abbey Hatfield
```

What's the difference? This version of the code creates two Employee objects. One is stored in the Emp1 variable and the other in Emp2. They are assigned different names and then the names are presented to the user.

When you create multiple copies, or *instances,* of a class, each has its own set of properties. That is, the `Emp1` and `Emp2` objects both have their own `FirstName` and `LastName` properties, and `Emp1.FirstName` can hold a different value from `Emp2.FirstName`. And the methods of `Emp1` (like `GetWholeName`) work with the properties of `Emp1`.

Get Out! This Is Private Property

To help you get a clearer understanding of classes, objects, properties, and methods, here's another example.

Suppose you want to create an object that works like a simple counter. It starts at 0 (zero). You can add one to it (increment) or you can subtract one from it (decrement). You can also check its current value. How would you create a class to implement that object?

Listing 8-3 shows one approach.

Listing 8-3:   The Counter Class

```
<%@ Page Explicit="True" Language="VB" Debug="True" %>
<html>
<head></head>
<script runat="server">

Class Counter
   Private CounterValue As Integer = 0

   Sub Increment
      CounterValue = CounterValue + 1
   End Sub

   Sub Decrement
      CounterValue = CounterValue - 1
   End Sub

   Function GetValue As Integer
      Return(CounterValue)
   End Function
End Class

</script>
<body>
<%
Dim Count1 As Counter
Count1 = New Counter
%>
Count1 = <%=Count1.GetValue%><br>
<%
```

```
Count1.Increment
Count1.Increment
Count1.Increment
Count1.Decrement
%>
Count1 = <%=Count1.GetValue%><br>
</body>
</html>
```

The `Counter` class is different from the `Employee` class in Listing 8-1. The `Counter` class has only one property: `CounterValue`. And instead of `Public` or `Dim`, I use the keyword `Private`.

In the earlier section, "Creating a Class," I mention that `Public` enables you to use an object's variable outside the object. `Private` means just the opposite. Only functions and subroutines inside the class can access properties that you declare as `Private`. But what good is a variable if you can't get to it?

Well, in this case, you're creating a simple counter. You don't want people to assign any value they want to the counter. It starts at 0 (zero), and then the developer who uses this class can increment or decrement it. The code provides two subroutines to do those tasks. You can call those subroutines from outside the object, and those subroutines can, in turn, change the private variable. So, there is a way to work with the value held by the private variable. But by providing access only through these subroutines, you specifically limit how the developer using your class works with the private variables.

But a counter isn't much good if you can't tell what number it's on right now, so the function `GetValue` returns the value of the private variable.

The body of the page code creates the object and puts it in the `Count1` variable. The code then uses the `GetValue` function to show that the counter starts at 0. Then, the `Increment` subroutine is called three times and the `Decrement` subroutine once, so the final value displayed is 2:

```
Count1 = 0
Count1 = 2
```

TRY THIS

Try adding this line anywhere in the body of your page code:

```
<% count1.CounterValue = 5 %>
```

When you try to access the private variable directly, you get an error that looks something like this:

```
'ASP.Default_aspx.Counter.CounterValue' is not
accessible in this context because it is 'Private'.
```

You can include both public and private variables in the same class. Public variables make it easy for anyone who uses your class to set the value directly. But if you want more control over the way the value is changed, use a private variable and then simply create functions that do the updating and retrieving of the value. For example, you can easily limit this counter so that it can never exceed 100. Simply change the `Increment` subroutine to check the current value with an `If...Then` condition (which I explain in Chapter 6):

```
Sub Increment
    If CounterValue < 100 Then
        CounterValue = CounterValue + 1
    End If
End Sub
```

Because those programmers who use the `Counter` class can change the value only through the `Increment` and `Decrement` methods, you know that this small change in the code will do the trick!

OOP folks have a word for the concept of creating private variables and then accessing and manipulating their values through methods. They call it *encapsulation*. It's an important feature of OOP because it helps you maintain control over your data.

Objects inside Objects inside . . .

I need to tell you about one more little wrinkle that you're likely to encounter. Sometimes, you find objects inside other objects. For example, suppose you have an object called `Customer`, which has these properties:

- ✔ Name: A string
- ✔ Address: A string

Also inside the `Customer` object, you have another object, `Order`, which represents an order made by that customer. `Order` has these properties:

- ✔ OrderNumber: An integer
- ✔ AmountTotal: A single

Because `Order` is inside `Customer`, you have to mention `Customer` when you access `Order`. You do that with dot notation:

```
Customer.Order.OrderNumber = 101
Customer.Order.AmountTotal = 35.75
```

In fact, you can have yet another object inside `Order`. Imagine an `Item` object with `Number` and `Name` properties:

```
Customer.Order.Item.Number = 101
Customer.Order.Item.Name = "Racquetball Racquet"
```

You might have objects inside objects inside other objects, as deep as you like. An object inside another object is often called a *nested* or *embedded* object.

You might be wondering how to create objects inside other objects. I don't show you how here. (You can find more information on how objects can be properties of other object in the .NET Framework documentation index. Just search for *properties*.) You need to know that objects can be inside other objects because you'll use objects like that which are included with the .NET Framework. But you probably won't need to create your own embedded objects until you start creating more complex Web applications.

Why OOP? Answer: The .NET Framework Class Libraries

Perhaps you're thinking, "This OOP stuff is interesting and all, but I'm not writing super-complex applications here. I'm not sure I'll need all these extra capabilities. I think I could probably get by just fine with functions and sub-routines." And, at least initially, you're probably right! You probably won't have an immediate need to create lots of classes in your ASP.NET 2.0 pages.

But you still need to understand what classes and objects are and how to use them. Why? Whether or not you create your own, you're going to work with lots of classes and objects when you start looking at the .NET Framework Class Libraries.

The .NET Framework Class Libraries are one of the more important parts of the .NET Framework. These libraries provide you with a whole lot of function-ality that you'd otherwise have to create yourself. They save time and effort and even make many programming tasks possible that you wouldn't be able to do any other way. (For examples of what you can do with the .NET Framework Class Libraries, see Chapter 17.)

Everything in the Framework works in an object-oriented way. So, as you begin to venture deeper into the capabilities of ASP.NET 2.0, the foundation this chapter provides is very helpful.

In fact, you might want to proceed directly to Chapter 9, where I demonstrate numerous interesting objects and the useful capabilities they provide to your ASP.NET 2.0 pages.

Chapter 9

Cool Stuff You Can Do with ASP.NET 2.0 Objects

In This Chapter

▶ Examining the ArrayList

▶ Displaying text on the page

▶ Jumping to a different page

▶ Sending information from one page to the next

▶ Exploring applications and sessions

Chapter 8 describes what objects are. This chapter helps you answer the question, "Why do I care?" You get a taste of how various .NET objects work and, at the same time, discover some practical, commonly used ASP.NET 2.0 techniques.

ArrayList: The Super, Handy-Dandy, Array-Type Thingy

In Chapter 6, I discuss arrays. Arrays enable you to store several pieces of information under one name. Then, you access those pieces of information by using an index number. If you haven't looked at that part of Chapter 6 or you're a little hazy on the details, go check it out before you read this section.

During the development of .NET, someone at Microsoft said, "You know, arrays are a nice thing. But wouldn't it be cool if we could create an object that worked like a really smart array? You wouldn't have to worry ahead of time about how many elements the array would have. And it could search itself to find a particular element you're looking for." That's how the ArrayList was born.

And that's a good way to think about the ArrayList — as an object that acts like a smart array.

Working over your friends

Listing 9-1 shows the example from Chapter 6, reworked to use an ArrayList.

Listing 9-1:   Friends — with an ArrayList

```
<html>
<body>
<%
Dim Friends As ArrayList = New ArrayList
Dim Found As Boolean
Dim FoundIndex As Integer

Friends.Add("Curtis Dicken")
Friends.Add("Dee Townsend")
Friends.Add("Brad Jones")
Friends.Add("Wayne Smith")
Friends.Add("TaKiesha Fuller")
Friends.Add("Mike Lafavers")
Friends.Add("Farion Grove")
Friends.Add("Troy Felton")
Friends.Add("Steve Barron")
Friends.Add("Marc Nelson")

Found = Friends.Contains("Mike Lafavers")
If Found = True Then
    FoundIndex = Friends.IndexOf("Mike Lafavers")
%>
<p>I found Mike Lafavers!</p>
<p>He's at <%=FoundIndex%>!</p>
<% Else %>
<p>I didn't find Mike Lafavers.</p>
<% End If %>
</body>
</html>
```

This code differs quite a bit from the Chapter 6 example. Starting at the top, ArrayList is an object. Actually, it's a class from which you can create your own objects:

```
Dim Friends As ArrayList = New ArrayList
```

This line creates the Friends variable, which has an ArrayList type. On the same line, using the New keyword, I create an ArrayList object and assign it to the Friends variable. In short, I create the Friends object by using the ArrayList class. (For more on classes and objects, see Chapter 8.)

ArrayList objects have an Add method. Instead of assigning a value to each individual element of the array by number, you simply call Add with whatever you want to add to the array — in this case, a name. I call Add again and again — once for each element:

```
Friends.Add("Curtis Dicken")
Friends.Add("Dee Townsend")
. . .
```

In a short program like the example from Chapter 6, in which I'm adding all the elements to the array in one place, using index numbers to fill in an array isn't a big deal. But in a larger program, you can easily lose track of the last number you filled in. With the ArrayList, the Add method keeps track of it for you and just adds the new element in wherever you left off.

One of the bigger benefits of the ArrayList, however, is that you don't have to use a loop to look at one element after another to find out whether it's in the array:

```
Found = Friends.Contains("Mike Lafavers")
If Found = True Then
   FoundIndex = Friends.IndexOf("Mike Lafavers")
. . .
```

The Contains method takes a value and looks it up in the array to see whether it's in there. This method returns True or False. If it returns False, you know your value isn't in the ArrayList. If it returns True, you can use the IndexOf method to get the index number where the value was found. (Finding the index number actually goes a step beyond the Chapter 6 example.)

Exploring additional ArrayList features

What else can you do with an ArrayList? Well, as with arrays, you can get the value of a specific element by using its index number:

```
PickFriend = Friends(2)
```

Keep in mind that an ArrayList is numbered starting at 0 (zero), not 1.

You can find out how many elements are in the ArrayList:

```
NumFriends = Friends.Count
```

Because an `ArrayList` is numbered starting at 0, the last element of the `ArrayList` is at index number `Count - 1`. In other words, if `Count` is 5, you know that you have elements numbered 0 through 4.

You also can easily remove elements from the `ArrayList` by index number:

```
Friends.RemoveAt(7)
```

This doesn't just make element number 7 blank. It removes that element altogether. All the elements above the removed element move down a notch. You can also remove elements based on their contents:

```
Friends.Remove("Dee Townsend")
```

If you want to remove all the elements, that's easy, too:

```
Friends.Clear
```

You can change the order of the elements. For example, you can reverse their order (you know, "The last shall be first and the first shall be last . . . "):

```
Friends.Reverse
```

Or, you can sort them:

```
Friends.Sort
```

In addition, if you want to process each element of an `ArrayList` individually, the `For Each` statement (which I describe in Chapter 6) works with an `ArrayList` in exactly the same way it works with an array.

The `ArrayList` isn't limited to storing strings. You can store virtually anything you like in it, including other objects. And you can even store different types of things in different elements of the same `ArrayList` — like an integer in one element and a string in another.

You might be thinking, "Gosh, with all the cool stuff I can do with an `ArrayList`, why would I ever use an array?" Well, an array is slightly more efficient and has less overhead (but, usually, not enough to really matter). Most people will probably opt for an `ArrayList` when they need to hold a list of values. However, some methods in the .NET Framework Class Library use arrays, so it's important to know how they work, too.

Are you interested in finding out more about the data structures available in the .NET Framework? Check out Bonus Chapter 4 on the CD. There I demonstrate something called a `HashTable`, which allows you to store and retrieve information based on its name (in the form of a string) rather than an index number as you do with the `ArrayList`.

Using Automatically Created Objects

The `ArrayList` is a class from which you can create your own objects that are useful for storing information. The other objects I discuss in this chapter are a little different. ASP.NET *automatically* creates them for you, so they are available whenever you need them. That means you can begin calling their methods without the need to instantiate them first.

Some objects require that you instantiate them, and some do not. I always let you know which is which when I introduce a new object.

The Input and Output Objects: Request and Response

The `Request` and `Response` objects represent information coming *into* the Web server from the browser and information going *out* from the server to the browser. So, from the server's perspective, you could call `Request` the *input* object, and you could call `Response` the *output* object. They are both available to you to use without the need to instantiate them. In this section, I present a few of these objects' more important properties and methods and the cool techniques they make possible.

Scribbling with Response.Write

`Response.Write` simply enables you to write text to the page.

This example is modified from one I presented in Chapter 6. It uses `Response.Write` to send HTML, as appropriate to the page:

```
<%@ Page Explicit="True" Language="VB" Debug="True" %>
<html>
<body>
<%
Dim Grade As Integer
Randomize
Grade = Int(Rnd * 100) + 1 ' Random number between 1 and
          100

Response.Write("<p>Your grade is " & Grade & ".</p>")
If Grade >= 60 Then
   Response.Write("<p>You passed!</p>")
```

```
Else
    Response.Write("<p>You failed...</p>")
End If
%>
</body>
</html>
```

In addition, if you want to display the value of a variable, you can just use the concatenation operator & to make it part of the string you send to the Write method. (See Chapter 5 for more on concatenation.)

Sending the user to another page with Response.Redirect

The Response object has an interesting method called Redirect, which enables you to send the user to a different page. This method can be quite handy, as the following example shows:

```
<%
Dim Username As String
...
If Username="Admin" Then
    Response.Redirect("adminhome.aspx")
Else
    Response.Redirect("home.aspx")
End If
%>
```

As you can see, if you want to send the user to another page in the same folder as the current page, you simply redirect the user with the page name. However, if you want to send the user to another site, you can use a complete URL:

```
Response.Redirect("http://www.edgequest.com")
```

Going long for the pass with Request.QueryString

The QueryString is a property of the Request object that allows you to do something very handy — pass information from one page to the next. Typically, when you create a variable on a page, you can only use that variable in functions and subroutines on that page. You can't access a variable you created in one page from another page. So using QueryString to pass information provides a way around that problem.

To give you a simple example of using `Request.QueryString` to pass information from one page to the next, I've created a simple trivia page that asks a question and provides several possible answers in the form of HTML links. All the links send the user to the same page: `GazilAns.aspx`, but they each pass a different value for `Answer` after the question mark.

Create a page called `GazilQues.aspx`. Listing 9-2 shows what it should contain.

Listing 9-2:   So Ya Wanna Be a Gazillionaire Trivia

```
<%@ Page Explicit="True" Language="VB" Debug="True" %>
<html>
<body>
<h1>So Ya Wanna Be A Gazillionaire</h1>
For one gazillion dollars, answer this question:<br>
<b>Who was the second man to walk on the moon?</b><br>
<a href="GazilAns.aspx?Answer=Armstrong">
Neil A. Armstrong</a><br>
<a href="GazilAns.aspx?Answer=Collins">
Michael Collins</a><br>
<a href="GazilAns.aspx?Answer=Aldrin">
Edwin E. Aldrin, Jr.</a><br>
<a href="GazilAns.aspx?Answer=Lightyear">
Buzz Lightyear</a><br>
</body>
</html>
```

Actually, this page has no ASP.NET code, so you could just as easily name it with an `.htm` or an `.html` extension (as long as you removed the `@ Page` declaration at the top). But leaving the `.aspx` extension doesn't hurt anything.

The question is displayed with standard HTML and the user responds by clicking a link. Each link passes a different value for the `Answer` variable after the `?` on the URL line. For example, if the user clicks `Edwin E. Aldrin, Jr.`, the user is sent to the `GazilAns.aspx` page with a URL line that looks like this:

```
http://localhost/Gazillionaire/GazilAns.aspx?Answer=Aldrin
```

The URL begins with `http://` as it usually does, then comes the domain name, then the page name. (Yours may differ, depending on what Web server you are using and the name you've given to this Web site.)

Then comes something unusual: a question mark. This is an example of passing information on the URL line itself, commonly referred to as a *QueryString*. The information is passed from the `GazilQues.aspx` page to the GazilAns. aspx page. The syntax here is important: after the question mark comes a *name=value*. The `GazilAns.aspx` page can now access the value passed by using `Request.QueryString` and referring to the name, *Answer*. When it does, it will receive the value passed, *Aldrin*.

In fact several values can be passed on the URL line by separating them with an & (ampersand). Here's what a URL line would look like that passes an employee ID and an employee name to a page called ProcEmp.aspx.

```
http://localhost/EmpLst/ProcEmp.aspx?EmpID=1101&EmpName=Fr
          ed
```

Getting back to the Gazillionaire example, what happens in the GazilAns.aspx page? Create a page called GazilAns.aspx. It should look like Listing 9-3.

Listing 9-3:   Responding to the User's Answer

```
<%@ Page Explicit="True" Language="VB" Debug="True" %>
<html>
<body>
<h1>So Ya Wanna Be A Gazillionaire</h1>
The Question Was:<br>
<b>Who was the second man to walk on the moon?</b><br>
<br>
<%
Dim Chosen As String
Chosen = Request.QueryString("Answer")
Select Case Chosen
Case "Armstrong"
    Response.Write("No, sorry! Neil Armstrong was actually
          ")
    Response.Write("the <i>first</i> man to walk on the ")
    Response.Write("moon.")
Case "Collins"
    Response.Write("No, sorry! Michael Collins never ")
    Response.Write("actually made it to the moon's
          surface.")
Case "Aldrin"
    Response.Write("Yes! You're right! Edwin Aldrin, Jr. ")
    Response.Write("was the second man to walk on the
          moon.")
Case "Lightyear"
    Response.Write("Nope. You've been watching way too ")
    Response.Write("many Disney movies.")
End Select
%>
</body>
</html>
```

You retrieve the value from the URL line by using the QueryString property of the Request object. Inside the parentheses after QueryString, you put the name that you've given the information. QueryString retrieves the value from the URL line and enables you to store the information in a string variable named Chosen.

A `Select Case` statement then uses this value to decide how to respond. A different response is provided for each possible answer. `Response.Write` lines are used to put the text on the page. (For information on `Select Case`, see Chapter 6.)

If you're interested in finding out more about the capabilities of the `Request` and `Response` objects, check out Bonus Chapter 4 on the CD. There you can find:

- ✔ How to creating and retrieving browser cookies
- ✔ The `Request.Browser` object that lets you find out what the user's browser is and what it's capable of
- ✔ A list of `Request` object properties that provide interesting information

The Application and Session Objects: More Variable Scope Options

The `Application` and `Session` objects work similarly, and you use them for similar tasks. The `Application` object holds information about the ASP.NET application. The `Session` object keeps track of each person who accesses the application, individually. Both objects are always available to your code — you don't need to instantiate them.

The application versus the session

To explain the difference between the `Application` and `Session` objects, here's an example.

The application:

Imagine your Web server has a cool real-estate ASP.NET application that enables users to look at a variety of homes, pick one, and then calculate what the mortgage payment would be if they bought it. Only one copy of this application exists on the Web server. The application starts up the first time someone accesses a page for that application. It doesn't end until the Web server is shut down. That's the `Application` object's domain: the entire application for its entire life.

The session:

The session is much different. Suppose Sparky logs on to your real-estate application and begins looking through the homes. Soon after, Judd pulls up a page and begins looking at houses, too. Now, two different people are running the same application. You don't have two different *applications,* but you do have two different *sessions.* Each time a new person accesses your ASP.NET application, a new session is created. If Sparky gives up for the night and comes back tomorrow, he will be in a different session from the one he was in previously.

It's a bird. It's a plane. No, it's a super-global Session variable!

After you've experimented with ASP.NET pages for a while, you'll find yourself wishing for a *super-global* variable — a variable that keeps its value from one page to the next.

What you really want is a Session variable:

```
Session("HouseCost") = 175000
```

This code creates a new variable called HouseCost and assigns it the value 175000. If the variable already exists, this code just changes its value. This variable is a session-level variable that your code can access from any page as long as the current user continues to use this application.

You access a Session variable in the same way:

```
If Session("HouseCost") > 150000 Then
```

Unlike variables declared with Dim, Session variables don't have a specified data type. They get their data type from the information you store in them.

Because you don't actually declare Session variables (you just begin using them), misspelling a variable name can confuse ASP.NET into thinking you're trying to create another variable. The compiler has no way of catching this kind of error with Session and Application variables, so be careful!

Using even-more-super Application variables

As you might expect, you can also create application-level variables. You work with them just as you do with session-level variables:

```
Application("NumberOfHits") = 0
```

How does the Web server know what a session is?

The World Wide Web uses HTTP as its protocol language for communication. Unfortunately, HTTP is what techie-types call a *stateless* protocol, which means that, unlike other networks, you don't log on and log off machines to use them. When you ask for a page, that is an independent request. The server sends you the page and then forgets about you. If you click a link to go to another page on that server, the request is sent, and the server sends that page to you — without any realization at all that you are the same person who asked for a page a minute ago.

So, if this is true, how can you talk about a session? Well, ASP.NET has a couple of different methods that it can use to keep track of sessions. By default, it uses cookies to keep track of sessions by uniquely identifying each person when that user first makes a request. Then, after that user makes another request in the near future, the server recognizes the user and accepts this new request as part of the same session. After a request, the server waits up to 20 minutes for a new request. If a new request doesn't happen in that time, the server assumes that the user has gone to some other site or gotten off the Internet entirely, the cookie vanishes and the server considers the session ended.

If many of your users' browsers don't support cookies, or cookie support is turned off, you can change the ASP.NET configuration to track users without the use of cookies. (For information on how to configure your application to track sessions without cookies, use the .NET Framework documentation index to locate information on the `<session>` tag in the `web.config` file.)

Only one application exists, no matter how many people use it. So, when you change an `Application` variable's value, it's possible that another session may be trying to change it at exactly the same time. This can cause your application variables to become corrupted. To avoid this, use the `Application` object's `Lock` and `Unlock` methods. Instead of just setting a value, as I do in the preceding code line, do this:

```
Application.Lock
Application("NumberOfHits") = 0
Application.Unlock
```

While the `Application` object is locked, any other sessions that try to change it are forced to wait until your changes are complete. Of course, you should not keep the `Application` object locked any longer than necessary. Always put the `Lock` and `Unlock` methods immediately before and immediately after the line that changes the Application variable.

You don't need to use the `Lock` and `Unlock` methods when you simply want to access an `Application` variable's value:

```
If Application("NumberOfHits") > 1000 Then
```

Understanding the difference between session-level and application-level variables

Here's the big difference between session-level variables and application-level variables: If five people are using your real-estate Web application at the same time, five copies of the `HouseCost` session-level variable are present — one for each session. Only one copy of the `NumberOfHits` variable exists. If you want to create a super-global variable to share information from one page to another, you definitely want to use the session-level variables.

Typically, application-level variables are used much less frequently. But they are great for keeping track of the number of hits a page has taken or other application-level statistics. You also can use them to share information among several sessions.

For a real-world example of using an application-level variable to share information between sessions, see the Café Chat Room application in Bonus Chapter 1. In this application, several people take part in a common conversation. The key to sharing the same conversation among many different participants is an application-level variable that is displayed — and redisplayed as it is updated — in the browsers of all participants.

Part V
Creating Interactive Web Applications

In this part . . .

After you have the Visual Basic 2005 language under your belt, you're ready to go interactive! In this part of the book, you discover how to create pages for filling out forms, taking part in surveys, calculating mortgage payments, and much more. In other words, this is the part where your applications come to life and really start doing something for the people who visit your site.

In addition, you find out how to help your users discover mistakes they've made when filling out a form—forgetting to fill in a required text box or accidentally typing in a value that can't possibly be right. ASP.NET 2.0 provides an innovative approach to this common task.

Chapter 10

Interfacing with Your Users

In This Chapter

▶ Discovering .NET Web Forms and how they work

▶ Exploring server control events and properties

▶ Working with all the different kinds of properties

Are you ready to get *interactive?* In this chapter, you find out how to create pages that not only display information for the user to see, but which also ask for input and respond intelligently. Discover how your pages can make the leap from boring documents to living applications!

If you've done much work creating Web pages in the past, you might be familiar with HTML forms. *HTML forms* are a set of tags that you use to make things like text boxes and radio buttons appear on the page so that the user can respond to questions or provide input. If you've ever worked with HTML forms, I have a small favor to ask of you: Please, right here and now, forget everything you know about them. Why? Because ASP.NET Web Forms work very differently, and if you try to compare them to HTML forms, you'll only get confused.

Examining Web Forms and Server Controls

Server controls (also simply called *controls*) are the primary building blocks for creating the user interface for your Web application. Examples include text boxes, check boxes, and command buttons. Controls are familiar to anyone who has used Windows or Web pages. So, understanding how to create and use controls is the first step in making your pages interactive.

When the Microsoft developers began thinking about how to create the best environment for interactive Web pages, they realized that the code you write in ASP.NET runs on the server. So, it makes sense that the controls you put on your page should run on the server, too. That way, you can easily access and manipulate them in your code. And if the controls and the code both reside on the server, your code can respond more easily when things happen, like when the user clicks a button.

That notion led to the development of .NET *Web Forms.* A Web Form is just a page that uses .NET server controls. Here are some of the most commonly used server controls. I discuss each of these in some detail in later chapters:

- ✔ Label
- ✔ TextBox
- ✔ Button
- ✔ ListBox
- ✔ DropDownList
- ✔ CheckBox
- ✔ RadioButton
- ✔ Image
- ✔ Link

Creating a simple form

Here's an example of a Web Form that uses .NET server controls. Create a page called age.aspx and enter the lines in Listing 10-1.

Listing 10-1:   If You Were a Dog Page

```
<%@ Page Explicit="True" Language="VB" Debug="True" %>
<html>
<body>
<form runat="server">
<h1>If You Were A Dog</h1>
How old are you?<br>
<asp:textbox id="Age" runat="server"/>
<asp:button text="OK" runat="server"/>
</form>
</body>
</html>
```

Figure 10-1 shows how this page looks in the browser.

Web Forms, server controls, and Visual Web Developer 2005 Express

You can use several methods to enter and test the examples throughout this book in Visual Web Developer 2005 Express. You can create a new page (making sure the *Place code in separate file* check box in the Add New Item dialog is deselected, as discussed in Chapter 4), and then clear the automatically generated tags and type in the text as it appears in the example you're testing. Or if you prefer, you can leave the automatically generated tags in there and just drag the appropriate server controls from the Toolbox window along the left. Either way, when the page is complete, you can click the Start Debugging button in the toolbar at the top to see your page in a browser. For more information and detailed step-by-step directions for entering and running the examples in this book with Visual Web Developer 2005 Express, see Chapter 4.

Figure 10-1:
The If You Were a Dog page.

The <form> tags surround all the server controls on your page. Standard HTML tags can appear between the <form> tags, too. The <form> tag's attribute, runat="server", indicates that the form is a Web Form, not an HTML form, and it is to be processed on the server.

The page shown in Figure 10-1 also has some text asking the user for his age, followed by a line that creates a textbox server control:

```
<asp:textbox id="Age" runat="server"/>
```

Although this looks like a normal HTML tag, two important clues tell you that it isn't:

✔ The tag name has the prefix `asp:`, which identifies `textbox` as an ASP.NET tag.

✔ Just as it does in the `<form>` tag, the attribute `runat="server"` tells you that the tag will be evaluated on the server before it is sent to the browser.

You see the `asp:` prefix and the `runat="server"` attribute on all ASP.NET 2.0 server controls.

You might have noticed that the `<asp:textbox>` tag and the other server control tags on the page end with a `/>`. It basically means that you want to bundle the opening tag and the closing tag into one tidy unit. So, if you were to see `<head></head>`, you could express it this way instead: `<head/>`. Both mean the same thing. The single-tag version just saves a few keystrokes. So, when you see `<asp:textbox . . . />`, it's the same as `<asp:textbox . . . ></asp:textbox>`, with nothing in between.

The `id` attribute gives this text box a name that you can use to refer to it in code (which I demonstrate in the section "Capturing events and changing properties," later in this chapter).

Next in Listing 10-1 is another server control — a button:

```
<asp:button text="OK" runat="server"/>
```

The `text` attribute determines what text appears on the face of the button.

However, if you click the button in your browser, nothing happens. I show you how to fix that situation in the next section.

Capturing events and changing properties

The preceding sections show you how to create ASP.NET Web Forms and how to use server controls, such as `textbox` and `button`. But a form that doesn't *do* anything isn't a very interesting form. So, I want to show you one more important feature: responding to server control *events*.

An event is something that occurs in an application. Usually, the events that you care about are triggered by the user. For example, clicking a button kicks off an event. Your code can *capture* that event; that is, you can write code that is tied to the event so that it gets executed when the event occurs. To show you how it's done, try adding a few lines to the If You Were a Dog example, from Listing 10-1. In Listing 10-2, the lines you need to add are bold.

Going behind the scenes with server controls

Perhaps you're thinking, "If the server controls run on the server, why do they show up in my browser?" Good question.

The server controls *do* run on the server, and that enables you to access and work with them in your ASP.NET 2.0 code (as I show you in this chapter). That's very handy. But when the server creates the page that's sent to the browser, you want these server controls to show up on your page as real controls that the user can interact with. To make this interaction happen, each server control uses HTML tags to paint a picture of itself in the user's browser.

This all happens automatically. The result is that the server control appears on the page just as you'd expect it to look.

If you've worked with HTML forms before and want to see exactly how this works, choose View➪Source from the menus in your browser while looking at the If You Were a Dog page, shown in Figure 10-1. You see `<input>` tags for the text box and button. You also see another hidden input tag called `__VIEWSTATE`, which ASP.NET 2.0 uses internally to keep track of information from one round trip to the server to the next.

Listing 10-2:   If You Were a Dog Page with Event Code

```
<%@ Page Explicit="True" Language="VB" Debug="True" %>
<html>
<script runat="server">
Sub OKButton_Click(Sender As Object, E As EventArgs)
    Dim UserAge, DogAge As Integer
    UserAge = Age.Text
    DogAge = UserAge / 7
    Message.Text="If you were a dog, you'd be " & _
        DogAge & " years old."
End Sub
</script>
<body>
<form runat="server">
<h1>If You Were A Dog</h1>
How old are you?<br>
<asp:textbox id="Age" runat="server"/>
<asp:button text="OK" onclick="OKButton_Click"
runat="server"/><br>
<asp:label id="Message" runat="server"/>
</form>
</body>
</html>
```

This code includes three new items:

- ✔ A `<script>` tag and a subroutine within it
- ✔ A new `label` control with its `id` attribute set to `Message`
- ✔ A new `onclick` attribute on the `button` control

First, take a look at the new attribute on the `button` server control:

```
<asp:button text="OK" onclick="OKButton_Click"
runat="server"/><br>
```

The `onclick` attribute captures the event that happens when the user clicks this button. How? By specifying the name of a subroutine to execute when the event happens. So, in this case, you write code in the `OKButton_Click` subroutine. Then when the user clicks the OK button, the subroutine is called, and code there is executed.

If you're using Visual Web Developer 2005 Express, you can use a couple of different techniques to automatically create subroutines to handle an event. You can simply double-click the button in Design view to switch to Source view and automatically create the `Click` event subroutine. Or if you are already in Source view, you can use the drop-down list boxes at the top of the Editor window to select the button control and then select the `Click` event. This also automatically creates the new subroutine. For more information and step-by-step directions, see Chapter 4.

The subroutine in Listing 10-2 accepts two arguments: `Sender` and `E`. All subroutines that respond to system events receive these arguments. You have to specify them here because that's what the event requires. But you don't have to use them. For now, you can ignore them.

First, you create a couple of integer variables. Then, you assign a value to one of them. The value is `Age.Text`:

```
UserAge = Age.Text
```

As you might expect, `Age` is an object, and `Text` is a property of the `Age` object. But what does `Age` refer to? Look at the `textbox` server control:

```
<asp:textbox id="Age" runat="server"/>
```

The `id` attribute is set to `Age`. That enables you to refer to `Age` as an object from your ASP.NET 2.0 code. When you work with server controls, the server creates the objects for you automatically so that you can immediately access the control's properties.

In this case, the `Age` text box object's `Text` property holds the information in the `textbox` control. The text in the `textbox` control is then placed in the `UserAge` variable.

The `DogAge` variable is then calculated by dividing `UserAge` by 7.

Finally, the result is displayed:

```
Message.Text="If you were a dog, you'd be " & _
    DogAge & " years old."
```

This time, you refer to another object: `Message`. `Message` is another server control. It's the new `label` control in this listing:

```
<asp:label id="Message" runat="server"/>
```

A `label` control is a lot like a `textbox` control, except it's designed only for showing text. You can't edit the text in a label. In this case, you use the label to display the result of the calculation. You simply assign a value, using `&` to stick the strings together with the variable `DogAge`.

Manipulating Server Control Properties

Properties and methods are the primary ways you work with server controls on your page. So, understanding which properties and methods are available for each control helps you understand what you can do with the controls. I spend the next few chapters helping you do just that.

But before I dive into each control and its members, you should know a few things about properties and giving them values. Not all of them work as simply as the `label` control's `Text` property. But after you get the hang of these few variations, you can work with any property on any control without trouble!

Don't skip these sections; otherwise, you might be baffled by the different ways properties are handled in subsequent chapters.

Changing properties in code and in the tag

To assign a value to a property from ASP.NET 2.0 code, you simply refer to the server control object by its name (specified in the `id` attribute of the server control tag), and to the appropriate property name. So to set the `Message` label's `Text` property you write this:

```
Message.Text = "Hello There!"
```

You can also specify a value for a server control's property in one other place: in the tag itself. For example, if you want the `Message` label to start out holding the text `"I'll calculate your age in dog-years"`, just change the server control tag to look like this:

```
<asp:label id="Message" runat="server"
text="I'll calculate your age in dog-years" />
```

You can specify almost any property of a server control either way. Put the property in the tag if you want it to come up that way first on the page. Change the property in the code (an event subroutine, for example) if you want to manipulate it based on user input.

In VWDE, setting the properties of a control using the Properties window is exactly the same as setting its attributes in the tag. In fact, if you change a control property and switch to Source view, you'll see that the attribute has been added to the corresponding tag.

Using enumeration properties to assign values

When you're working with the tag, you can almost always assign a string value to a property that will be interpreted correctly. For example, to set the color of a label's text to red, you change the tag to look like this:

```
<asp:label id="Message" runat="server" forecolor="Red"
text="I'm so embarrassed!"/><br>
```

So, your natural inclination would be to change the property in code by using a line like this:

```
' Sorry - this doesn't work!
Message.ForeColor = "Red"
```

Unfortunately, this line of code doesn't work. Instead, you have to assign a special value that represents the color red to the ForeColor property when you're setting it from code.

However, you don't have to remember some complex number that represents the color red every time you want to set a color. Instead, the .NET Framework provides objects with a special kind of property called an *enumeration*. Enumerations are properties that hold a specific value that you'll commonly need to use. The values for colors, for example, are stored in an object called Drawing.Color. So, if you want to set the foreground color of Message to red, you do it this way:

```
Message.ForeColor = Drawing.Color.Red
```

Of course, the Drawing.Color object has values for blue, green, and many, many other colors you might need. (For more information, see Chapter 12.)

Enumeration property values

If you're using Visual Web Developer 2005 Express, you can use the Properties window to change properties. Whether in Design view or Source view, you just click the server control you want to change and then change the property value in the Properties window. If the property accepts an enumeration, you often can select the options from a drop-down list box. Or, in the case of colors, you can just type the name of the color.

Changing property values by using the Property window is exactly the same as setting the property in HTML. (In fact, when you use the Property window, the server control tag in the Source view is immediately updated.) So any values you set determine the look and behavior of that control when it first appears on the page. For more information on using the Property window, see Chapter 4.

I refer to objects that have enumeration properties as *enumeration objects.* Enumeration objects are everywhere in the .NET Framework. As I show you different properties that use enumeration values in the coming chapters, I always provide the name of the enumeration object and a list of its common enumeration properties for you to use.

Using enumeration object methods

Some enumeration objects, such as `Drawing.Color`, also offer *methods* to help in assigning a value to a property — for example:

```
Message.ForeColor = Drawing.Color.FromARGB(255,255,255)
```

`FromARGB` is a method that enables you to specify a color by indicating the amount of red, green, and blue you want mixed in, each on a scale of 0 to 255. For more information on `FromARGB`, see Chapter 12.

Working with subobject properties

Some server controls have properties that are actually objects themselves. In Chapter 8, I describe how you access an object that's inside another object: You simply use dot notation. For example, to set a label's font to bold, you use the `Bold` property of the `Font` object that's inside a `label` server control. If the `label` control is named `MyLabel`, your code should look like this:

```
MyLabel.Font.Bold = True
```

But it works a little differently for server control tags. Here's an example of setting the font to bold in the tag itself:

```
<asp:label id="MyLabel" runat="server"
font-bold="true" Text="I'm FLASHY!"/><br>
```

Here, you use the subobject name and its property name together, separated by a *dash*. This example demonstrates how you handle all subobject properties in server control tags.

Chapter 11

Turning the Page

● ●

● ●

*I*n this chapter, I introduce you to a couple common problems and confusing situations that you can get yourself into with Web Forms. Then, I show you the slick features ASP.NET 2.0 offers to handle those situations. It all starts with the `Page` object.

Page Me!

The `Page` object represents not just a single control, but the whole Web page. The `Page` object — like any object — has its own properties and methods. It also has an event or two that you'll find helpful. The following sections demonstrate how the `Page` object helps you solve a common problem that you're likely to encounter.

The first topic I discuss is the `Page_Load` event. As its name implies, this is an event that is associated with the page itself and occurs when the page is retrieved. I'll demonstrate a common problem, initializing server controls, and show you how to use the event to solve it.

The second topic is related to page variables and how they are used and accessed from one server round-trip to the next. It doesn't work like you'd expect!

The problem: Initializing controls with a function

When a page is first retrieved, often its controls are blank — ready for the user to enter her own information. Initialization means setting a control to a default value that appears when the page is first retrieved. Default values mean the user doesn't have to type in typical responses.

To set a control's default value, you can simply add the value to the tag, as demonstrated in Chapter 10. Here's an example:

```
<asp:textbox id="Country" runat="server"
text="USA"/>
```

When the page is displayed, this text box appears with USA already in it. Users can then leave it alone or change it if they like.

However, initialization is not always that simple. You can only initialize controls using tag attributes with static values. If you want to call a function or do a calculation to determine the default value, you have to find another way. As an example, suppose that you're creating a page on which people can register the software they just bought from your company. The registration page asks all the familiar stuff — name, e-mail address, product purchased, and so on. But your problem comes when asking for the purchase date. Because most people register their software right away (if they register it at all), using today's date as the default for this text box makes sense. Then, even if the purchase date was yesterday or the day before, users can easily change the value in the text box. But how do you use today's date as the default value? To initialize the textbox with the current date, you need to use the VB 2005 function `Today()`. But where do you call the function? The answer is the `Page_Load` event, which I conveniently discuss in the following section.

Why can't you just use the `<%=` syntax in the server control to call the function? Remember that server control tags are *not* HTML tags. Server control tags are evaluated and created on the server long before the `<%=...%>` code on the page is evaluated. So the following code doesn't work:

```
<!-- This doesn't work! -->
<asp:textbox id="DatePurchased" runat="server"
text=<%=Today%>/>
```

If you try this approach, you get an error message that looks like this:

```
Server tags cannot contain <% ... %> constructs.
```

The solution: Using the Page_Load event

The problem I describe in the preceding section has a solution, and it lies in the Page object. The Page object has an event called Page_Load. Page_Load is the *first* event triggered when a page is retrieved, and it's triggered *every* time the page is loaded.

The example in Listing 11-1 demonstrates how you can use the Page_Load event to fix the problem I present in the preceding section.

Listing 11-1: Initializing the Date Purchased

```
<%@ Page Explicit="True" Language="VB" Debug="True" %>
<html>
<script runat="server">
Sub Page_Load(Sender As Object, E As EventArgs)
DatePurchased.Text = Today
End Sub
</script>
<body>
<h1>Software Registration Form</h1>
<form runat="server">
Name:<br><asp:textbox id="Name" runat="server"/><br>
E-mail:<br><asp:textbox id="Email" runat="server"/><br>
Product:<br><asp:textbox id="Product" runat="server"/><br>
Date Purchased:<br>
<asp:textbox id="DatePurchased" runat="server"/><br>
<asp:button text="OK" runat="server"/>
</form>
</body>
</html>
```

This code produces a form that looks like Figure 11-1.

The Page_Load event is similar to the button's onclick event. It is triggered at a particular time and enables you to write a subroutine that will execute in response to it. And, like the onclick event, it accepts the Sender and E as arguments. (For more information on the button's onclick event, see Chapter 10.)

However, the onclick and Page_Load events differ in a couple ways:

✔ Page_Load isn't triggered directly by something the user does. The system triggers this event when it loads the page to be processed. (Yeah, yeah, technically, you could say that the user requested the page and thus caused the system to process the page, but I did say *directly.*)

✔ You can give any name to the subroutine triggered from a button's `onclick` event. You just have to specify that name as the value for the `asp:button onclick` attribute. `Page_Load` isn't specified in any tag's attribute. It must always have the name `Page_Load`, and it's automatically triggered (if you've written a subroutine with that name) when the page is loaded.

The `Page_Load` event is a perfect place to initialize the `textbox` with values that you couldn't enter in the tag itself — as in this case. It's also a good place to do any general preparation or startup stuff you want done before the rest of the page executes. However, the example in Listing 11-1 does still have one more problem. I describe the problem and its solution in the next section.

Figure 11-1:
The Software Registration Form has a date that defaults to the current day.

Page_Load: Is it triggered the first time or every time?

The example that I present in the preceding section has a small problem: The information that gets submitted isn't always the information the user entered. To see this problem, change the example to look like Listing 11-2, adding the parts in bold.

Listing 11-2:   Checking the Information Entered

```
<%@ Page Explicit="True" Language="VB" Debug="True" %>
<html>
<script runat="server">
Sub Page_Load(Sender As Object, E As EventArgs)
DatePurchased.Text = Today
End Sub

Sub OK_Click(Sender As Object, E As EventArgs)
Header.Text="You Entered:"
LabelName.Text = Name.Text
LabelEmail.Text = Email.Text
LabelProduct.Text = Product.Text
LabelDatePurchased.Text = DatePurchased.Text
End Sub
</script>
<body>
<h1>Software Registration Form</h1>
<form runat="server">
Name:<br><asp:textbox id="Name" runat="server"/><br>
Email:<br><asp:textbox id="Email" runat="server"/><br>
Product:<br><asp:textbox id="Product" runat="server"/><br>
Date Purchased:<br>
<asp:textbox id="DatePurchased" runat="server"/><br>
<asp:button text="OK" runat="server"
onclick="OK_Click" /><br>
<asp:label id="Header" runat="server" /><br>
<asp:label id="LabelName" runat="server"/><br>
<asp:label id="LabelEmail" runat="server"/><br>
<asp:label id="LabelProduct" runat="server"/><br>
<asp:label id="LabelDatePurchased" runat="server"/><br>
</form>
</body>
</html>
```

When you try out the page, fill in all the information, but change the date. Now click the OK button. After you click, all the information is displayed below the OK button with one small error: The date you entered is changed *back* to the current date. In fact, if you look back up at the text boxes, the value has been changed there, too! What's going on?

Well, when you click the OK button, the page is actually loaded again on the server. When the page is loaded again, because a button is clicked or some other event occurs, it's referred to as a *post back*. But regardless of whether this is the first time the page was requested or this a post back, the Page_Load event is the first thing that happens. So, regardless of what you type into the DatePurchased text box, the current date always overwrites it.

What you *really* want to do is set DatePurchased to Today only the *first* time the page is loaded. Fortunately, you can easily determine whether this is the first time the page is loaded.

Change the Page_Load subroutine to look like Listing 11-3.

Listing 11-3: Checking Page.IsPostBack

```
Sub Page_Load(Sender As Object, E As EventArgs)
If Page.IsPostBack=False Then
   DatePurchased.Text = Today
End If
End Sub
```

This time, the page should work as you expect it to, retaining the value in the date when you click OK.

IsPostBack is a property of the Page that holds a Boolean value (either True or False). The first time a page is loaded, IsPostBack is set to False. Every time the page *returns* to the server to do something, such as executing the OK_Click subroutine, ASP.NET 2.0 automatically sets IsPostBack to True. So, you can use this value to find out whether this is the first time the page was loaded or whether this is a post-back.

In this case, the code checks to see whether IsPostBack is False — that is, whether this is the first time the page has been loaded. If it is, the code initializes the textbox with the current date. Later, when the OK button is clicked, IsPostBack will be True, and the initialization line won't execute again.

Here's another way to do the same thing:

```
If Not Page.IsPostBack Then
```

Because IsPostBack is a Boolean variable, you can use it directly in an If...Then statement without the =True part, if you like. But in this case, the Not reverses the Boolean value, so the statements inside the If...Then are only executed if IsPostBack is false. So, this works exactly like the code in Listing 11-3.

It's a common approach, and a very good idea, to include all your preparation and initialization code inside an If statement that checks for IsPostBack=False (or Not IsPostBack) in the Page_Load event.

Making Your Head Spin with Server Round-Trips

When you create page variables and then try to access them in the various event subroutines on your page, you may find that the value seems to get reset every time there's a round-trip to the server. In this section I describe how to deal with this problem and, in the process, I introduce you to a handy feature of ASP.NET 2.0 called `ViewState`.

A puzzling example: The no-count counter

Listing 11-4 demonstrates how page variables get reset every time the page makes a round-trip to the server. This code initializes a variable called `Counter` to 1 and displays it on the page with a `label` control. Then, each time you click a button, the counter is increased by 1 and then displayed. At least, that's the way it's supposed to work.

Listing 11-4:   The No-Count Counter

```
<%@ Page Explicit="True" Language="VB" Debug="True" %>
<html>
<script runat="server">
Dim Counter As Integer

Sub Page_Load(Sender As Object, E As EventArgs)
If Not IsPostBack Then
    Counter = 1
    ShowCounter.Text = Counter
End If
End Sub

Sub PushMe_Click(Sender As Object, E As EventArgs)
Counter = Counter + 1
ShowCounter.Text = Counter
End Sub
</script>
<body>
<form runat="server">
Counter: <asp:label id="ShowCounter" runat="server" /><br>
<asp:button id="PushMeButton" text="Push Me"
runat="server" onclick="PushMe_Click"/><br>
</form>
</body>
</html>
```

Here's what you see when you show this page in your browser:

```
Counter: 1
```

Under this label is a button labeled Push Me. Push the button. Nothing happens. Push it again. Still nothing. What happened? Why doesn't the counter's value increase by 1 each time? Although Counter is a page-level variable and is accessible from all of the code on the page, its value resets each time the page returns to the server.

The body of the page in Listing 11-4 includes a label and a button — nothing special.

At the top of the page, Counter is declared as a global variable (see Chapter 7 for more information on global, local, and body variables):

```
<script runat="server">
Dim Counter As Integer
. . .
```

Now, a global variable should be available to be used anywhere on the page — in a subroutine or function inside the <script> section or in the body of the page. So, in the Page_Load event, you give the Counter variable a value:

```
Sub Page_Load(Sender As Object, E As EventArgs)
If Not Page.IsPostBack Then
   Counter = 1
   ShowCounter.Text = Counter
End If
End Sub
```

You want the code to set Counter to 1 only the first time the page is loaded, so you enclose it inside an If Not Page.IsPostBack Then statement (see the preceding section).

Now the page appears in the browser for the first time. The user sees it and pushes the button. The button is associated with the PushMe_Click subroutine. So the page returns to the server to execute it:

```
Sub PushMe_Click(Sender As Object, E As EventArgs)
Counter = Counter + 1
ShowCounter.Text = Counter
End Sub
```

So what's wrong? All is revealed in the next section.

Discovering the answer to the mystery

Global variables *are* accessible from anywhere on the page. I don't lie to you. However, global variables do *not* remember their value from one round-trip to the server to the next.

When the page is first requested, the value for the `Counter` variable is set in the `Page_Load` event and displayed. That all happens in the *first* trip to the server. Clicking the button causes the page to go *back* to the server a second time. This time, the global variable is essentially *created anew* and has a value of `0`.

So when the `PushMe_Click` subroutine adds 1 to `Counter`, its new value is 1! This value is then displayed in the label. Likewise, every time the user clicks the button, the variable is re-created with the value `0`, its value is increased to `1`, and the page displays the value.

ViewState to the rescue

Your Web page contains a hidden field called `ViewState`. ASP.NET 2.0 uses `ViewState` to store all the information about the server controls on the page — not only their contents, but also whether they're enabled, what color they are, and so on. Then, when ASP.NET 2.0 is ready to create the page again on a future round-trip to the server, it has the information it needs. You can think of `ViewState` as the scrap paper on which ASP.NET 2.0 writes down everything it needs to remember about this page.

That's a very nice feature. And it all happens automatically. But, wouldn't it be nice if you could tap into that feature somehow to store the value of global variables you want your code to remember? Well, the good folks at Microsoft thought so, too.

In Listing 11-5, you can fix the problem by using `ViewState`. The lines you see in bold are new.

Listing 11-5:   Counting on ViewState

```
<%@ Page Explicit="True" Language="VB" Debug="True" %>
<html>
<script runat="server">
Dim Counter As Integer
```

(continued)

Listing 11-5 *(continued)*

```
Sub Page_Load(Sender As Object, E As EventArgs)
If Not Page.IsPostBack Then
    Counter = 1
    ShowCounter.Text = Counter
    ViewState("Counter") = Counter
End If
End Sub

Sub PushMe_Click(Sender As Object, E As EventArgs)
Counter = ViewState("Counter")
Counter = Counter + 1
ShowCounter.Text = Counter
ViewState("Counter") = Counter
End Sub
</script>
<body>
<form runat="server">
Counter: <asp:label id="ShowCounter" runat="server" /><br>
<asp:button id="PushMeButton" text="Push Me"
runat="server" onclick="PushMe_Click"/><br>
</form>
</body>
</html>
```

When you try this page, it should work as you'd expect.

To get ASP.NET 2.0 to store your values in the `ViewState` hidden field, you create `ViewState` variables. This works just like it does for the `Session` and `Application` variables I describe in Chapter 9. You create a new `ViewState` variable by simply choosing a name, putting it in quotes inside parentheses, and then assigning a value to it.

You can see this at the end of the `Page_Load` event. You store the global variable in a `ViewState` variable with the name `Counter`:

```
ViewState("Counter") = Counter
```

(The `ViewState` variable name doesn't have to match your global variable name, but if it does, it can help you keep things straight!) Then when you need it, you simply get it out, as you do first thing in the `PushMe_Click` subroutine:

```
Counter = ViewState("Counter")
```

If you had other event subroutines on the page where you wanted to use the `Counter` variable, you'd have to include this line at the top of each of them, too.

Finally, because you changed the value of the `Counter` global variable in the `PushMe_Click` subroutine, you need to store it back into the `ViewState` at the end of the subroutine so that it's remembered next time around:

```
ViewState("Counter") = Counter
```

As you can see, this solves the problem. The only catch is that you have to put the `ViewState` values back into their associated global variables at the top of any event subroutine where you want to use them. And if you change the global variable, you must be sure to put the value back into the `ViewState` variable.

An easier way to store and retrieve page variables in ViewState

The approach to the problem in the previous section works perfectly well. However, if you have quite a few event subroutines in which you use global variables, you're going to have to retrieve the global variables out of `ViewState` at the beginning of each subroutine and then put them all back in at the end of each subroutine. All this shuffling of information can become annoying! Wouldn't it be nice if you had one place where you could put all the global variables into `ViewState` and one place where you could get them all back out of `ViewState`? You do — check out Listing 11-6.

Listing 11-6:   Storing and Retrieving Variables from ViewState

```
<%@ Page Explicit="True" Language="VB" Debug="True" %>
<html>
<script runat="server">
Dim Counter As Integer
Dim StringVar As String
Dim SingleVar As Single

Sub Page_Load(Sender As Object, E As EventArgs)
If Not Page.IsPostBack Then
    Counter = 1
    StringVar = "Hello"
    SingleVar = 3.5
    ShowCounter.Text = Counter
    ShowStringVar.Text = StringVar
    ShowSingleVar.Text = SingleVar
Else
    Counter = ViewState("Counter")
    StringVar = ViewState("StringVar")
    SingleVar = ViewState("SingleVar")
```

(continued)

Listing 11-6 *(continued)*

```
End If
End Sub

Sub Page_PreRender(Sender As Object, E As EventArgs)
ViewState("Counter") = Counter
ViewState("StringVar") = StringVar
ViewState("SingleVar") = SingleVar
End Sub

Sub PushMe_Click(Sender As Object, E As EventArgs)
Counter = Counter + 1
StringVar = StringVar & "!"
SingleVar = SingleVar + 0.1
ShowCounter.Text = Counter
ShowStringVar.Text = StringVar
ShowSingleVar.Text = SingleVar
End Sub
</script>
<body>
<form runat="server">
Counter: <asp:label id="ShowCounter" runat="server" /><br>
StringVar: <asp:label id="ShowStringVar"
runat="server" /><br>
SingleVar: <asp:label id="ShowSingleVar"
runat="server" /><br>
<asp:button id="PushMeButton" text="Push Me"
runat="server" onclick="PushMe_Click"/><br>
</form>
</body>
</html>
```

This is essentially the same page that I use in Listing 11-5, except that I add two global variables: `StringVar` and `SingleVar`. I also add labels to display the values and have changed the values in a noticeable way in the `PushMe_Click` subroutine. I added them to show that this solution can work for a whole group of global variables. When you try the page, you see that all the values are updated each time you click the button.

When the page is first requested, the following process kicks off:

1. The `Page_Load` event is triggered, and `Page.IsPostBack` is false. This causes the code inside the `If Not IsPostBack Then` statement to execute, initializing the global variables.

2. Just before the page is sent to the browser, the `Page_PreRender` event is triggered. (This event is associated with the page, and it happens *after* all the other server control events are done and *before* the page is sent off to the browser. What a perfect opportunity to save off all the global variables into `ViewState`!)

3. The page is created and sent to the browser. The user clicks the button.

4. The `Page_Load` event is triggered, and `Page.IsPostBack` is true, which causes the code inside the `Else` part of the `If` statement to execute. Here, all the information in `ViewState` is pulled out and put into the appropriate global variables.

5. The `PushMe_Click` event happens. Here, I can use, display, and even change the value of global variables without worrying about them being preserved. (That's true for all the other events that you'd put on a page, too.) After this structure is in place, the events can simply assume that the global variables are available anytime, anywhere.

6. The `Page_PreRender` event happens just before the page is created and sent back to the browser. Any changes made in the global variables are stored safely in `ViewState`.

7. The page is created and sent to the browser. If the user clicks the button again, the process continues with Step 4 again.

Writing the code this way gets the global variables out once (before any event occurs) and puts them away once (after all other events are done). If you add a new global variable to the page, you have to remember to add entries in the `Page_Load` and `Page_PreRender` events to ensure that your page remembers the global variable.

Chapter 12

Basic Server Controls: Labels, Text Boxes, and Buttons

. . . .

In This Chapter

▶ Creating and manipulating the `label` server control

▶ Working with text boxes and their properties

▶ Pushing buttons

. . . .

*I*n this chapter, I take you through each of the important server controls individually so that I can show you all the cool stuff that's built in! But trust me — I don't give you a regurgitation of the documentation. Chapters 12 through 14 offer a quick survey, with liberal examples, showing all the important stuff. Nevertheless, if you're in a hurry, you can skim through the information in these chapters and come back to it later when you need the details.

Don't Label Me!

The humble label is one of the simpler server controls. It does nothing but display text. And, unlike the text box, the user can't mess with the text in the label. But that doesn't mean the label is boring — far from it! In the following sections, I explore some of the more interesting properties you can manipulate.

I explain the `Text` property of the `label` control in Chapter 10.

Adding a splash of color

The label has two important color properties. In fact, these same properties are available on most controls, and they work the same way for those controls as they do for labels:

✔ ForeColor: Holds the color of the text.

✔ BackColor: Holds the color of the background.

Setting colors in the server control tag

Here's an example that shows how you set a label's text and background colors:

```
<%@ Page Explicit="True" Language="VB" Debug="True" %>
<html>
<body>
<form runat="server">
<asp:label id="FlashyLabel" runat="server" forecolor="Red"
backcolor="Yellow" text="I'm FLASHY!"/><br>
</form>
</body>
</html>
```

When you try this page, you see the words I'm FLASHY! in the upper-left corner of your browser window — red text on a yellow background.

Setting colors in code with enumeration properties

You set the colors in the code by using string values in the server control tag. To do this, you have to use enumeration properties. (For more information on how enumeration properties work, see Chapter 10.) The values for colors are stored in an object called Drawing.Color. So, here's how you set the foreground color of FlashyLabel to red:

```
FlashyLabel.ForeColor = Drawing.Color.Red
```

You can't set the colors in code:

```
' Sorry - this doesn't work!
FlashyLabel.ForeColor = "Red"
FlashyLabel.BackColor = "Yellow"
```

Any time you need to specify a color in your code, you'll probably use the Drawing.Color object's enumerated properties. Table 12-1 lists some of the color properties available in that object. Because that object has well over a hundred color properties available, I don't list them all, but I do list the common ones. The words in parentheses after some colors mean that you can prefix those words on the color's name to give it a different nuance. So, Gray (Dark, Light, Dim) means that Gray, DarkGray, LightGray, and DimGray are all options.

Table 12-1	The Drawing.Color Object's Common Enumeration Color Properties	
Red (Dark, Indian, Orange, PaleViolet)	Green (Light, Dark, DarkOlive, Forest, Lawn, Lime, Pale, Yellow)	Black
Blue (Light, Dark, Medium, Alice, Cornflower, Dodger, Midnight, Powder, Royal)	SeaGreen (Light, Dark, Medium)	White (Floral, Ghost, Navajo)
SkyBlue (Deep, Light)	SpringGreen (Medium)	Gray (Light, Dark, Dim)
SlateBlue (Dark, Medium)	Cyan (Light, Dark)	SlateGray (Dark, Light)
SteelBlue (Light)	Salmon (Light, Dark)	Silver
Yellow (Light, Green, LightGoldenrod)	Pink (Light, Deep, Hot)	Brown (Rosy, Saddle, Sandy)
Purple (Medium)	Beige	Tan
Violet (Blue, Dark)		

Setting colors in code with the FromARGB method

The `Drawing.Color` object provides another way for you to specify what color you want: the `FromARGB` method.

`FromARGB` works like you would if you were mixing a palette of red, green, and blue paints together — the higher the number (up to 255), the more paint you use. A little red and no green or blue (100,0,0) makes a dark red or maroon. No red but lots of blue and green (0,200,200) makes cyan. They don't mix exactly like paints do, though. For example, to get white, you mix all three colors together completely (255,255,255). Likewise, mixing nothing (0,0,0) makes black. This example shows how to change a label's text color to gray:

```
' Give FlashyLabel's text a gray color
FlashyLabel.ForeColor =
        Drawing.Color.FromARGB(128,128,128)
```

Settling a border dispute

Like the color properties, the border properties aren't specific to the label. These properties are available on most of the server controls:

✔ `BorderStyle`: Style of border.

✔ `BorderColor`: Color of the border.

BorderColor works just like the other color properties that I describe in the earlier section, "Adding a splash of color."

BorderStyle has its own set of enumerated properties. To make this one easy to remember, the object holding the enumerated properties is called BorderStyle. So, if you want a red-on-yellow label with a green-dotted border, you can do it this way in the tag:

```
<asp:label id="FlashyLabel" runat="server" ForeColor="Red"
BackColor="Yellow" BorderColor="Green"
          BorderStyle="Dotted"
Text="I'm FLASHY!"/><br>
```

Or, you can do it this way in code:

```
FlashyLabel.ForeColor = Drawing.Color.Red
FlashyLabel.BackColor = Drawing.Color.Yellow
FlashyLabel.BorderColor = Drawing.Color.Green
FlashyLabel.BorderStyle = BorderStyle.Dotted
```

BorderStyle offers lots of fun possibilities. You can set it to any of the following enumeration values:

✔ Dashed

✔ Dotted

✔ Double

✔ None

✔ NotSet

✔ Solid

You can even give your page a more 3D look with these options for BorderStyle:

✔ Inset: Inset border, sunken control.

✔ Outset: Outset border, raised control.

✔ Groove: Grooved, sunken border.

✔ Ridge: Ridged, raised border.

Finding the font of youth

A *font* is the typeface of your text. It determines whether your text looks simple and readable or extravagant and outlandish. The Font object is built into the label control (and pretty much every other control that can display text).

You can use the properties of the Font object to determine exactly what the text in the label will look like. Here's a list of the important Font properties:

- ✔ Names: A list of one or more names identifying the typeface you want to use. The browser uses the first one in the list that it finds on the computer where the browser is running. Common typefaces are Arial, Times New Roman, and Courier New.
- ✔ Size: The size of the text.
- ✔ Bold, Italic, Underline: True/false settings indicating whether you want those styles added to the text.

To access the property of a subobject from a server control tag, you use a dash between the subobject name and the property within the subobject. (For more information on setting subobject properties, see Chapter 8.) Here's an example:

```
<asp:label id="FlashyLabel" runat="server"
font-names="Arial" font-size="30pt" font-bold="true"
Text="I'm FLASHY!"/><br>
```

This technique works whenever you're assigning a value to the property of a subobject in a server control tag.

To assign these values in code, the Bold, Underline, Italic, and Names properties work as you'd expect them to:

```
FlashyLabel.Font.Bold = True
FlashyLabel.Font.Underline = True
FlashyLabel.Font.Italic = True
FlashyLabel.Font.Names = "Arial"
```

But assigning the Font object's Size property is a little trickier. You use an enumeration object called FontUnit. Just as when you're assigning colors, you have two different options: enumeration properties or a method. The following line is an example of using the enumeration property:

```
FlashyLabel.Font.Size = FontUnit.Large
```

Options for the enumerated properties are XXSmall, XSmall, Smaller, Small, Medium, Large, Larger, XLarge, and XXLarge. You also can use these values inside quotes when specifying the size in the server control tag:

```
<asp:label id="FlashyLabel" runat="server"
font-names="Arial" font-size="Smaller" font-bold="true"
Text="I'm FLASHY!"/><br>
```

Another option for specifying the size in code is to use the Point method:

```
FlashyLabel.Font.Size = FontUnit.Point(12)
```

This example sets the text in the label to a size of 12 points.

Font is a subobject — a property of an object, like a label, that is, itself, an object with its own properties. In VWDE, subobjects like Font appear as a single entry in your Properties window with a + beside them. If you click the plus sign, the Font opens up, and you see all its properties beneath it, such as Name, Size, Bold, Underline, and so on. You can then set them as you would any other property. For more information on the Property window, see Chapter 4.

Sizing up your label with the Height and Width properties

The Height and Width properties set the size of the label. You don't usually have to mess with these settings directly because when you set the size of your label's font to something large, the size of the label expands to fit it.

But if you ever do need to resize the label, you must set both Height and Width by using an enumeration object method. The object's name is Unit. The methods you can use are Pixel (to give it a size in pixels) or Point (to give it a size in points). For example:

```
MyLabel.Height = Unit.Pixel(50)
MyLabel.Width = Unit.Pixel(100)
```

These lines change the size of the label to 50 x 100 pixels.

ToolTip: Don't run with scissors

A ToolTip is a little yellow box that appears with a helpful description in it when your mouse pointer hovers over something on the screen for a second or two. Not-so-coincidentally, the Label provides a property named ToolTip, which allows you to specify the text that appears in the little yellow box. You usually see ToolTips used with toolbar buttons, but you can use them with nearly any control — even a label:

```
<asp:label id="FlashyLabel" runat="server"
tooltip="This is one flashy label, no doubt!"
Text="I'm FLASHY!"/><br>
```

Now when you hover over the label, the little yellow ToolTip box appears with your text in it. This tool is simple, yet potentially quite informative. For an example of using ToolTips with text boxes, see "The TextBox's TextChanged event and AutoPostBack property," later in this chapter.

The Enabled and Visible properties

The `Enabled` and `Visible` properties contain simple *Boolean* values — they take a value of either `true` or `false`. However, these little values have a big impact on your control.

`Visible` is `true` by default. When you set it to `false`, the control seems to disappear off the page. The user can't see or interact with the control when it isn't visible. You can set it back to visible by assigning `true` to the property.

`Enabled` determines whether the visitor to your site can use the control. It is `true` by default, but when you set it to `false`, the control is visible, but dead. The effect is much clearer on a text box: The user simply can't enter any text. But for a label, the effect is subtler: Any text inside the label simply turns gray. If you use a label to prompt the user to enter information in a nearby text box, setting the label's `Enabled` property to `false` at the same time you set the textbox's `Enabled` property to `false` gives users an extra visual clue that they can't use the text box right now (because both the text box and its label are grayed out).

Shadowboxing? No, Text Boxing!

The text box is probably the most commonly used server control. It enables users to enter small amounts of text, such as a first name, or large amounts of text, such as a description of a car for sale. In this section, you discover the more important text box properties and how to use them in your own Web applications.

All the label-related properties that I describe in the previous sections — for example, how to manipulate the color, border, font, and so on — are available on the text box as well, and they work in just the same way. So, if you want information on those properties, see the previous sections in this chapter. I cover them in this section only if they work differently or if you use them differently with a text box.

You can find out about the `Text` property of the `textbox` control in Chapter 10.

He's only half illiterate — He's ReadOnly

By assigning a value of `true` or `false` to `ReadOnly`, you indicate whether the user can edit the text box (`false`) or not (`true`). By default, `ReadOnly` is `false`.

If you find yourself using `ReadOnly` in the server control tag, ask yourself whether you really want a label.

If you want the text box to be `ReadOnly` at some times and not at others, think about using the `Enabled` property instead. The `Enabled` property grays out the control so that the user knows the text box is unavailable. `ReadOnly` does not.

Put TabIndex A in SlotIndex B

If you have a form that includes lots of controls, users can click each one in turn to get around the page, if they like. But most users prefer to use the Tab key to jump from one control to the next if they already have their fingers on the keyboard.

The computer determines the order of the controls as the user presses the Tab key based on the order in which you created the controls. It's likely that the order of creation won't be exactly what you want the order of the Tab key movements to be. That's where the `TabIndex` property comes in.

You can set the `TabIndex` property to any integer value. The value for any individual control isn't so important. What's important is where that value falls in the list of `TabIndex` values for all the other controls on the page. When the user presses the Tab key, the cursor jumps to the control with the next highest `TabIndex`. So, if you have three controls — A, B, and C — that have `TabIndex` values of 5, 10, and 1 respectively, the cursor starts out on C, jumps to A when the user presses Tab, and then jumps to B when the user presses Tab again.

The many faces of the TextMode property

The text box is a flexible control. The `TextMode` property has three different possible values that enable you to create three very different kinds of text boxes. To specify these values, `TextMode` uses an enumeration object named `TextBoxMode`. The following bullet list tells you about the three enumeration values you can assign to `TextMode` and the kinds of text boxes that are created as a result:

✔ `SingleLine`: A text box designed to get a single word or a single line of text. `SingleLine` is the default value of `TextMode`.

✔ `Password`: A special kind of single-line text box that causes the characters to come up looking like asterisks. This keeps Nosy Ned from reading a password over your user's shoulder as she enters it. (Another option

> for accepting user IDs and passwords is the Login control, which I discuss in Chapter 22.)
>
> ✔ MultiLine: A text box for entering multiple lines of text, like a memo field.

In the next two sections, I show examples of the single-line text box and the multiple-line text box, and I point out important properties to keep in mind.

SingleLine size matters with the MaxLength and Columns properties

If you're working with a SingleLine text box, a couple properties are important for sizing: MaxLength and Columns.

By setting the MaxLength property to an integer value, you limit the number of characters that users can enter. If you don't set it (or you set it to 0), users can enter any number of characters in the text box. If you set this property, you usually do it in the control tag:

```
<asp:textbox id="UserName" runat="server"
maxlength="8"/><br>
```

Likewise, you can set the Columns property to any integer. This value determines how long the text box is — that is, how much space it takes up on the page.

So, if you set Columns to 20 and Maxlength to 40, what happens? When you type in the text box, it begins to scroll sideways until you get to the maximum length. Try it out!

```
<%@ Page Explicit="True" Language="VB" Debug="True" %>
<html>
<body>
<form runat="server">
<asp:textbox id="Name" runat="server"
columns="20" maxlength="40" />
</form>
</body>
</html>
```

Now try reversing it: Give Columns a value of 40 and Maxlength a value of 20. Although the text box takes up lots of room, you can use only about half of it to enter text!

Multiple-line text boxes

The third option for the TextMode property is the MultiLine enumeration, which enables you to create a memo-like text field for entering several lines of information all at once. Give it a try:

```
<%@ Page Explicit="True" Language="VB" Debug="True" %>
<html>
<body>
<form runat="server">
<asp:textbox id="Memo" runat="server"
textmode="multiline" /><br>
</form>
</body>
</html>
```

This page produces a two-line text box with a scroll bar along the right side. Try typing some text. When you get to the end of a line, the text box automatically wraps words down to the next line. If you type more than two lines, it begins scrolling up.

Just as with the single-line text box, you can use the Columns property to set the width. You also can use a Rows property to set the height. Change the text box line in the preceding code to look like this:

```
<asp:textbox id="Memo" runat="server"
textmode="multiline" columns="40" rows="10" /><br>
```

This makes the multiline text box much bigger.

The TextBox's TextChanged event and AutoPostBack property

In Chapter 10, I demonstrate a way to capture the button's click event so that you can write a subroutine that will react intelligently. The text box also has an event that you can capture. It's called TextChanged.

The TextChanged event happens when the user changes the text in the text box and then presses Tab or uses the mouse to click elsewhere.

Listing 12-1 demonstrates using the TextChanged event to automatically enable or disable other text boxes, as appropriate.

Listing 12-1:   Using TextChanged and AutoPostBack

```
<%@ Page Explicit="True" Language="VB" Debug="True" %>
<html>
<script runat="server">
Sub HaveCell_TextChanged(Sender As Object, E As EventArgs)
If HaveCell.Text <> "yes" Then
   LabelCellPhone.Enabled = False
   CellPhone.Enabled = False
   CellPhone.ToolTip = "No Cell Phone"
```

```
Else
    LabelCellPhone.Enabled = True
    CellPhone.Enabled = True
    CellPhone.ToolTip = "Please enter your cell phone
            number"
End If
End Sub
</script>
<body>
<h1>Add Phonebook Entry</h1>
<form runat="server">
<asp:label id="LabelName" text="Name"
runat="server"/><br>
<asp:textbox id="Name" runat="server"
tooltip="Please enter your name"
tabindex="10"/><br>

<asp:label id="LabelHomePhone" text="Home Phone"
runat="server"/><br>
<asp:textbox id="HomePhone" runat="server"
tooltip="Please enter your home phone number"
tabindex="20"/><br>

<asp:label id="LabelHaveCell"
text="Do you have a cell phone?"
runat="server"/><br>
<asp:textbox id="HaveCell" runat="server"
tooltip="Do you have a cell phone? Answer yes or no."
ontextchanged="HaveCell_TextChanged"
autopostback="true" tabindex="30"/><br>

<asp:label id="LabelCellPhone" text="Cell Phone"
runat="server"/><br>
<asp:textbox id="CellPhone" runat="server"
tooltip="Please enter your cell phone number"
tabindex="40"/><br>

</form>
</body>
</html>
```

When you try this page, it looks much like Figure 12-1.

Before you type anything, allow your mouse pointer to hover over each of the text boxes. You should see the text specified for ToolTip for each one. These handy ToolTips give the user more information about what to enter than you've provided on the page.

Next, begin entering a name and home phone for someone. When you get to the question about a cellphone, type **no** and then press Tab or click in another text box. The page returns to the server. Because of the value specified in ontextchanged in the HaveCell text box, the server executes the

`HaveCell_TextChanged` subroutine. In doing so, it notices what you've entered for the cellphone question and therefore disables the cellphone text box. It even changes the cellphone text box's ToolTip.

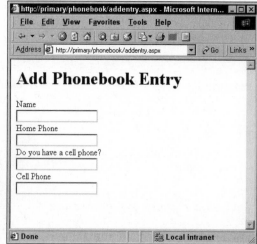

Figure 12-1:
The Add
Phonebook
Entry page.

If you try typing something else in the `HaveCell` text box, it goes back to the server each time you move the cursor away. This happens because you set the `AutoPostBack` property of the `HaveCell` text box to `true`. If you didn't set this property to `true`, the page would not return to the server when you move the cursor away and it wouldn't immediately trigger the `TextChanged` event.

So, whenever you want to capture the `TextChanged` event, you must set the `AutoPostBack` property to `True`; otherwise, the event on the server will not be executed right away. This is true for text box events, drop-down list box events, and the events of many other controls. The only control event that automatically goes back to the server when it's triggered (without having an `autopostback` property set to `true`) is the `button` control's `Click` event.

Of course, the only way to get the `CellPhone` text box enabled again is by typing **yes** in the `HaveCell` text box and then pressing the Tab key.

You might have noticed that the code in the subroutine disables *both* the text box and the label. I do this so the label appears grayed out and offers a visual cue to the users, indicating that they can't use the associated text box.

Finally, I set the `TabIndex` property for each text box and numbered them by tens. Why? Simple — That leaves room to add new controls in the middle, if necessary, in later updates to this form.

Button, Button — Who's Got the Button?

The button is a very simple control. Its primary purpose in life is to kick off a process or make something happen.

All the properties that I describe for the label (see the "Don't Label Me!" section in this chapter) also apply to the button. Only a few are different enough to discuss here:

- ✔ `Height` and `Width`: Buttons need to stand out more than labels do. Giving buttons a consistent size, shape, and placement is often important to creating a clean, well-organized page. You can use the `Unit.Pixel` method to set a button's `Height` and `Width` properties in the code. But usually, you'll set these properties in the server control tag. You'd need to change these properties in code only in an unusual situation.

- ✔ `ToolTip`: Although you almost never use a `ToolTip` on a label, you will very often use them for buttons. If you have a button with only a graphic (as on a button bar) or with only one or two words on it, the `ToolTip` is a good place to provide some additional information about what the button does.

- ✔ `Text`: This property contains the text that appears on the button. Make the text clear, concise, and consistent. Go with the Windows standards of using OK and Cancel wherever appropriate, because people are used to seeing and responding to that.

- ✔ `Font`: You use the `Font` object to change the text that appears on the button. Typically, you should choose a font and size and use them consistently for all your buttons.

- ✔ `Enabled` and `Visible`: You will often use these properties with buttons. If a particular command is unavailable for some reason, you simply disable the associated button. Disabling a button is better than making it invisible. Seeing buttons appear and disappear can be confusing to the user.

Of course, the most important event in a button's life is its `Click` event:

```
<asp:button onclick="OK_Click"
text="OK" runat="server" />
```

It's customary to name the subroutine that's executed based on the button's ID and the event, separated by an underscore (`OK_Click`, for example). Although this is a good idea (to help keep your subroutines straight), it isn't required. Whatever you put inside the quotes assigned to the `onclick` attribute is the subroutine name that is executed when the `Click` event occurs.

The button doesn't have an `AutoPostBack` property. It doesn't need one. The button's `Click` event always triggers a round-trip to the server.

For examples that use the `button` server control, see Chapter 10 and the following sections in this chapter: "Adding a splash of color," and "The TextBox's TextChanged event and AutoPostBack property."

Chapter 13

Making a List Control (And Checking It Twice)

*I*f necessary, you could build a user interface with the labels, text boxes, and buttons that I describe in Chapter 12. But you'd have a tough time creating a really interesting or exciting user interface. Fortunately, those controls are only the beginning of your many options. In this chapter, I add several new options to your server control toy box: check boxes, radio buttons, list boxes, and drop-down lists.

Checking for Check Boxes

Check boxes give users a list of one or more possible options. The user can then select any or all options that apply — or leave them all deselected. Check boxes can provide an easy way for a user to answer a yes/no or an on/off or a true/false question.

The ASP.NET server controls provide two different ways to present check boxes to your user: the `CheckBox` control and the `CheckBoxList`. The `CheckBox` control provides a single check box whereas the `CheckBoxList` provides several check boxes together in a list.

A CheckBoxList example: Know your primes

You present check boxes to the user with the CheckBoxList server control. Listing 13-1 demonstrates how this control works.

Listing 13-1: Know Your Primes

```
<%@ Page Explicit="True" Language="VB" Debug="True" %>
<html>
<script runat="server">
Sub OK_Click(Sender As Object, E As EventArgs)
Dim ItemNum As Integer
Chose.Text = "You chose "
For ItemNum=0 To Primes.Items.Count - 1
   If Primes.Items(ItemNum).Selected = True Then
      Chose.Text = Chose.Text & _
         Primes.Items(ItemNum).Text & " "
   End If
Next
End Sub
</script>
<body>
<h1>Know Your Primes</h1>
Do you know what a prime number is? Simple!
It's any number that can't be divided by another
number (besides 1 and itself). For example, 4 is
not a prime number because you can divide it by
2. But 7 is prime because it can only be divided by 1
and 7.<br><br>
<form runat="server">
So which of the following numbers are prime
numbers?<br>
<asp:checkboxlist id="Primes" runat="server">
   <asp:listitem>2</asp:listitem>
   <asp:listitem>5</asp:listitem>
   <asp:listitem>18</asp:listitem>
   <asp:listitem>27</asp:listitem>
   <asp:listitem>149</asp:listitem>
</asp:checkboxlist>
<br>
<asp:button id="OKButton" text="OK" runat="server"
onclick="OK_Click" /><br>
<asp:label id="Chose" runat="server" /><br>
<asp:label id="RightOrWrong" runat="server" /><br>
</form>
</body>
</html>
```

When you try this page, your browser looks a lot like Figure 13-1.

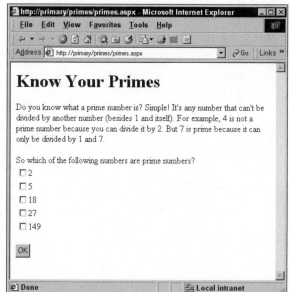

Figure 13-1:
The Know
Your Primes
page.

Try selecting a few of the check boxes, and then click the OK button. You see the label at the bottom of the page display a line that looks like this:

```
You chose 5 18 27
```

The `<asp:checkboxlist>` server control tag looks a little different from `<asp:textbox>` or `<asp:label>`:

```
<asp:checkboxlist id="Primes" runat="server">
   <asp:listitem>2</asp:listitem>
   <asp:listitem>5</asp:listitem>
   <asp:listitem>18</asp:listitem>
   <asp:listitem>27</asp:listitem>
   <asp:listitem>149</asp:listitem>
</asp:checkboxlist>
```

The `<asp:checkboxlist>` tag has an `id` and the ever-present `runat=`
`"server"`, but it also has another set of tags inside it: `<asp:listitem>`.
The `<asp:checkboxlist>` tag represents the whole list, and the `<asp:`
`listitem>` tags represent individual check boxes within the list. Inside each
`<asp:listitem>` tag is the text that will label the check box. In this case, a
number appears next to each check box, but you could just as easily use text,
including text with HTML tags.

The CheckBoxList in Visual Web Developer 2005 Express

VWDE provides a visual way of setting the items in your check box list. You can drag the `CheckBoxList` control from the Toolbox and drop it on your page or type the tag. Either way, click the `CheckBoxList` control and then go to the Property window. Scroll down to the `Items` property and click it. When you do, a tiny button with a "..." on it appears. Click the button, and you see the ListItem Collection Editor window appear. (See the figure.)

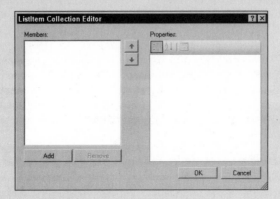

Now you can use the Add and Remove buttons to add and remove items from the list on the left. You can use the Up and Down buttons in the middle to change the order of the items in the list. And you can change the individual items by selecting the item on the left and then changing the item properties on the right.

The `RadioButtonList`, `ListBox`, and `DropDownList` controls (each of which I discuss in this chapter) all have an `Items` property and all work in the same way.

When the user clicks the button, the `OK_Click` subroutine is executed. (For more information on subroutines, see Chapter 7. For more information on event subroutines, see Chapter 10.) Take a look at the code in the `OK_Click` subroutine:

```
Sub OK_Click(Sender As Object, E As EventArgs)
Dim ItemNum As Integer
Chose.Text = "You chose "
For ItemNum=0 To Primes.Items.Count - 1
    If Primes.Items(ItemNum).Selected = True Then
        Chose.Text = Chose.Text & _
            Primes.Items(ItemNum).Text & " "
    End If
Next
End Sub
```

I refer to the list of check boxes as one control, named `Primes`. The `Primes` server control is a `CheckBoxList` and it contains an object called `Items`. `Items` is actually a *collection*. A collection is simply an object that contains several other objects, which you can access by number, like an array. (See Chapter 6 for more on arrays.) The `collection` object also typically has a few properties, including one called `Count`, which tells you how *many* objects are in the collection. So, in this case, the subroutine checks to see how many objects are in the collection and then loops through each object.

Like arrays and array lists, the items in a collection are numbered starting with 0 (zero). So, if `Primes.Items.Count` holds a value of 5, the items in that collection are numbered 0 through 4. That's why the loop goes from 0 to `Primes.Items.Count - 1`.

Each time through the loop, an `If...Then` statement checks the `Selected` property of the current item in the list. This property is `True` or `False`, indicating whether the check box for that item is selected. If it is selected, the `Text` property of this item (the number, in this case) is added to end of the `Chose.Text` string with a space following it.

Responding to the user's answer

The example in the preceding section demonstrates how to use check boxes, but it doesn't tell users whether they correctly guessed which numbers were prime! So, to provide a more complete example and to give you some tips on how to use control properties to interact with your users, here's a more complete Know Your Primes example.

Add the following highlighted code to the `OK_Click` subroutine in Listing 13-1:

```
    . . .
    End If
Next
If (Primes.Items(0).Selected = True) And _
    (Primes.Items(1).Selected = True) And _
    (Primes.Items(2).Selected = False) And _
    (Primes.Items(3).Selected = False) And _
    (Primes.Items(4).Selected = True) Then
        RightOrWrong.Text = "You are exactly right!"
        OKButton.Enabled = False
Else
    RightOrWrong.Text = "Nope. You got one or more wrong."
    OKButton.Text = "Try Again!"
End If
End Sub
</script>
```

Now try it. You see something that looks like this:

```
You chose 5 18 27
Nope. You got one or more wrong.
```

Also, the OK button's text has changed! Instead of OK, it now says `Try Again!` That prompts users to go ahead and change the check boxes and click the button again and again until they get it right:

```
You chose 2 5 149
You are exactly right!
```

And to ensure that users don't *continue* clicking the button after they get it right, the button is disabled.

Changing the `Text` and the `Enabled` properties of buttons on your page can help users understand their options as well as which options are available or not at different times.

Using common CheckBoxList properties

The `CheckBoxList` represents the whole group of check boxes. When you set properties for this object, they typically affect the list or all the individual check boxes. The `CheckBoxList` has a collection property called `Items`, which enables you to access all the individual check boxes. You can check or set the properties of individual check boxes through this collection.

In the following sections, I tell you about many of the common properties for `CheckBoxList`. (The earlier sections in this chapter tell you about the `Items(x).Selected` and `Items(x).Text` properties. You can also use the `Enabled`, `Visible`, `ToolTip`, `ForeColor`, `BackColor`, `BorderColor`, `BorderStyle`, `Font`, `Height`, `Width`, and `Visible` properties, which I cover in Chapter 12.)

TextAlign

The `TextAlign` property determines whether the text appears on the right or left side of the check box. The one you choose simply depends on the layout of your page and what you think looks best. Figure 13-2 shows two short lists: The first is `Right` aligned (the default), and the second is `Left` aligned. Remember that `Right` and `Left` refer to the *text,* not the check box.

Repeat after me . . .

The `RepeatColumns`, `RepeatDirection`, and `RepeatLayout` properties give you some flexibility and options when deciding how your check box list should look.

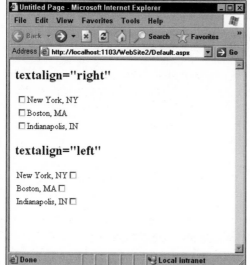

Figure 13-2:
Right-
aligned (the
default) and
left-aligned
CheckBox
Lists.

RepeatColumns determines how many columns you want to use for organizing the check boxes. ASP.NET 2.0 does the math to figure out how many items
should be in each column to balance it out. Here's an example:

```
<asp:checkboxlist id="States" runat="server"
repeatcolumns="3">
    <asp:listitem>1. Honda Accord</asp:listitem>
    <asp:listitem>2. Honda Civic</asp:listitem>
    <asp:listitem>3. Toyota RAV4</asp:listitem>
    <asp:listitem>4. BMW 3-Series</asp:listitem>
    <asp:listitem>5. Volkswagen Jetta</asp:listitem>
    <asp:listitem>6. Ford Escape</asp:listitem>
    <asp:listitem>7. Toyota Camry</asp:listitem>
</asp:checkboxlist>
```

Figure 13-3 shows the result.

If you use RepeatColumns, you can use the RepeatDirection and Repeat
Layout to fine-tune how your column are displayed. RepeatDirection
determines whether the check boxes are organized horizontally or vertically
within the columns you create. The default is vertical. That's what you
see in Figure 13-3. Figure 13-4 shows how the page differs if you add repeat
direction="horizontal" to the <asp:checkboxlist> tag.

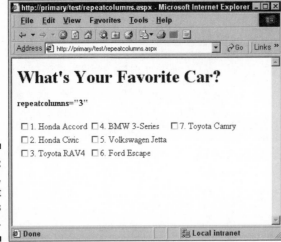

Figure 13-3:
For this list,
Repeat
Columns is
set to 3.

Figure 13-4:
The check
boxes from
Figure 13-3
now have
Repeat
Direction
set to
horizontal.

By default, an HTML table organizes your check boxes into neat rows and columns. That's why the check boxes in Figures 13-3 and 13-4 look so tidy. However, you can turn this off, if you want. That's what the RepeatLayout property does. You can set it to one of two values: table (the default) or flow. Figure 13-5 shows what setting repeatlayout to "flow" does to the appearance.

CellPadding and CellSpacing

CheckBoxList organizes the individual check boxes into an invisible HTML table to help lay them out appropriately. HTML tables have two attributes that control how the content in them is spaced out: CellPadding and

CellSpacing. These attributes appear as properties on the CheckBoxList control. They work like this: Each cell in a table is a box that contains one check box and its associated text. CellPadding determines how big that box is and thus how much space exists around the check box and text. CellSpacing, on the other hand, determines how far apart each box is from the other boxes (or cells) in the table.

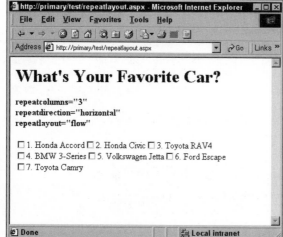

Figure 13-5:
The check boxes have RepeatLay-out set to flow.

Because you can't actually see the table when using the CheckBoxList control, CellPadding and CellSpacing both end up having the net effect of moving your check boxes farther away from each other.

AutoPostBack and SelectedIndexChanged

If you want respond with code in a subroutine immediately when the user changes a check box in the list, use the AutoPostBack property and the SelectedIndexChanged event. As with the textbox control, if AutoPost Back gets set to True, the page returns to the server every time the user makes a change to any of the check boxes in the list. This gives the server a chance to catch the SelectedIndexChanged event and then execute the subroutine you specify. Here's an example:

```
<asp:checkboxlist id="FavoriteFoods"
onselectedindexchanged="Favorite_Change"
autopostback="true" runat="server">
   <asp:listitem>T-Bone Steak</asp:listitem>
   <asp:listitem>Mashed Potatoes</asp:listitem>
   <asp:listitem>Broccoli</asp:listitem>
</asp:checkboxlist>
```

These foods appear as a list of check boxes. Whenever the user selects or deselects a box, the page returns to the server (because `autopostback` is set to `true`). When this happens, the server sees that a value has been set for `onselectedindexchanged` and then executes the `Favorite_Change` subroutine. For a complete example demonstrating the corresponding properties for a text box (which work exactly the same way), see the section on the `TextChanged` event and the `AutoPostBack` property in Chapter 12.

The CheckBox control

`CheckBoxList` is a great option if you want to ask users several yes/no or true/false questions. But in some cases, you might need to present the user with only one check box. In other cases, you might need to present several check boxes, but you want to control the formatting and HTML that appears between them. In those cases, using the individual `CheckBox` server control is usually easier. Listing 13-2 gives you an example.

Listing 13-2:   Electronic Newsletter Signup Page

```
<%@ Page Explicit="True" Language="VB" Debug="True" %>
<html>
<script runat="server">
Sub OK_Click(Sender As Object, E As EventArgs)
If Hollywood.Checked=True and Music.Checked=True Then
   Feedback.Text = "You subscribed to both. Thanks!"
ElseIf Hollywood.Checked=True Then
   Feedback.Text = _
      "You subscribed to Hollywood Gossip. Thanks!"
ElseIf Music.Checked=True Then
   Feedback.Text = "You subscribed to Music Gossip.
         Thanks!"
Else
   Feedback.Text = "You didn't subscribe to either!"
End If
End Sub
</script>
<body>
<h1>Sign Up For Our Electronic Newsletters</h1>
Are you sad because you don't receive enough junk in your
e-mail box? Let us help. Sign up for our electronic
newsletters and you'll get a full Inbox every day!<br><br>
<form runat="server">
<h2>Hollywood Gossip</h2>
Get all the dirt on all your favorite actors and
actresses.<br>
<asp:checkbox id="Hollywood" runat="server"
text="Sign Me Up For Hollywood Gossip!"/><br>
<h2>Music Gossip</h2>
Get all the dirt on all your favorite musicians.<br>
```

```
<asp:checkbox id="Music" runat="server"
text="Sign Me Up For Music Gossip!"/><br><br>
<asp:button id="OKButton" text="OK" runat="server"
onclick="OK_Click" /><br><br>
<asp:label id="Feedback" runat="server" /><br>
</form>
</body>
</html>
```

You can see the result in Figure 13-6.

Figure 13-6:
Electronic
Newsletter
Signup
page.

CheckBox is a pretty simple control. When you create it, you assign the text property, which becomes the label for the check box. Then, you look at the Checked property in your code to find out what the user chose.

Using common CheckBox properties

In this section, I highlight the important CheckBox control properties. Common properties of the CheckBox control include Text, Checked, and TextAlign properties (which I cover earlier in this chapter) as well as many of the properties that I discuss in Chapter 12 (namely, the Enabled, Visible, ToolTip, ForeColor, BackColor, BorderColor, BorderStyle, Font, Height, Width, Visible properties).

The next two sections focus on a couple properties that work a little differently with `CheckBox` than they do with `CheckBoxList`.

AutoPostBack and CheckChanged

The `AutoPostBack` property works for an individual check box the same way it does for the `CheckBoxList`. If `AutoPostBack` is set to `True`, then whenever the user changes the check box, the page returns to the server to see whether it needs to execute any events. *However,* the event name you need to capture for `CheckBox` differs from the one for `CheckBoxList`. With `CheckBoxList`, the event name was `SelectedIndexChanged`. With `CheckBox`, the event is `CheckChanged`. In this example, when the user changes the check box, the page returns to the server and executes the `Agree_Change` subroutine:

```
<asp:checkbox id="Agree"
Text="I agree to the terms stated above."
oncheckchanged="Agree_Change"
autopostback="true" runat="server"/>
```

Checked or selected?

You might have noticed another inconsistency between the `CheckBoxList` and `CheckBox` controls. If you want to see whether an item in a `CheckBoxList` has a check mark beside it, you use the `Selected` property:

```
If Primes.Items(ItemNum).Selected = True Then
```

But if you want to find out whether a `CheckBox` has a check mark beside it, you use the `Checked` property:

```
If Hollywood.Checked=True and Music.Checked=True Then
```

Why? I don't know. But this is also true of the `RadioButtonList` and `RadioButton` server controls, and it's important to remember!

Radio for Help on Radio Buttons

Radio buttons are very similar to check boxes. The only difference is that users may choose only one radio button in a list. This characteristic makes them ideal for multiple-choice questions.

A RadioButtonList example: More gazillionaire trivia

In Chapter 9, I show you an example of using HTML links and the `Query String` property to create a trivia question page and another page that tells you whether you got the question right. In this section, I show you how to use the `RadioButtonList` control to do the same thing in one simple page. Take Listing 13-3 for a spin around the browser.

Listing 13-3:   Gazillionaire Trivia, Version 2.0

```
<%@ Page Explicit="True" Language="VB" Debug="True" %>
<html>
<script runat="server">
Sub OK_Click(Sender As Object, E As EventArgs)
If Deadly.SelectedItem.Text = "Cowardice" Then
   Message.Text = "You're right! You really know your
          sins!"
   OKButton.Enabled = False
Else
   Message.Text = "No, sorry. " & Deadly.SelectedItem.Text
          & _
      " is one of the Seven Deadly Sins."
   OKButton.Text = "Try Again!"
End If
End Sub
</script>
<body>
<h1>So Ya Wanna Be A Gazillionaire</h1>
For one gazillion dollars, answer this question:<br><br>
<b>Which of the following is <i>not</i> one of the
Seven Deadly Sins?</b><br>
<form runat="server">
<asp:radiobuttonlist id="Deadly"
repeatcolumns="2" runat="server">
   <asp:listitem selected="true">Gluttony</asp:listitem>
   <asp:listitem>Greed</asp:listitem>
   <asp:listitem>Envy</asp:listitem>
   <asp:listitem>Cowardice</asp:listitem>
   <asp:listitem>Anger</asp:listitem>
</asp:radiobuttonlist><br>
<asp:button id="OKButton" text="OK" runat="server"
onclick="OK_Click" /><br><br>
<asp:label id="Message" runat="server" /><br>
</form>
</body>
</html>
```

You can see the result in Figure 13-7.

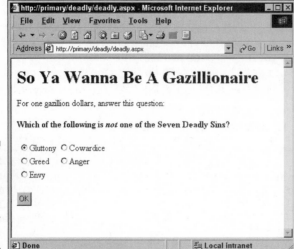

Figure 13-7:
Gazillionaire
trivia
question #2:
Know Your
Deadly Sins!

The `<asp:radiobuttonlist>` tag looks and works almost exactly like the `<asp:checkboxlist>` tag. The specific items are listed within the `<asp:radiobuttonlist>` tag using `<asp:listitem>`. The text in each list item is used to label each radio button.

In the first list item in this example, notice that `selected` is set to `"true"`. That's how you specify a default selected value for a list of radio buttons.

Always have a default radio button selected in a `RadioButtonList` control. Otherwise, you run the risk that the user won't pick *any* of the possibilities, and then you'll have to check for that possibility separately. If you start with a default, the user has to either stay with the default or choose a different option. After one of the radio buttons is selected, the user can't deselect it without selecting another one.

In Listing 13-3, I use the `repeatcolumns` property to organize the radio buttons into two columns. (See the earlier section "Repeat after me . . ." for more information on `repeatcolumns`.)

When the user chooses an option and clicks the button, the `OK_Clicked` subroutine is executed:

```
Sub OK_Click(Sender As Object, E As EventArgs)
If Deadly.SelectedItem.Text = "Cowardice" Then
    Message.Text="You're right! You really know your sins!"
    OKButton.Enabled=False
```

```
Else
   Message.Text="No, sorry. " & Deadly.SelectedItem.Text &
       —
       " is one of the Seven Deadly Sins."
   OKButton.Text="Try Again!"
End If
End Sub
```

`Deadly` is the name that was given to `RadioButtonList`. `SelectedItem` is a property that holds the currently selected item in the list. So, the code simply checks the `Text` property of that item to see whether it's the right one. If so, the subroutine congratulates the user and disables the button.

If not, the subroutine apologizes and informs the user that the selected option is, in fact, a deadly sin. The code does this by using the `&` concatenation operator to add the `Text` property of the radio button item chosen. Then, the code changes the OK button's text to `"Try Again!"`

A RadioButton example: Notification options

In much the same way as you can create individual check boxes with the `CheckBox` server control, you can create individual radio buttons with the `RadioButton` server control.

Typically, you won't ever use a single radio button on a page (because the point of radio buttons is to allow the user to select one option from several possibilities), but using a set of individual `RadioButton` controls gives you more control over the layout and arrangement of the radio buttons than you get with a `RadioButtonList`. Listing 13-4 gives you an example.

Listing 13-4:   Notification Options Page

```
<%@ Page Explicit="True" Language="VB" Debug="True" %>
<html>
<script runat="server">
Dim UserEmail As String = "bradjones@edgequest.com"
Dim UserMail As String = "613 S. Grove St., Marion, IN"

Sub OK_Click(Sender As Object, E As EventArgs)
If Mail.Checked=True Then
   Feedback.Text = "You'll be notified by mail."
Else
   Feedback.Text = "You'll be the first to know via
          email!"
```

(continued)

Listing 13-4 *(continued)*

```
End If
End Sub
</script>
<body>
<h1>Notification Options</h1>
Please tell us how you'd prefer to be notified of updates
to our software:<br><br>
<form runat="server">
<asp:radiobutton id="Mail" runat="server"
text="Mail, Delivered To:" groupname="notification"/><br>
<b><%=UserMail%></b><br><br>
<asp:radiobutton id="Email" runat="server"
text="Email, Delivered To:" groupname="notification"/><br>
<b><%=UserEmail%></b><br><br>
<asp:button id="OKButton" text="OK" runat="server"
onclick="OK_Click" /><br><br>
<asp:label id="Feedback" runat="server" /><br>
</form>
</body>
</html>
```

In this page, information from variables is used within the radio button list. This isn't possible with the RadioButtonList control. Using individual RadioButton controls provides for more flexible formatting.

But you still need to have the radio buttons work together. That is, when one in the list is selected, you want all the rest to be deselected. You accomplish this with the groupname property. By setting it to contain the same value for both radio buttons (for example, in Listing 13-4, groupname="notification"), ASP.NET 2.0 knows that you want them to work together as a group. You can include several groups of radio buttons on a page, as long as each group has a unique name.

As with a RadioButtonList, it's a good idea to select one of the RadioButton controls in a group to be the default.

Using common RadioButtonList and RadioButton properties

For a list of common properties used with RadioButtonList and RadioButton, see "Using common CheckBoxList properties" and "Using common CheckBox properties," earlier in this chapter. All the properties and events work the same and have the same names.

Only two properties exist that you're likely to use with `RadioButtonList` that you wouldn't likely use with `CheckBoxList`:

- ✔ `SelectedIndex`: A number indicating which radio button in the `Items` list is selected.
- ✔ `SelectedItem`: The actual radio button item that's selected.

These properties provide the most convenient way to determine which option the user chose. For a complete example of using `RadioButtonList` and the `SelectedItem` property, see the section "A RadioButtonList example: More gazillionaire trivia," earlier in this chapter.

There's only one property you're likely to use with `RadioButton` that you don't use with `CheckBox`: `GroupName`. The `GroupName` property determines the other radio buttons on the page with which this one should work. For an example of `GroupName` in action, see "A RadioButton example: Notification options," earlier in this chapter.

Your Kiss Is on My ListBox

Similar to a list of check boxes or radio buttons, a list box enables the user to pick one or more options from a long list. But because a list box can scroll its list of options, you can put many more possibilities in the list without taking up most of a page.

A ListBox example: The Personalize Your PC page

In the code in Listing 13-5, you provide your users with a list box full of options they can add to the new PC they're buying from you. The page then adds up the price and provides the user with a total.

Listing 13-5: Creating a Personalized PC

```
<%@ Page Explicit="True" Language="VB" Debug="True" %>
<html>
<script runat="server">
Sub OK_Click(Sender As Object, E As EventArgs)
Dim Total, ItemIndex As Integer
Message.Text = "You chose:<br>"
Total = 1000
```

(continued)

Listing 13-5 *(continued)*

```
For ItemIndex = 0 To PCOptions.Items.Count -1
    If PCOptions.Items(ItemIndex).Selected = True Then
        Message.Text = Message.Text & _
            PCOptions.Items(ItemIndex).Text & "<br>"
        Total = Total + PCOptions.Items(ItemIndex).Value
    End If
Next
Message.Text = Message.Text & "Your total is $" & Total
End Sub
</script>
<body>
<h1>Personalize Your PC</h1>
Thanks for deciding to purchase our choice,
one-of-a-kind Generic PC for a base price of only
$1,000. Now you can pick from the following options
you'd like to add:<br>
<form runat="server">
<asp:listbox id="PCOptions" selectionmode="multiple"
runat="server">
    <asp:listitem value="100">
    CD-ROM Drive - $100</asp:listitem>
    <asp:listitem value="200">
    19 Inch Monitor - $200</asp:listitem>
    <asp:listitem value="150">
    Ink Jet Printer - $150</asp:listitem>
    <asp:listitem value="50">
    Joystick - $50</asp:listitem>
    <asp:listitem value="100">
    128MB More RAM - $100</asp:listitem>
</asp:listbox><br><br>
<asp:button id="OKButton" text="OK" runat="server"
onclick="OK_Click" /><br><br>
<asp:label id="Message" runat="server" /><br>
</form>
</body>
</html>
```

This page ends up looking like Figure 13-8.

The format of the <asp:listbox> tag is similar to the <asp:checkboxlist> and <asp:radiobuttonlist> tags that I discuss earlier in this chapter. The outer tag surrounds several <asp:listitem> tags that include the text that will appear on each line within the list box.

Several new attributes inside the tag deserve attention. In the <asp:listbox> tag, notice that I set the selectionmode property to multiple. This setting enables users to choose multiple items in the list box by holding down the Shift or Control key as they click. You need to include this setting because the default value for selectionmode is single.

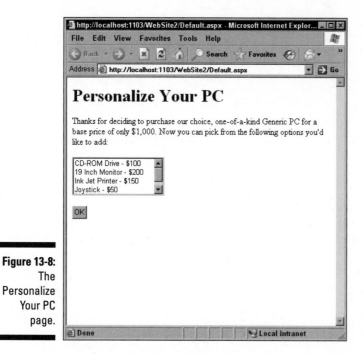

Figure 13-8:
The
Personalize
Your PC
page.

The <asp:listitem> tags also contain something new: value. The value attribute enables you to specify some information about each line that you want to keep, but don't necessarily want to display as part of the line in the list box. You don't have to use value at all, but it is handy in cases like this. If you didn't have the value, you'd have to keep a separate list of the prices in an array or try to grab the last few characters of each string and figure it out from there.

When the user selects a few of the options and clicks OK, the OK_Click subroutine is executed:

```
Sub OK_Click(Sender As Object, E As EventArgs)
Dim Total, ItemIndex As Integer
Message.Text = "You chose:<br>"
Total = 1000
For ItemIndex = 0 To PCOptions.Items.Count -1
   If PCOptions.Items(ItemIndex).Selected = True Then
      Message.Text = Message.Text & _
         PCOptions.Items(ItemIndex).Text & "<br>"
      Total = Total + PCOptions.Items(ItemIndex).Value
   End If
Next
Message.Text = Message.Text & "Your total is $" & Total
End Sub
```

The loop goes through all the items in the list box. (For more information on walking through a collection of items with a `For...Next` loop, see the section "A CheckBoxList example: Know your primes," earlier in this in chapter.)

If the current item is selected, the label `Message` has this item's name appended to it, followed by a `<br>` tag. In addition, the value of this item is added to the total.

Finally, after the loop ends, the `Message` label gets one more string(s) added to the end: a total for the items selected. The following example shows the results that are returned to the user:

```
You chose:
CD-ROM Drive - $100
Ink Jet Printer - $150
Your total is $1250
```

Using common ListBox properties

For details and examples of how to use the `Items(x).Selected`, `Items(x).Text`, and `SelectionMode` properties, see the section "A ListBox example: The Personalize Your PC page," earlier in this chapter. For a description of standard properties of the `ListBox` that are common with other controls, see Chapter 12.

In the following sections I describe properties of the `ListBox` that I don't describe in earlier sections and some properties that I do describe earlier, but which work a little differently for the `ListBox`.

Rows and Columns

The `Rows` property determines how tall the list box is so that it can display the number of rows specified. If the list box contains more than that number of items, the scrollbar enables you to see the rest.

The `ListBox` control doesn't have a `Columns` property. By default, the `ListBox` control makes itself wide enough to display the text of its longest item.

SelectedIndex and SelectedItem

As with radio buttons, the `SelectedIndex` and `SelectedItem` properties are quite handy for list boxes in which users can select only one item. `SelectedIndex` gives you the index number of that property, and `SelectedItem` actually returns the `ListItem` object itself.

AutoPostBack and SelectedIndexChanged

As with check boxes and radio buttons, the list box has an `AutoPostBack` property, which, when set to `True`, causes the browser to return to the server every time the user changes the items selected. If your page specifies a `SelectedIndexChanged` event for the `ListBox` control, the event is then executed.

Using common ListBox.Items methods

The `ListBox` control includes a collection called `Items`, which holds all the items in the `ListBox` control. Some properties are associated with *individual* items, like `Selected`, `Text`, and `Value`. However, numerous methods are associated with the *entire list.* You can use these methods to add items to the list, remove items from the list, clear the list entirely, and even search the list. The following sections summarize these methods.

Items.Add and Items.Insert

When you want to add a new item to a list box, you have a couple different options:

- ✔ **If you don't care about placement or you want the item placed at the bottom of the list,** you can use `Items.Add`, as in this example:

```
FavoriteFruit.Items.Add("Apple")
```

- ✔ **If you want the new item added at a specific index,** you can use `Items.Insert`, as shown in the following example:

```
FavoriteFruit.Items.Insert(2, "Apple")
```

Before this line is executed, your list might look like this:

```
Pear
Grape
Lime
```

Here's what the list looks like after the line with `Items.Insert` is executed:

```
Pear
Grape
Apple
Lime
```

The index number is zero-based, so element number 2 is actually the third element in the list.

Items.Remove and Items.RemoveAt

To take items out of the list, use one of the Remove functions: Items.Remove and Items.RemoveAt. The only difference between the two is how you indicate which item you want to remove. With Items.Remove, you pass a string that matches the text of the one you want to remove — for example:

```
FavoriteFruit.Items.Remove("Grape")
```

There's another way you can indicate which item to get rid of with the Remove method: Send the ListItem object itself. Here's a common example:

```
FavoriteFruit.Items.Remove(FavoriteFruit.SelectedItem)
```

This line grabs the currently selected item and sends it to the Remove function.

The Items.RemoveAt method requires you to send the index number of the item you want to remove. For example, assume that you have the following list:

```
Pear
Apple
Grape
Lime
```

You'd use the following line to remove the Grape item:

```
FavoriteFruit.Items.RemoveAt(2)
```

Again, the index to a collection always begins counting with zero.

Items.Clear

The Items.Clear method is probably the simplest of them all. You don't pass any arguments. It simply removes all the items in the list at once:

```
FavoriteFruit.Items.Clear
```

The item sleuths: Items.FindByText and Items.FindByValue

If you're looking for a particular item in the list, you can always use a For...Next loop to go through all the items and compare Items(x).Text to whatever you're looking for. But there's a faster and easier way: the Items.FindByText method. Here's an example:

```
FoundItem = FavoriteFruit.Items.FindByText("Lime")
```

The `Items.FindByText` method doesn't return the index of the item found. It returns the item *itself.* So, before you can receive the item back into a variable, you have to declare the variable to hold an object of type `ListItem`, as the following example shows:

```
Dim FoundItem As ListItem
FoundItem = FavoriteFruit.Items.FindByText("Lime")
If Not IsNothing(FoundItem) Then
    Response.Write("I found this item: " & FoundItem.Text)
End If
```

This code declares the variable, receives the object back, and displays it. There's just one gotcha: What if the item *isn't* found? Well, in that case, `FoundItem` contains *nothing.* If you declare an integer, its initial value is set to 0. If you declare a variable to hold an object, like `ListItem`, what does it contain? Nothing. The VB 2005 built-in `IsNothing` function enables you to check whether an object variable holds an object. If not, `IsNothing` returns `true`. In this example, you need to check that. If you try to get the page to display the value returned by the `FoundItem.Text` method and `FoundItem` contains nothing, you get an error.

The `Items.FindByValue` method works exactly like the `Items.FindByText` except, as you might expect, it looks through all the `Items(x).Value` properties for the string you pass. For more information on the `Value` property of the `ListBox`, see "A ListBox example: The Personalize Your PC page," earlier in this chapter.

An Add/Remove/Clear example: The Grocery List page

To demonstrate some of the important `Items` methods, try the example in Listing 13-6, which enables you to enter your grocery list.

Listing 13-6:   Your Online Grocery List

```
<%@ Page Explicit="True" Language="VB" Debug="True" %>
<html>
<script runat="server">
Sub Add_Click(Sender As Object, E As EventArgs)
GroceryList.Items.Add(AddText.Text)
End Sub
Sub Remove_Click(Sender As Object, E As EventArgs)
GroceryList.Items.Remove(GroceryList.SelectedItem)
End Sub
```

(continued)

Listing 13-6 *(continued)*

```
Sub Clear_Click(Sender As Object, E As EventArgs)
GroceryList.Items.Clear
End Sub
</script>
<body>
<h1>Your Online Grocery List</h1>
Welcome to your very own online grocery list.
I've included some items for you to get started. Feel
free to add and remove items as you see fit. Clear
erases the whole list, so be careful with that button!<br>
<form runat="server">
<asp:listbox id="GroceryList" rows="3" runat="server">
    <asp:listitem>5 Apples</asp:listitem>
    <asp:listitem>Orange Juice</asp:listitem>
    <asp:listitem>2 Gal. Milk</asp:listitem>
    <asp:listitem>2 Loaf Bread</asp:listitem>
    <asp:listitem>Potato Chips</asp:listitem>
</asp:listbox><br><br>
<asp:textbox id="AddText" runat="server" />
<asp:button id="AddButton" text="Add" runat="server"
onclick="Add_Click" /><br>
<asp:button id="RemoveButton" text="Remove" runat="server"
onclick="Remove_Click" />
<asp:button id="ClearButton" text="Clear" runat="server"
onclick="Clear_Click" /><br><br>
<asp:label id="Message" runat="server" /><br>
</form>
</body>
</html>
```

The result looks like Figure 13-9.

Figure 13-9:
The Grocery
List page.

Just type something in the text box and click the Add button. The new item should be added to the bottom of the list. (You might have to scroll down to see it.) Then, click an item that you want to get rid of and click the Remove button. Or just click the Clear button to remove all the items.

In Listing 13-6, each button has its own subroutine, which is called when you click the button:

✔ **When you click the Add button,** the `Add_Click` subroutine is executed:

```
Sub Add_Click(Sender As Object, E As EventArgs)
GroceryList.Items.Add(AddText.Text)
End Sub
```

This subroutine takes the text and uses it as the argument for the `Add` function.

✔ **Clicking the Remove button** calls the `Remove_Click` subroutine:

```
Sub Remove_Click(Sender As Object, E As EventArgs)
GroceryList.Items.Remove(GroceryList.SelectedItem)
End Sub
```

Here, the `SelectedItem` property gets the currently selected item and sends it to the `Remove` method. The item is deleted.

✔ **When you click the Clear button,** the `Clear_Click` subroutine is executed:

```
Sub Clear_Click(Sender As Object, E As EventArgs)
GroceryList.Items.Clear
End Sub
```

Calling the `Clear` method removes all the items from the list box.

Searching the grocery list with FindByText

You can enhance the Grocery List page with a Find capability by using the `FindByText` method. Add these lines to the bottom of the code from Listing 13-6, just before `</form>` (but don't run the application yet — you have more to add!):

```
<asp:textbox id="FindText" runat="server" />
<asp:button id="FindButton" text="Find" runat="server"
onclick="Find_Click" /><br><br>
<asp:label id="FindMessage" runat="server" /><br>
```

This code creates the text box, the Find button, and a label for displaying the results of the find.

Now add this subroutine immediately after the opening `<script>` tag at the top of Listing 13-6 to respond to the `FindButton` click event:

```
Sub Find_Click(Sender As Object, E As EventArgs)
Dim FoundItem As ListItem
FoundItem = GroceryList.Items.FindByText(FindText.Text)
If Not IsNothing(FoundItem) Then
    FindMessage.Text = "Yes! Found it: " & FoundItem.Text
Else
    FindMessage.Text = "Nope! Sorry, didn't find it."
End If
End Sub
```

The `Items.FindByText` method is sent the text in the `FindText` text box. If the item is found, it's returned into the `FoundItem` variable. Using the `IsNothing` function, the `If...Then` statement checks whether `FoundItem` contains an object. The `Not` before `IsNothing` reverses the `true/false` status, so if `FoundItem` is not nothing, the `FoundItem` object's text is displayed.

Dropping In on the DropDownList

The drop-down list is a hybrid beast that looks like a text box with a button beside it. When you click the button, you see something that looks like a list box. But, when you're designing your user interface, the drop-down list works more like a set of radio buttons: It enables a user to pick one option from a list.

With a drop-down list, however, the option the user chooses remains clearly visible, but the other options don't appear on the screen unless you click the button. In this way, a drop-down list saves space and enables you to create a nicer-looking page.

Typically, you use the drop-down list on Web pages for two different purposes. Like a list box or a list of radio buttons, it enables the user to pick an option. Then, later, when the user pushes a button, the chosen option can be noted, displayed, or stored.

But Web *applications* have another common use for the drop-down list: kicking off an action, much like a button does. Instead of simply putting one predefined action in motion, the drop-down list can start up one of several actions.

A DropDownList example: Site navigation

The drop-down list is often used as a navigational tool, listing the popular destinations of your Web site. When users choose a destination from the drop-down list, they are immediately whisked away to that page.

As with the `TextBox`, `CheckBoxList`, `RadioButtonList`, and `ListBox` controls, the `DropDownList` control has an `AutoPostBack` property. This property, in coordination with the `SelectedIndexChanged` event, provides the key to making this example work. Check out Listing 13-7.

Listing 13-7:   Drop-Down List Navigation

```
<%@ Page Explicit="True" Language="VB" Debug="True" %>
<html>
<script runat="server">
Sub JumpTo_Change(Sender As Object, E As EventArgs)
Response.Redirect(JumpTo.SelectedItem.Text & ".aspx")
End Sub
</script>
<body>
<h1>Jump Page</h1>
<form runat="server">
Jump To:<br>
<asp:dropdownlist id="JumpTo" runat="server"
onselectedindexchanged="JumpTo_Change"
          autopostback="true">
   <asp:listitem></asp:listitem>
   <asp:listitem>News</asp:listitem>
   <asp:listitem>Articles</asp:listitem>
   <asp:listitem>Links</asp:listitem>
</asp:dropdownlist><br>
</form>
</body>
</html>
```

The page contains an `<asp:dropdownlist>` server control named `JumpTo`. The `autopostback` property is set to `true`, and `onselectedindex changed` is set to the name of the subroutine that's at the top of the listing, inside the `<script>` tag.

If no list item is selected, the first one is selected by default. But notice here that the first item doesn't contain any text. Consequently, nothing is displayed in the box by default. This is important because the `SelectedIndex Changed` event gets triggered only if the selection *changes.* So, you need to start with a blank default.

Then, when the user chooses one of the other options, `AutoPostBack` causes the page to return to the server, and the `JumpTo_Change` subroutine is executed. That subroutine has only one line: a `Response.Redirect` method call that gets the text of the currently selected item and then appends `.aspx` to the end. So, if the user chooses `News`, the page attempts to redirect to `News.aspx`.

Providing a drop-down list to navigate your site or kick off one of multiple possible actions is very handy for your users.

Using common DropDownList properties and methods

All the properties and methods of the `ListBox` control and the `ListBox`. `Items` collection are available and work in the same way for the `DropDown List` control. You need to be aware of only a few differences:

- ✔ `DropDownList` has no `SelectionMode` property. By its nature, a `DropDownList` allows the user to pick one and only one option. If the user needs to pick more than one option, use a `ListBox` or a `Check BoxList` control.

- ✔ `DropDownList` has no `Columns` or `Rows` properties. The control is automatically sized as needed.

- ✔ As demonstrated in the preceding section, the `AutoPostBack` property and the `SelectedIndexChanged` event are much more useful with `DropDownList` than they are with `ListBox`.

Chapter 14

More User Interface Goodies (And How to Make Your Own!)

. . . .

In This Chapter

▶ Exploring image, link, and button controls

▶ Discovering the rich calendar control

▶ Creating your own user controls

. . . .

*P*revious chapters in this part of the book explore common user interface elements that you can use to create interactive pages. In this chapter, I introduce three additional user interface topics.

First, I briefly discuss several additional controls that don't fit neatly anywhere else. They give you more flexibility by providing additional design options when creating your pages.

Next, I show you one of the coolest, most useful controls yet — the Calendar control. It provides a very flexible calendar that you can customize to meet almost any timekeeping need.

Finally, I demonstrate how you can easily combine several controls with your own code to create your own user control.

A Few Image, Link, and Button Controls

In these sections, I describe some simple but interesting controls that provide a few more options when you're creating your pages.

Your image consultant

If you've worked with HTML for long, you're familiar with the tag that's used to display pictures on a Web page. Here's an example:

```
<img src="stoplight.jpg" alt="Always Obey Stoplights!"
align="left">
```

The `<img>` tag displays the image specified by the `src` attribute and aligns the image with the other text on the page as specified by its `align` attribute. The `alt` attribute provides text that's displayed instead of the image in browsers that don't support images, or have them turned off.

Of course, you can use the `<img>` tag in the body of your ASP.NET 2.0 pages, just as you can any HTML tag. But what do you do if you want your ASP.NET 2.0 code to change the picture that's displayed with an `<img>` tag? That would take some work . . . unless you use the `Image` server control instead of the `<img>` tag.

Suppose that you have two images: one of a stoplight that's green and another of a stoplight that's red. You want the page to display one of the images and switch to the other every time the user clicks a button. Listing 14-1 shows you that it's a piece of cake!

Listing 14-1:   Stop in the Name of the Code

```
<%@ Page Explicit="True" Language="VB" Debug="True" %>
<html>
<script runat="server">
Sub Switch_Click(Sender As Object, E As EventArgs)
If Stoplight.ImageURL="stoplightgo.bmp" Then
    Stoplight.ImageURL="stoplightstop.bmp"
Else
    Stoplight.ImageURL="stoplightgo.bmp"
End If
End Sub
</script>
<body>
<form runat="server">
<asp:image id="Stoplight" runat="server"
imageurl="stoplightgo.bmp"
alternatetext="Always Obey Stoplights!"
imagealign="top" /><br><br>
<asp:button id="Switch" text="Switch" runat="server"
onclick="Switch_Click"/>
</form>
</body>
</html>
```

ON THE CD

You can find the beautifully rendered bitmaps created by my art department (uh, that's me) and used on this page on the CD-ROM in the back of this book.

This code produces a very simple page with the image and a button, as shown in Figure 14-1. Try clicking the button a few times. The image should switch back and forth.

Figure 14-1:
The
stoplight
page.

The <asp:image> tag creates the server control. The imageurl attribute contains the path and filename of the image, and the alternatetext attribute displays the text that appears in browsers that don't support images. And finally, imagealign determines how the image appears alongside the rest of the text on the page.

You see the real benefit of using this control over the HTML <img> tag in the code at the top of the page in the Switch_Click subroutine. An If...Then statement checks for the current value of the ImageURL property and then switches it to the other value. You simply assign a new value to the ImageURL property, and the new image appears.

Click me, I'm beautiful: ImageButton

In some cases, it makes sense for the user to click an image, rather than a button, to kick off some action. For example, if you show a picture of your family, you might enable users to click each person in the image to see information about the person displayed on the page.

You can't capture the click event for an Image server control. But another server control does provide a click event: the ImageButton. In fact, it not only informs you when the user clicks the image, but it also tells you the precise location within the image where the user clicked!

Listing 14-2 extends the page from Listing 14-1. You no longer need a button; you click directly on the stoplight image. The image doesn't simply go back and forth between red and green anymore, either. If you click the top of the image, it turns red; if you click the bottom of the image, it turns green.

Listing 14-2:   Stop, Version 2.0

```
<%@ Page Explicit="True" Language="VB" Debug="True" %>
<html>
<script runat="server">
Sub Stoplight_Click(Sender As Object, _
    E As ImageClickEventArgs)
If E.Y < 32 Then
    Stoplight.ImageURL="stoplightstop.bmp"
Else
    Stoplight.ImageURL="stoplightgo.bmp"
End If
End Sub
</script>
<body>
<form runat="server">
<asp:imagebutton id="Stoplight" runat="server"
imageurl="stoplightgo.bmp"
alternatetext="Always Obey Stoplights!"
imagealign="top"
onclick="Stoplight_Click" /><br><br>
</form>
</body>
</html>
```

As shown in Figure 14-2, the result is a page that contains only the image. If you click the top part of the image, the red light bitmap is displayed. And if you click the bottom part of the image, the green light bitmap appears.

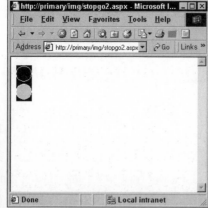

Figure 14-2:
The revised
stoplight
page.

The `<asp:image>` tag is replaced with the `<asp:imagebutton>` tag. All the attributes are the same, with the addition of `onclick`. This event triggers the `Stoplight_Click` subroutine at the top of the page.

You might have noticed that this event's second argument is a bit different from normal. Usually, you'd expect to see this: `E As EventArgs`. Because this event provides specific information through this argument, you must use `ImageClickEventArgs` as the type for `E` instead.

How does the `ImageClickEventArgs` event use the `E` argument? Well, two important pieces of information are passed as properties of `E`: the X and Y coordinates of the mouse pointer when the user clicked. If you think of the image as a tiny grid of dots, `E.X` identifies how many dots from the left the user clicked. `E.Y` indicates how many dots from the top the user clicked.

In this page, I care only about how far from the top the user clicked. Because 32 is roughly between the two circles, I check to see whether the user clicked above or below that line. If above, I use the red light image; if below, I use the green light image.

 How did I figure out that 32 was the magic number? I just created a page that displayed `E.Y` in a label every time I clicked the image. That way, I could find a number that was in the middle. Of course, if you have image-editing software, you can use that to measure more precisely.

 If you're looking for a more sophisticated way of creating images that have regions that users can click to do different things, you definitely want to check out a new server control that has been added in ASP.NET 2.0: `ImageMap`. The `ImageMap` allows you to add *hotspots* of various shapes and sizes on the image that react when the user clicks them. For more information on the `ImageMap`, see the .NET Framework documentation

A button disguised as a link: LinkButton

Usually, when users click a link, they expect to be whisked away to another page. But in some cases, you'd like a link to do what a button normally does: return to the server and execute code you've written to respond to the event. That's what the `LinkButton` does.

Think of the `LinkButton` as a normal button dressed up to look like a link. Why would you want such a thing? It simply provides more flexibility when designing your user interface. Often a link is more appropriate in certain situations or with certain site designs. In addition, you might actually want to send the user to another page, but you want to do some processing first. In that case, you could use a `LinkButton`, do the processing in the `Click` event, and then use the `Response.Redirect` method to take the user to the new page.

In the example in Listing 14-3, a user types his name and then clicks a link. Instead of sending him to another page, as he might expect, this page executes a subroutine and uses a label to respond to the user.

Listing 14-3: The Tricky LinkButton

```
<%@ Page Explicit="True" Language="VB" Debug="True" %>
<html>
<script runat="server">
Sub NormalLink_Click(Sender As Object, E As EventArgs)
Message.Text = "Fooled you, " & Name.Text & _
    "! Thought you were going somewhere, didn't you?"
End Sub
</script>
<body>
<form runat="server">
Enter Your Name:<br>
<asp:textbox id="Name" runat="server" /><br><br>
Then click on the link below:<br>
<asp:linkbutton id="NormalLink" runat="server"
onclick="NormalLink_Click">
This looks like a normal link
</asp:linkbutton><br><br>
<asp:label id="Message" runat="server" />
</form>
</body>
</html>
```

After the user types his name and clicks the link, the page looks something like Figure 14-3.

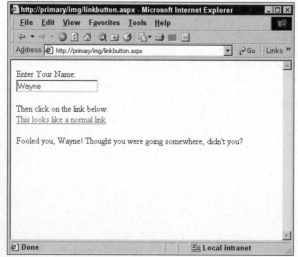

Figure 14-3: Looks like a link, acts like a button: the LinkButton.

_____ Chapter 14: More User Interface Goodies (And How to Make Your Own!) **213**

The `<asp:linkbutton>` tag doesn't have any unusual attributes. The text that appears as a link is the text between the open and close tag. The `onclick` attribute sends you to the `NormalLink_Click` subroutine. There, the label's text is filled in, making use of the name the user entered.

Handling the hysterical HyperLink

Just like a normal HTML `<a>` tag, a `HyperLink` server control enables you to display some text that users can click to go to another page. However, because `HyperLink` is a server control, you also can access and manipulate it from code just as you do with the `Image` server control (see "Click me, I'm beautiful: ImageButton," earlier in this chapter).

For example, in your code, you can dynamically change the target of a `HyperLink` control.

By using the `HyperLink` server control, you can create a simple Web Roulette page that randomly sends the user to a page picked at random from a list. It looks like Listing 14-4.

Listing 14-4: Web Roulette

```
<%@ Page Explicit="True" Language="VB" Debug="True" %>
<html>
<script runat="server">
Sub Page_Load(Sender As Object, E As EventArgs)
Dim Sites As ArrayList = New ArrayList
Dim Num As Integer
Randomize
Sites.Add("http://www.microsoft.com")
Sites.Add("http://www.borland.com")
Sites.Add("http://www.netscape.com")
Sites.Add("http://www.sun.com")
Sites.Add("http://www.ibm.com")
Sites.Add("http://www.lotus.com")
Sites.Add("http://www.discovery.com")
Sites.Add("http://www.comedy.com")
Sites.Add("http://www.ebay.com")
Num = Int(Rnd * Sites.Count)
RouletteLink.NavigateURL = Sites(Num)
End Sub
</script>
<body>
<h1>Welcome to Web Site Roulette</h1>
<p>Care to take a spin on the wheel? Round and round
she goes! Where she stops - Well, you'll find out...</p>
<p>When you're ready, just click...</p>
```

(continued)

Listing 14-4 *(continued)*

```
<form runat="server">
<asp:hyperlink id="RouletteLink" runat="server" >
<center><h3>SPIN!</h3></center>
</asp:hyperlink>
</form>
</body>
</html>
```

The page looks like Figure 14-4. Click the link. Go back. Click Refresh. Then click the link again. Keep it up. You go to a randomly selected site each time.

Figure 14-4:
Web
Roulette.

Although this page and the one in Chapter 9 look similar to the user, they work very differently. The one in Chapter 9 decides which page to go to after the user clicks. This page decides when it is first loaded. In fact, in Internet Explorer, you can hover your pointer over the link and look down at the browser status bar to see where the link will take you. Each time you click Refresh, it changes.

Why? Well, the <asp:hyperlink> control appears in the body with only id and runat attributes. The important attribute — NavigateURL, which identifies the destination Web site — isn't filled in until the code in the Page_Load event is executed (when the page is requested). This code picks a random element from the array list and assigns it to NavigateURL, thus setting the destination to a different spot every time the page is refreshed.

Marking Time with the Calendar Control

All the server controls that I show you in previous pages of this book are used to create relatively standard user interface elements that are pretty familiar to you. But Microsoft didn't stop there. Just to show what's possible with server controls, Microsoft has created *rich* user interface controls. *Rich* in this context means that they have lots of built-in functionality, and they provide a broad range of properties, events, and methods that enable you to customize how they work.

I've picked out one of the coolest and most useful rich controls to show you here — the Calendar. By including just a single tag and setting a couple attributes, you can create a fully functional monthly calendar that users can easily navigate. (For information on other rich controls, see Chapter 22 on the security controls, Chapter 24 on the Web parts controls, and the online .NET Framework documentation on the Ad Rotator control.)

A Calendar example: Unborn Baby Age Calculator

To demonstrate the Calendar server control, I have created the Unborn Baby Age Calculator, as you see in Listing 14-5.

Listing 14-5: Unborn Baby Age Calculator

```
<%@ Page Explicit="True" Language="VB" Debug="True" %>
<html>
<script runat="server">
Sub DateSelected(Sender As Object, E As EventArgs)
Dim WeeksUntilDue,WeeksOld As Integer
TodayDate.Text = "Today's Date: <b>" & Today & "</b>"
DueDate.Text = _
    "Due Date: <b>" & BabyAgeCalendar.SelectedDate & "</b>"
WeeksUntilDue = _
    DateDiff("w",Today,BabyAgeCalendar.SelectedDate)
If WeeksUntilDue > 40 Then
    Message.Text = "<i>If that's your due date, " & _
        "then you haven't conceived yet!</i>"
ElseIf WeeksUntilDue < -5
    Message.Text = "<i>You really should have " & _
        "delivered this child by now!</i>"
Else
    WeeksOld = 40 - WeeksUntilDue
    Message.Text = _
        "Your baby is <b>" & WeeksOld & "</b> weeks old"
```

(continued)

Listing 14-5 *(continued)*

```
End If
End Sub
</script>
<body>
<h1>Unborn Baby Age Calculator</h1>
<p>So you're expecting! Congratulations! Find out how many
weeks old the baby forming inside you is right now. Just
click on your due date!</p>
<form runat="server">
<center>
<asp:calendar id="BabyAgeCalendar" runat="server"
onselectionchanged="DateSelected"/><br>
</center>
<asp:label id="TodayDate" runat="server" /><br>
<asp:label id="DueDate" runat="server" /><br>
<asp:label id="Message" runat="server" /><br>
</form>
</body>
</html>
```

If you're pregnant (or know someone who is), just click the little arrows in the upper-left and upper-right corners of the calendar to navigate to the month and year when the baby is due. Then click the due date and find out exactly how many weeks old the little one is, as shown in Figure 14-5.

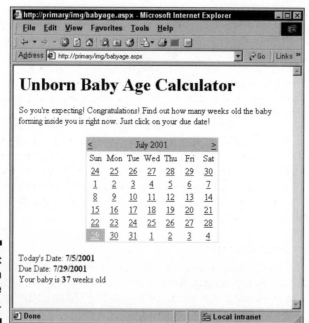

Figure 14-5:
The Unborn
Baby Age
Calculator.

This control is amazingly cool and functional, and getting it to work takes incredibly little effort. As you can see, the `<asp:calendar>` tag requires only an `id` and a `runat` attribute. And, if you want to capture the user's click as an event, you need `onselectionchanged`.

After the user clicks a date, the `DateSelected` subroutine is executed. The `SelectedDate` property returns the date the user clicked. This, along with today's date, is displayed in the appropriate labels.

After that comes the real calculation:

```
WeeksUntilDue = _
    DateDiff("w",Today,BabyAgeCalendar.SelectedDate)
```

`DateDiff` is a built-in VB 2005 function. It accepts two dates and returns the number of days, weeks, months, or years between the dates. Because I included a `"w"` as the first argument, it gives me the difference in weeks.

The only other little bit of information you need to know is that the average pregnancy lasts about 40 weeks. So, subtracting `WeeksUntilDue` from 40 gives you the age of the child!

Using common Calendar members

The `Calendar` example in the preceding section looks simple but works quite well. However, its look and feel might appear out of place on your site. Fortunately, the folks at Microsoft made this control very customizable. They did this by providing a whole host of properties and methods.

I don't have the space to introduce and explain each of those properties here. You can look them up for yourself as you need them. But I do point out a few highlights in the following sections.

Visual Web Developer 2005 Express makes it even easier to create beautiful calendars with a predefined selection of designs that you can use as-is or customize. Just click over to Design mode and select the Calendar control. Then right-click to display the contextual menu and choose Auto Format to show the Auto Format window. There you can select the design you want and immediately see what it looks like.

Global Calendar properties

You can change the look of the whole calendar by setting a couple properties. The `FirstDayOfWeek` property, for example, enables you to determine which day of the week shows up in the first column of the calendar. The `ShowGridLines` property determines whether lines appear to separate the days. (This property is `false` by default.)

Parts is parts: The pieces of a calendar

Most of the changes you can make to the calendar involve the individual sections of the control:

- ✔ **Title:** The part at the top that contains the month and year. The Title includes the Next/Prev Month arrows.

- ✔ **Next/Prev Month arrows:** The little arrows on either side of the month/year that enable you to navigate to the next and previous month.

- ✔ **Day header:** The first row of column headers, with the day names.

- ✔ **Days:** All the individual days listed on the calendar.

- ✔ **Weekend Days:** The days on the calendar that represent Saturday and Sunday.

- ✔ **Selected Days:** The day or days that have been selected by the user.

You can turn the display of some of these parts on or off by using these calendar properties: `ShowTitle`, `ShowNextPrevMonth`, and `ShowDayHeader`. You can change the formatting of some of these parts by changing these properties: `TitleFormat`, `NextPrevFormat`, and `DayNameFormat`.

In addition, numerous subobjects inside the calendar represent the style of these different parts of the calendar control. By manipulating the properties of these subobjects, you describe how you want that part to look. These are some of the important style subobjects: `TitleStyle`, `NextPrevStyle`, `DayHeaderStyle`, `DayStyle`, `WeekendDayStyle`, and `SelectedDayStyle`.

How do these subobjects work? Well, you can find various style properties for nearly any visible server control. Examples include `ForeColor`, `BackColor`, `BorderStyle`, `BorderWidth`, and the `Font` object with all its properties. They're available for the calendar control itself, and when you set them, the settings affect the whole control.

But each of these individual style objects also has *its own set* of those same properties. If you set them, you affect just *that part* of the calendar control.

For example, change the calendar control in the Unborn Baby Age Calculator example from Listing 14-5 to look like this:

```
<asp:calendar id="BabyAgeCalendar" runat="server"
showgridlines="true" backcolor="skyblue"
titlestyle-backcolor="yellow"
dayheaderstyle-backcolor="red"
onselectionchanged="DateSelected"/>
```

Notice that `backcolor` for the calendar control is set to `skyblue`. That affects the whole calendar. But the `titlestyle` subobject's `backcolor` is set to `yellow`, and the `dayheaderstyle` subobject's `backcolor` is set to `red`. So when you see the calendar, everything is blue but the title and day headers. Figure 14-6 shows the new calendar, but doesn't quite capture all the subtle hues I describe.

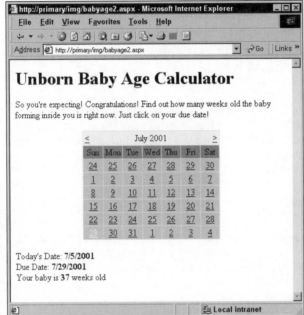

Figure 14-6: The colorful Unborn Baby Age Calculator.

Subobject syntax

When you refer to the properties of subobjects in the `<asp:calendar>` tag, you use the subobject name, then a dash, and then the property name. I describe this syntax in Chapter 8, but because you might not have run into it very often, I mention it again here.

Of course, if you're referring to the subobject property in code, you use dot notation and enumeration properties (which I also cover in Chapter 8), as in the following example:

```
BabyAgeCalendar.TitleStyle.BackColor =
           Drawing.Color.Yellow
```

The Calendar has lots of subobjects, each with numerous properties. If you're setting several properties on several subobjects, you might find it easier to use this alternative syntax:

```
<asp:calendar id="BabyAgeCalendar" runat="server"
showgridlines="true" backcolor="skyblue"
onselectionchanged="DateSelected">

<titlestyle backcolor="yellow"
forecolor="blue" font-bold="true" />

<dayheaderstyle backcolor="red"
forecolor="yellow" font-italic="true"/>

</asp:calendar>
```

Here, instead of immediately closing the <asp:calendar> tag, I've put additional tags inside it. These additional tags *are* the subobjects. Then, within each subobject's tags, you can set *its* individual properties. If the subobject itself has a subobject, as in the case of font, you can use the dash notation: font-bold="true".

Calendar events

Finally, in addition to the SelectionChanged event that I use in the Unborn Baby Age example, you might find one more event useful: VisibleMonthChanged. It happens, as you might expect, when the user clicks the next or previous links to change the displayed month.

Doing It Yourself: User Controls

Microsoft has obviously provided a bunch of interesting server controls to make designing the user interface of your Web applications a fruitful task. But wouldn't it be nice if you could package up parts of your page and reuse those parts in other pages, as if they were a new server control? That's exactly what *user controls* enable you to do.

Creating a reusable page header

When you design a Web site, you might want to create a header that goes across the top of virtually every page on your site. This page header prominently displays the name of your site at the left and perhaps provides some commonly accessed links along the right.

You could simply create the header and then copy and paste the HTML into each page where it's needed. That works and doesn't require too much effort. But suppose you change your color scheme. Or, you change the name or location of one of those pages listed among the header's links. Now you have to revisit every page with a header and change it. That's a major pain!

A better way exists. You can create a user control that contains the header and then drop that user control on each page where it should appear. In the future, when you change the user control, all the pages that use it are automatically updated.

Here's an example of just such a header created as a user control:

Enter the code from Listing 14-6 into a file and save the file with the name `Header.ascx`. Notice the extension: `.ascx`. It's different from a typical page. (You won't be able to access this page directly in a browser. You must create a page that uses the control, which I show you how to do in the next section of this chapter.)

Listing 14-6:   A User Control Page Header

```
<%@ Control Explicit="True" Language="VB" Debug="True" %>
<table width="100%" cellpadding="10"
          bgcolor="blue"><tr><td>
<asp:label id="HeaderLabel" runat="server"
backcolor="blue" forecolor="yellow"
font-size="18 pt" font-name="Arial" font-bold="true"
text="EdgeQuest"/></td>
<td align="right" ><b>
<asp:hyperlink id="HomeLink" runat="server"
navigateurl="home.htm">
<font color="yellow">Home</font>
</asp:hyperlink> *
<asp:hyperlink id="NewsLink" runat="server"
navigateurl="news.htm">
<font color="yellow">News</font>
</asp:hyperlink> *
<asp:hyperlink id="ArticlesLink" runat="server"
navigateurl="articles.htm">
<font color="yellow">Articles</font>
</asp:hyperlink> *
<asp:hyperlink id="LinksLink" runat="server"
navigateurl="links.htm">
<font color="yellow">Links</font>
</asp:hyperlink>
</b></tr></table>
```

This is a user control. It looks and works very much like a normal ASP.NET 2.0 page: HTML tags and server controls are mixed freely throughout the page. Specifically, this control has five server controls: one `label` control for the site name and four `hyperlink` controls to provide quick access to key areas on the site. These server controls are organized into an HTML table to format them and add a bit of color.

You can even have a `<script runat="server">` section in a user control, if you like. However, a user control differs from a normal ASP.NET page in a few important ways:

- ✔ The name of the file has an extension of `.ascx` rather than `.aspx`. That ensures that no one will try to retrieve the user object page directly.

- ✔ The `@ Page` directive at the top is replaced with the `@ Control` directive. The attributes you specify within the directive are the same.

- ✔ The user control contains *no* `<html>`, `<body>`, or `<form>` tags. Never use these tags in a user control. The page where you use the control supplies these tags.

That's all there is to creating a user control!

I use a page header as a simple example in this section to introduce you to the basic features of a user control and demonstrate how it works. Another option for creating common headers and other page elements is to use Master Pages. To find out more about Master Pages, see Chapter 21.

Using the page header

Listing 14-7 shows you a simple page that makes use of the header from Listing 14-6.

Listing 14-7:   Using the Header User Control

```
<%@ Page Explicit="True" Language="VB" Debug="True" %>
<%@ Register TagPrefix="ASPFD" TagName="Header"
Src="header.ascx" %>
<html>
<body>
<form runat="server">
<aspfd:header runat="server"/>
<h1>Really Important News</h1>
<p>Blah blah blah. Blah blah blah blah blah blah. Blah
          blah
blah. Blah blah blah blah blah.</p>
</form>
</body>
</html>
```

The first thing you notice is the @ Register directive, which appears right below the @ Page directive. You must include an @ Register directive line for *each different type* of user control you use on this page. The @ Register directive provides two important bits of information: the *name* (including prefix) you want the control to have in this page and the *file* where the user control can be found. I've given the control a prefix of ASPFD (an abbreviation for the title of this book) and a name of Header. You can pick any prefix and name you want. If the user control's .ascx file is in a different folder, you can specify a path in the Src attribute, along with the filename. In this case, the file is in the same folder as the page that uses it.

Finally, after the user control is registered, you can use it one or more times anywhere in the page, just as you would a server control:

```
<aspfd:header runat="server"/>
```

When you want to add a user control to your page in Visual Web Developer 2005 Express, simply open the page, click to select the user control's .ascx filename in the Solution Explorer, and drag and drop the control onto your page. The @ Register directive is created along with the user control tag. In Design mode, you see the user control as it will appear on the final page.

Rolling your own dice

User controls can do much more than simply package server controls and HTML to be dropped on a page. They can help make your pages come to life!

Here's an example: Suppose you want to create one or more Web games that use standard dice. Wouldn't it be nice to have a die user control that you could just drop into a page whenever you need it?

I thought so. So I created the one in Listing 14-8, which I call die.ascx. (I omit some parts of the code. For the complete listing, see the application on the CD.)

Listing 14-8:   The Die User Control

```
<%@ Control Explicit="True" Language="VB" Debug="True" %>
<script runat="server">
Public Showing As Integer

Private Sub ClearDie
UpLeft.Text = " "
UpMid.Text = " "
UpRight.Text = " "
. . .
```

(continued)

Listing 14-8 *(continued)*

```
End Sub

Public Sub Roll
Showing = Int(Rnd * 6) + 1
ClearDie
Select Case Showing
Case 1
    MidMid.Text = "O"
Case 2
    UpLeft.Text = "O"
    LowRight.Text = "O"
Case 3
    UpLeft.Text = "O"
    MidMid.Text = "O"
    LowRight.Text = "O"
. . .
End Sub

</script>
<table width="75" height="75" border="1"
cellspacing="0"><tr><td>
<table width="100%"><tr>
<td align="center">
<asp:label id="UpLeft" runat="server" /></td>
<td align="center">
<asp:label id="UpMid" runat="server" /></td>
<td align="center">
<asp:label id="UpRight" runat="server" /></td>
</tr><tr>
<td align="center">
<asp:label id="MidLeft" runat="server" /></td>
<td align="center">
<asp:label id="MidMid" runat="server" /></td>
<td align="center">
<asp:label id="MidRight" runat="server" /></td>
</tr><tr>
<td align="center">
<asp:label id="LowLeft" runat="server" /></td>
<td align="center">
<asp:label id="LowMid" runat="server" /></td>
<td align="center">
<asp:label id="LowRight" runat="server" /></td>
</tr></table></td></tr></table>
```

Unlike Listing 14-7, this listing does include a `<script runat="server">` section. But before I get to that, take a look at the table in the bottom part of the page. Actually, there are two tables. The first is just a one-cell table that has a one-pixel border and a set height and width. This defines the box within which I create a die.

Inside the box is another table. This one has no border and is designed to fill the space inside the outer table. The inner table has three rows and three columns for a total of nine cells. Inside each cell is a label with a name appropriate to its location: UpLeft, MidRight, LowRight, and so on. Think of it like a tic-tac-toe board. I place dots in these labels as appropriate to mimic the way a die looks for each roll. (I use a capital *O* to create the dots. You can change it to *, +, or whatever you prefer.)

Now look in the <script> section. There's a subroutine called Roll, which, appropriately enough, rolls this die. It does that by picking a random number between 1 and 6. That's the easy part. The tougher part is showing the result.

First, I call the ClearDie subroutine. This subroutine simply goes through all the labels and puts an   (a *non-breaking space*) inside each one. This is a character that you can use in HTML to force a space to appear in a location. HTML typically ignores regular spaces, but it doesn't ignore this kind of space.

Notice that the ClearDie subroutine is labeled as Private. This means that only other subroutines *in this user control* can call it. It can't be called from the page that uses this user control. On the other hand, the Roll method is not labeled Private, so it is available to be called from the page.

After I call the ClearDie method, I can use a Case statement to fill in the appropriate dots for each possible outcome:

```
Select Case Showing
Case 1
    MidMid.Text = "O"
Case 2
    UpLeft.Text = "O"
    LowRight.Text = "O"
. . .
Case 6
    UpLeft.Text = "O"
    MidLeft.Text = "O"
    LowLeft.Text = "O"
    UpRight.Text = "O"
    MidRight.Text = "O"
    LowRight.Text = "O"
End Select
```

And that's all there is to the die user control. It's completely self-contained: a random number generator and an intuitive way to display the results.

Yacht. See?

You can create a page that puts the `die` user control (from Listing 14-8) to work. One of the more popular dice games in the United States is called Yacht (commercially sold as Yahtzee). Although creating a full-blown Yacht game would take more time and space than I can offer to the project in these pages, in Listing 14-9 I create a miniature version that uses only three dice and has only one goal: to get three of a kind with three dice!

Listing 14-9:   Creating a Yacht Game with the Die User Control

```
<%@ Page Explicit="True" Language="VB" Debug="True" %>
<%@ Register TagPrefix="ASPFD" TagName="Die"
Src="die.ascx" %>
<html>
<script runat="server">
Sub Roll_Click(Sender As Object, E As EventArgs)
Message.Text = ""
Die1.Roll
Die2.Roll
Die3.Roll
If Die1.Showing = Die2.Showing And _
   Die2.Showing = Die3.Showing Then
      Message.Text = _
         "You WIN! You got three of a kind with " & _
         Die1.Showing
End If
End Sub
</script>
<body>
<form runat="server">
<h1>Mini-Yacht</h1>
<table><tr>
<td><aspfd:die id="Die1" runat="server" /></td>
<td><aspfd:die id="Die2" runat="server" /></td>
<td><aspfd:die id="Die3" runat="server" /></td>
</tr></table><br>
<asp:button runat="server" text="Roll!"
onclick="Roll_Click" /><br><br>
<asp:label id="Message" runat="server" />
</form>
</body>
</html>
```

I placed three `die` user controls on this page. And to get them to line up nicely beside each other, I use a simple one-row, three-column table (with no border). Initially, the dice appear as blank boxes. But when you click the Roll! button, the boxes are filled with the values rolled, as shown in Figure 14-7.

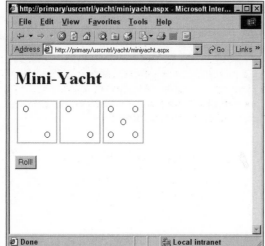

Figure 14-7:
The Mini-
Yacht game
in action.

Clicking the button causes the `Roll_Click` subroutine to be executed.

The `Roll` method of each die is called. Then, the `Showing` property is used to see the value showing on each die. If you look at the code for the user control, you can see the `Showing` property at the top of the `<script>` section:

```
. . .
<script runat="server">
Public Showing As Integer

Private Sub ClearDie
UpLeft.Text = " "
UpMid.Text = " "
. . .
```

Because the `Showing` variable is identified as `Public`, it effectively becomes a property of this user control. This enables the page that uses the control to access its value. Each die uses the `Showing` variable to hold the random number generated:

```
Sub Roll
Showing = Int(Rnd * 6) + 1
ClearDie
Select Case Showing
```

If all three dice show the same number, the user wins and is informed by the `Message` label:

```
If Die1.Showing = Die2.Showing And _
   Die2.Showing = Die3.Showing Then
      Message.Text = _
         "You WIN! You got three of a kind with " & _
         Die1.Showing
End If
```

Otherwise, the user can keep clicking the button until the dice show a winning combination. Sometimes, that takes a lot of clicks.

Chapter 15

Getting It Right: Validating User Input

"To err is human . . ." If that's true, then users are the most human people I've ever met.

– An anonymous ASP.NET developer

Face it — everyone makes mistakes! That's why validation is so important. *Validation* is the process of making sure that users typed the correct information into a form.

Of course, if you ask for a name and the user types `Elmer Fudd`, your page can't figure out whether the user is yanking your chain.

But if your page asks for a phone number, and the user types in only three digits or nothing at all, your page *can* catch that error and ask the user to complete the information. So, validation is really about just trying to get the best information you can before you accept it.

Putting RequiredFieldValidator to Work

The simplest of the validation controls is the `RequiredFieldValidator`. This one simply makes sure the user doesn't leave anything blank that you want filled in.

Using RequiredFieldValidator with a text box

You can use the `RequiredFieldValidator` with various controls, but a couple of examples should give you the general feel for how it works. Listing 15-1 shows how it works with a text box.

Listing 15-1: Requiring an E-Mail Address

```
<%@ Page Explicit="True" Language="VB" Debug="True" %>
<html>
<body>
<form runat="server">
What's Your E-mail Address?<br>
<asp:textbox id="Email" runat="server" /><br>
<asp:requiredfieldvalidator id="EmailRequired"
controltovalidate="Email" runat="server" >
Whoops! You forgot to enter an e-mail address!
</asp:requiredfieldvalidator><br>
<asp:button id="OK" text="OK" runat="server" />
</form>
</body>
</html>
```

In this example, the text box is followed by the `<asp:requiredfield validator>` control. This validation control has several important attributes:

- ✔ id: Gives the validation control a name.
- ✔ `controltovalidate`: Identifies the server control it validates.
- ✔ runat: Identifies it as a server control.

In addition, inside the tag is an error message. This message appears only when the server control identified in the `controltovalidate` attribute is empty.

When you first bring up this page, click the OK button before entering anything in the text box. The error message immediately appears, as shown in Figure 15-1.

Figure 15-1:
Missing
the e-mail
address.

Now type some text in the text box and click the button again. The error message goes away.

Using RequiredFieldValidator with a drop-down list

You can also use `RequiredFieldValidator` with a drop-down list, as you see in Listing 15-2.

Listing 15-2:   Picking a Color

```
<%@ Page Explicit="True" Language="VB" Debug="True" %>
<html>
<body>
<form runat="server">
What Color Do You Prefer?<br>
<asp:dropdownlist id="Color" runat="server" >
    <asp:listitem>Pick A Color</asp:listitem>
    <asp:listitem>Red</asp:listitem>
    <asp:listitem>Green</asp:listitem>
    <asp:listitem>Blue</asp:listitem>
</asp:dropdownlist><br>
```

(continues)

Listing 15-2 *(continued)*

```
<asp:requiredfieldvalidator id="ColorRequired"
controltovalidate="Color" runat="server"
initialvalue="Pick A Color">
Whoops! You forgot to choose a color!
</asp:requiredfieldvalidator><br>
<asp:button id="OK" text="OK" runat="server" />
</form>
</body>
</html>
```

By default, the first item in a `DropDownList` control initially appears in the box. Often, instead of offering a real choice, this item includes instructions for the user. In this case, the user must "Pick A Color." The `RequiredField Validator` control includes a property called `initialvalue`, which lets the validation control know that this value appears initially in the `DropDownList` control and shouldn't be counted as a real selection.

If you retrieve this page, you immediately see `Pick A Color` in the drop-down list. As shown in Figure 15-2, if you click the OK button, the validation control displays the error because you haven't chosen a real value from the list.

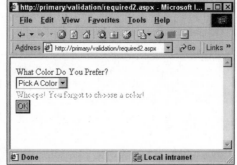

Figure 15-2:
You forgot
to choose
a color!

Using CompareValidator

The `CompareValidator` is a relatively simple validation control. It enables you to compare the value in a control to a value that you specify or to the value held in another control.

Comparing with a value

In Listing 15-3, the validation control requires that the temperature entered is greater than 32.

Listing 15-3:   Is It Freezing?

```
<%@ Page Explicit="True" Language="VB" Debug="True" %>
<html>
<body>
<form runat="server">
Enter the temperature:<br>
<asp:textbox id="Temp" runat="server" /><br>
<asp:comparevalidator id="TempCompare"
controltovalidate="Temp" valuetocompare="32"
operator="GreaterThan" type="integer"
runat="server" >
The temperature must be above 32 degrees.
</asp:comparevalidator><br>
<asp:button id="OK" text="OK" runat="server" />
</form>
</body>
</html>
```

The `<asp:comparevalidator>` control has some of the same attributes as the `<asp:requiredfieldvalidator>` control (see "Putting RequiredField-Validator to Work," earlier in this chapter). The `id`, `controltovalidate`, and `runat` attributes work just as they do there. However, this example also introduces a few new attributes:

- ✔ `valuetocompare`: As the name implies, it provides the value to use when comparing the contents of the control.

- ✔ `operator`: Describes how the comparison should be done. Common values: `Equal`, `NotEqual`, `GreaterThan`, `GreaterThanEqual`, `LessThan`, and `LessThanEqual`. This attribute is *optional*, and if you do not include it, it defaults to `Equal`.

- ✔ `type`: Identifies the type of the data being compared. Common values: `Integer`, `String`, and `Date`.

In this example, the contents of the `Temp` control (which holds an integer) must be greater than the integer value `32`. If not, you get an error message, as shown in Figure 15-3.

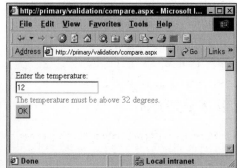

Figure 15-3:
Getting the
temperature
right.

Comparing with another control

You can use the `CompareValidator` to compare the contents of a control being validated with the contents of another control, as Listing 15-4 demonstrates.

Listing 15-4: Comparing Ages

```
<%@ Page Explicit="True" Language="VB" Debug="True" %>
<html>
<body>
<form runat="server">
How old are you?<br>
<asp:textbox id="YourAge" runat="server" /><br>
How old is your youngest son/daughter?<br>
<asp:textbox id="ChildAge" runat="server" /><br>
<asp:comparevalidator id="AgeCompare"
controltovalidate="ChildAge" controltocompare="YourAge"
operator="LessThan" type="integer"
runat="server" >
Um, your child must be younger than you!
</asp:comparevalidator><br>
<asp:button id="OK" text="OK" runat="server" />
</form>
</body>
</html>
```

If you enter 33 for your age and 55 for your child's age, this page is smart enough to know that those values can't be right, as you see in Figure 15-4.

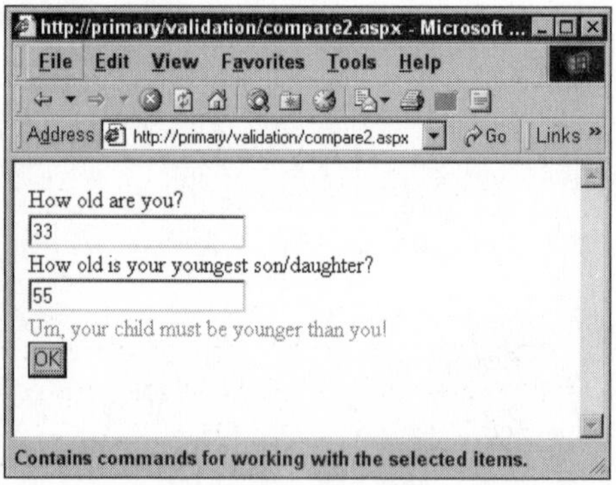

Figure 15-4:
You can't be
younger
than your
child.

The only real difference between this example and the one in the preceding section is that the `valuetocompare` attribute is replaced with the `control tocompare` attribute, and it holds the control's name. Otherwise, `operator`, `type`, and everything else work as they do in the previous example.

Keeping the User in Range with RangeValidator

RangeValidator goes a step further than the CompareValidator. It enables you to check to see whether a server control holds a value that falls within a specific range. This, too, is a very common type of validation.

Checking the range with two values

Earlier in this chapter, in the section titled "Comparing with a value," I show you how to use the CompareValidator to ensure that the user enters a temperature greater than the freezing point for water. In Listing 15-5, I extend that example to check that the water temperature is above freezing level and below the boiling point.

Listing 15-5:   Checking the Temperature

```
<%@ Page Explicit="True" Language="VB" Debug="True" %>
<html>
<body>
<form runat="server">
Enter the temperature:<br>
<asp:textbox id="Temp" runat="server" /><br>
<asp:rangevalidator id="TempRange"
controltovalidate="Temp"
minimumvalue="33" maximumvalue="219"
type="integer" runat="server" >
The Temperature Must Be Above 32 Degrees and
Below 220 Degrees.
</asp:rangevalidator><br>
<asp:button id="OK" text="OK" runat="server" />
</form>
</body>
</html>
```

Now, instead of a valuetocompare, you have a minimumvalue and a maximumvalue. Those numbers probably aren't quite what you'd expect them to be. Remember that you're specifying the lowest and highest *acceptable* values. So, to get values *between* 32 and 220, you must specify 33 and 219. If you enter a value that falls outside that range, you get the result shown in Figure 15-5.

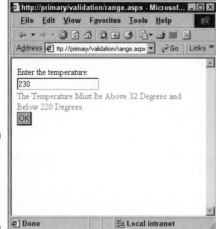

Figure 15-5:
Entering a
temperature
outside the
range.

Checking the range with other controls

Because CompareValidator has a controltocompare attribute, you might expect to find a minimumcontroltocompare and a maximumcontrolto compare for the RangeValidator. Unfortunately they don't exist.

However, you can check a range of values based on what the user entered in other controls. You just need a little code to help you accomplish it. I demonstrate that technique in Bonus Chapter 4 on this book's CD.

Displaying the Results with ValidationSummary

You might not necessarily want to display all your error messages beside their related controls. Doing so can make designing a good-looking page very difficult. A better approach is to collect all the error messages in one place — say, at the bottom of the form — and put a star or an exclamation point next to each control that contains invalid data.

Fortunately, ASP.NET 2.0 has a control that addresses this need directly: ValidationSummary.

Because you really need several validation controls on a page to see how ValidationSummary works, in Listing 15-6 I provide an example that demonstrates how you might create a page to accept information from a user who wants to create a login account on your site.

Listing 15-6:   Creating a New User Account

```
<%@ Page Explicit="True" Language="VB" Debug="True" %>
<html>
<head/>
<script runat="server">
Sub CreateButton_Click(Sender As Object, E As EventArgs)
If IsValid = True Then
   Status.Text = _
      "Everything Looks Good - Creating New Account"
   Create.Enabled = False
   ' Create new user account
End If
End Sub
</script>
<body>
<h1>Create a New Account</h1>
<form runat="server">

Enter a Username:<br>
<asp:textbox id="Name" runat="server" />
<asp:requiredfieldvalidator id="NameRequired"
controltovalidate="Name" runat="server"
errormessage="Please Enter a Username">
*
</asp:requiredfieldvalidator><br>

Enter a Password:<br>
<asp:textbox id="Password" textmode="password"
runat="server" />
<asp:requiredfieldvalidator id="PasswordRequired"
controltovalidate="Password" runat="server"
errormessage="Please Enter a Password">
*
</asp:requiredfieldvalidator><br>

Confirm Password:<br>
<asp:textbox id="Confirm" textmode="password"
runat="server" />
<asp:requiredfieldvalidator id="ConfirmRequired"
controltovalidate="Confirm" runat="server"
errormessage="Please Confirm Your Password">
*
</asp:requiredfieldvalidator>

<asp:comparevalidator id="PasswordCompare"
controltovalidate="Password" controltocompare="Confirm"
type="string" runat="server"
errormessage="Your Password and Confirmation Don't Match">
*
</asp:comparevalidator>
<br>
Enter Your Age:<br>
```

(continues)

Listing 15-6 *(continued)*

```
<asp:textbox id="Age" runat="server" />
<asp:rangevalidator id="AgeRange" controltovalidate="Age"
minimumvalue="18" maximumvalue="120"
type="Integer" runat="server"
errormessage="Please Enter an Age Between 18 and 120">
*
</asp:rangevalidator><br><br>
<asp:button text="Create" id="Create"
onclick="CreateButton_Click" runat="server"/><br>

<asp:label id="Status" runat="server" /><br>

<asp:validationsummary id="Summary"
displaymode="bulletlist" runat="server"
headertext="Validation Errors"/>

</form>
</body>
</html>
```

If you simply bring up the page and immediately click the Create button, your screen lights up with red error messages, as shown in Figure 15-6.

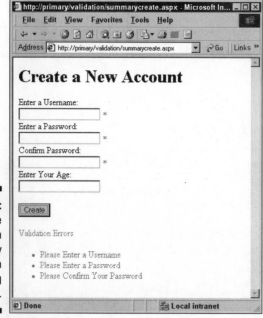

Figure 15-6: The Validation Summary control in action using bullet list.

I use the `RequiredFieldValidator` control to ensure that the user enters the username, password, and confirmation. The `CompareValidator` control ensures that the password text box and the confirmation text box both contain the same value. (Notice that I don't specify an operator, so `Equals` is assumed by default.)

Finally, I use `RangeValidator` to ensure that the `Age` text box contains a value between (and including) 18 and 120.

Another option for creating a page that accepts user registration information is the `CreateUserWizard`. This control is part of the security controls provided with ASP.NET 2.0. For more information on these controls, see Chapter 22.

Using Page.IsValid to ensure that all is well

Unlike the other small examples in previous sections of this chapter, Listing 15-6 includes a subroutine that gets executed when the user clicks the button on this page.

That subroutine checks something called `Page.IsValid` to see whether the page has any errors. `IsValid` is `true` if all the validation controls on this page have passed. If any of them fail, `IsValid` is set to `false` automatically by ASP.NET 2.0. This provides a very handy way to be sure that you don't process anything until everything is exactly as you want it.

Using the ValidationSummary to clean up the page

The `ValidationSummary` control appears at the bottom of the page in Listing 15-6. Instead of working with the text inside the validation controls on the page, the `ValidationSummary` control displays the value from each validation control's `errormessage` property.

The *text inside* each validation control appears on the page where the validation control itself is located, as it always has. In this case, however, that means that only a * is displayed.

The `ValidationSummary` control has a `headertext` property and a `displaymode` property. The `headertext` property is simply the text that appears at the top of the summary of error messages. The `displaymode`

Protecting yourself from hackers

Theoretically, some clever developers out there could create a form that submits information to *your* server. And if they do, it might not contain the JavaScript that checks to make sure all the data is okay first. That means the hacker could submit bad data to your server using his own form.

To combat this possibility, the validation server controls don't actually replace the server valida

tion with client validation when the user has a newer browser. The controls actually do both client *and* server validation. That way, they can be sure that no bad data gets submitted, even if some tricky developers try to send it from their own forms.

property can have one of several possible values: bulletlist, list, and singleparagraph. The value you see in Figure 15-6 is bulletlist. If you prefer, you can remove the bullets by using list. Alternatively, if you just want to run all the error messages together as several sentences in one big paragraph, you can use singleparagraph.

Client Versus Server Validation

These validation controls are very clever. They actually check to see which browser the user has, and they react differently based on the result. For example, if you have an older browser that doesn't support client-side JavaScript, these controls validate the data entered after it's submitted, on the server.

However, if the user has a newer browser that supports client-side JavaScript, the validation server controls create JavaScript code to do the validation in the browser. That way, you don't waste time sending bad data to the server. You catch it right away and give the user immediate feedback. Then, when it's all set, the data can be sent to the server.

I Want More!

Validation is an important topic — virtually every Web application needs it! As a result, I provide information on more advanced validation controls and more advanced techniques for using them in Bonus Chapter 5 on the CD. In addition, you also find tables summarizing all the validation controls and their commonly used properties. Check it out!

Part VI
Casting a Wider ASP.NET

In this part . . .

*I*n this part of the book, you develop an appreciation
of VB 2005's data-handling capabilities and you explore
the .NET Framework Class Libraries, discovering some neat
tricks along the way. You also find out about application-
level events and configuration settings that help make
large-scale application development easier. All the tools
and techniques you need to become a Web guru are within
your grasp!

Chapter 16

Variable Data Types: Preaching to the Converted

---

*A*SP.NET 2.0 makes your pages act intelligently by providing you with the ability to write VB 2005 code to respond to a user's actions. A VB 2005 program (like all computer programs) has data at its heart. Variables allow your application to hold and manipulate data. But all variables have some data type that determines the valid types of data that can be stored in the variable.

Earlier chapters tell you about the `Integer`, `Single`, and `String` data types. (If this sounds foreign to you, turn to Chapter 5, where I introduce the concept of variables and data types.) In this chapter, I point out a few other data types that you might run across, and I explain how to work with them and convert them to and from the types you already know. Trust me, it's much more exciting than it sounds!

Meeting the Elementary Data Types

Information comes in many shapes and sizes, and you have lots of different data types to accommodate them. In the next few sections, I describe different categories of what .NET Framework refers to as the *elementary data types*.

Elementary data types are the simple types you use in your everyday programming — things like integers, singles, doubles, strings and Booleans.

I introduce you to the really common ones in Chapter 5. In this chapter, I present a broader range of data types so you'll always have just the right type for storing your information.

Storing whole numbers

Data types that hold whole numbers are called *integral* (meaning *integer-like*). In Chapter 5, I introduce you to `Integer`. It can handle most of your needs for holding whole numbers. But you do have a few other options, just in case. Here's all of them:

- ✔ `Byte`: Holds values between `0` and `255`.

- ✔ `Short`: Stands for *short integer*. Holds values between `-32,678` and `32,767`.

- ✔ `Integer`: Holds values between `-2,147,483,648` and `2,147,483,647`.

- ✔ `Long`: Stands for *long integer*. Holds values between `-9,223,372,036,854,775,808` and `9,223,372,036,854,775,807`.

Unless you have a specific reason, you're usually better off using `Integer` any time you want to store whole numbers. Calculations with `Integer` are faster than with any other data type. When might you use the other whole-number types? You can use `Byte` and `Short` to (marginally) reduce the amount of memory your application requires. `Long` might be handy if you need to store a particularly large number that won't fit in an `Integer`.

Storing numbers with a decimal point

Data types that hold numbers with a decimal point are called *non-integral*. Here's the whole list:

- ✔ `Single`: Holds most decimal numbers you're going to encounter in everyday life. `Single` can handle most of your needs for decimal numbers. (I also discuss `Single` in Chapter 5.)

- ✔ `Double`: Holds very big and very small (lots of numbers to the right of the decimal point) numbers more accurately than `Single`. Developers often use `Double` in scientific applications.

- ✔ `Decimal`: Holds even bigger and even smaller numbers more accurately than `Double`. Because of the way `Single` and `Double` work, they can sometimes make very small rounding mistakes. These mistakes usually aren't a big deal, but when they are, you can use `Decimal` to make sure those mistakes don't happen. `Decimal` is usually used in finance and banking applications (where even small mistakes can't be tolerated).

If you're interested in the specific ranges of values held by these different data types, see the online help. Trust me — the numbers are large and ugly enough to scare a math teacher.

Storing values other than numbers

Here's a list of the types that round out the elementary data types:

- ✔ `String`: Holds a bunch of letters, numbers, and symbols all in a row — as long or short as you like. Can be used to hold names, words, sentences, or paragraphs.

  If you want more information on `String`, see Chapter 5. Also, Bonus Chapter 4 on the CD includes a section in which I present several VB 2005 functions that make working with strings easy.

- ✔ `Char`: Like a string with a length of 1, `Char` holds a single letter, number, or symbol. You're not likely to use the `Char` type unless you're working with objects or functions written in other languages that require it.

- ✔ `Boolean`: Holds one of two values: `True` or `False`. For more information on the `Boolean` data type, see Chapter 6.

- ✔ `Date`: Holds a date or a time or both.

- ✔ `Object`: Holds *anything!*

I don't discuss `Date` or `Object` anywhere else in this book, so I tell you a little about them in the following two sections.

Getting a date

The `Date` data type enables you to create variables that hold a specific date and time. A date variable actually always contains both a date and a time, but if you need to store only a date, you can ignore the time part, and vice versa.

You might be wondering why you need a `Date` data type at all. You can use strings to hold dates, as I explain in Chapter 5. But suppose you want to *compare* two dates. If you use the `String` data type for comparing dates, as in Listing 16-1, you might get unexpected results.

Listing 16-1: This Code Doesn't Work Quite Right

```
<%@ Page Explicit="True" Language="VB" Debug="True" %>
<html>
<body>
<%
Dim MyBirthday As String
Dim WifeBirthday As String
MyBirthday = "10/5/1967"
WifeBirthday = "5/6/1967"

If WifeBirthday < MyBirthday Then
    Response.Write("She was born first.")
Else
    Response.Write("You were born first.")
End If
%>
</body>
</html>
```

In this example, `MyBirthday` is actually five months after my wife's, which means she was born first. But when I try it out, it says

```
You were born first.
```

The code doesn't work right because the computer thinks of the two values it compares as `strings`, so it organizes them alphabetically as you would see in a dictionary. It looks at the first character in both strings — 1 and 5 — and decides that 5 is *not* less than 1 so the `Else` part is executed.

When you use a `Date` data type, the computer understands that the values are dates and compares them correctly.

Change the first four lines of the preceding VB 2005 code to look like this:

```
Dim MyBirthday As Date
Dim WifeBirthday As Date
MyBirthday = #10/5/1967#
WifeBirthday = #5/6/1967#
```

Notice that when you assign a literal date to a `Date` variable, you put it between # signs. This looks odd, but you use them just like you use double-quotes around a literal string when assigning it to a string variable.

The result is correct this time:

```
She was born first.
```

You can assign a time or both a date and time to Date variables in the same way:

```
LunchTime = #12:30 PM#
PlaneArrives = #12/7/2001 5:53 PM#
```

In Bonus Chapter 4, I describe several useful date- and time-oriented functions offered by VB 2005. In the examples I use to demonstrate these functions, I use string variables. This works because VB 2005 is usually pretty smart at converting between strings and dates when it needs to. But now that you know how the Date data type works, you're much better off using Date variables with these functions. They'll execute faster and you won't run into comparison problems like the one in the preceding example.

You're the Object of my affection

The Object data type is the simplest and most primitive type in all of .NET. If you declare a variable of type Object, that variable can hold any type of data — string, integer, date/time, whatever. It can also hold any type of object. You could create an array list and put it in there, it could hold a hash table — whatever!

The Object variable can be very useful for certain situations, but it can also be very dangerous. When a variable is defined as an Object, the system doesn't really know anything about it and can't warn you if you try to do something stupid! (Believe me, I've done stupid things often enough to know — I need all the warning I can get!)

Use Object variables only when you have a specific need to — that is, you have to work with data and you have no way of knowing what you'll be working with. For example, at times you might want to retrieve data from a database or an XML file and you might not know at first what type it is. Even then, try to identify the data as quickly as possible and put it in a variable of the appropriate type as soon as you can.

Using Automatic and Explicit Type Conversion

With all these different data types available, you might find yourself working with data of one type when you need it to be in another type. You can convert the data in one of two ways:

✔ **Automatic conversion:** Allowing VB 2005 to do the conversion for you. (Sometimes people call this *implicit* conversion.)

✔ **Explicit conversion:** Calling a specific function to convert the information in a variable to a new data type.

For an example of automatic conversion, the code in Listing 16-2 tells you how old you'd be if you were a dog. (It might be familiar to you if you've looked at Chapter 10.)

Listing 16-2: The Listing Formerly Known As Listing 10-2

```
<%@ Page Explicit="True" Language="VB" Debug="True" %>
<html>
<script runat="server">
Sub OKButton_Click(Sender As Object, E As EventArgs)
    Dim UserAge, DogAge As Integer
    UserAge = Age.Text
    DogAge = UserAge / 7
    Message.Text="If you were a dog, you'd be " & _
        DogAge & " years old."
End Sub
</script>
<body>
<h1>If You Were A Dog</h1>
<form runat="server">
How old are you?<br>
<asp:textbox id="Age" runat="server"/>
<asp:button text="OK" onclick="OKButton_Click"
runat="server"/><br>
<asp:label id="Message" runat="server"/>
</form>
</body>
</html>
```

When you get information from the Text property of a TextBox, it is always in the form of a string, even if you expect the user to enter a number, as I do here. To get around this problem, I put the string into an Integer variable before I divided it by 7:

```
UserAge = Age.Text
```

VB 2005 sees that I am putting a string into an integer variable, and VB automatically does the conversion for me. By default, VB 2005 does a lot of automatic conversions for you. And when you're first trying to figure out how VB 2005 works, that's handy. It's just one less thing that you have to think about.

However, as you get a little more experience, start paying attention to these details and start clearly specifying when you want to convert between data types by using data conversion functions. (That is, use explicit conversion, rather than just letting VB 2005 do it automatically.)

For example, here's a better way to code the preceding line:

```
UserAge = CInt(Age.Text)
```

CInt is one of a family of functions that does data type conversion. You can read this function's name as "convert to integer." It takes whatever you send it, converts that data into an integer, and returns the result. (To meet the rest of the CInt function's family, see the following sections.)

Strive to make all the type conversions that happen in your pages explicit. It makes your intentions clearer — to you, to VB 2005, and to any other developers who have to make changes to your pages in the future.

Amassing Your Conversion Function Arsenal

To make your conversions explicit, you have to know about the conversion functions that are available.

Standard conversion functions

A conversion function exists for each of the different data types available:

- **Converting to whole numbers:** CByte, CShort, CInt, and CLng
- **Converting to decimal point numbers:** CSng, CDbl, and CDec
- **Converting to String, Char, Boolean, or Date:** CStr, CChar, CBool, and CDate

All these functions take virtually anything that you care to send to them, and they do their best to convert it to the data type stated in their name and return the result.

Of course, just as you aren't likely to use all the data types available every day, so you aren't likely to use all these functions on a regular basis. The most commonly used are probably `CInt`, `CSng`, `CStr`, and `CDate`. (I present an example using `CInt` in the preceding section.)

`CStr` is useful for converting a number or a date to a string before it is displayed. For example, in Listing 16-2, you should explicitly convert the `Integer` variable `DogAge` to a `String` to concatenate it together with the other strings placed in the `Message` label:

```
Message.Text="If you were a dog, you'd be " & _
    CStr(DogAge) & " years old."
```

If you retrieve a date from a text box, convert it to a `Date` when you use it. Doing so ensures that all comparisons your code makes are made correctly. For example, this code compares the value in a text box with a `Date` variable called `DueDate`:

```
If CDate(DateCompleted.Text)  > DueDate Then
    Message.Text = "You're late!"
End If
```

The CType conversion function

The `CType` function is a generalized version of the functions that I describe in the preceding section. You pass `CType` two arguments: the value you want to convert and the type to which you want to convert it. Here's an example:

```
UserAge = CType(Age.Text, Integer)
```

Here, `CType` takes the place of `CInt` by converting the value in the Age text box into an `Integer`. And in the following code, it takes the place of `CStr` by converting `DogAge` into a `String`:

```
Message.Text="If you were a dog, you'd be " & _
    CType(DogAge, String) & " years old."
```

Using one of the conversion functions that I describe in the preceding section is usually simpler than using `CType`, but you will see `CType` used from time to time, especially with classes and objects. I explain classes and objects in Chapter 8.

Using the Int, Val, and Str conversion functions

Typically when you need to do a conversion, CInt, CStr, and the others are the easiest to remember, and they almost always do the job for you. However, VB 2005 provides a few additional functions that you'll see used from time to time:

- Int: Accepts a decimal point number and returns an integer. It's doesn't work in quite the same way as CInt. If you call Int(3.7), it returns 3. It truncates, or chops off the fractional part of the value. However, if you call CInt(3.7), it returns 4. CInt does something more akin to rounding.

- Val: Accepts a string and returns a number. The number it returns might be an integer or a decimal point number.

- Str: Accepts any kind of number and converts it into a string.

Be Strict: Spare the Rod, Spoil the Programmer

As I state earlier in this chapter, you should always make your conversions *explicit* — that is, use the conversion functions anytime you convert a value from one data type to another, rather than just letting VB 2005 do it for you automatically.

This is especially true for conversions where you could lose data. For example, if you store the value 33000 in an Integer variable and then try to assign that variable to a Byte variable, it doesn't work. A Byte variable can hold values only up to 255. This is sometimes referred to as a *narrowing conversion* because you're going from a bigger type, the Integer, to a smaller type, the Byte. VB 2005 usually lets you get by with narrowing conversions when you compile your applications. But when you run them, if the conversion really does cause you to lose data (as it would in my Integer and Byte example), you get a runtime error.

If you're ready to take your programming to the next level, you can use the Strict keyword in your page header:

```
<%@ Page Explicit="True" Strict="True" Language="VB"
Debug="True" %>
```

Setting Strict to True causes VB 2005 to catch you at compile time if you try to do a narrowing conversion without using a conversion function.

By forcing yourself to use the conversion functions on narrowing conversions, you're more likely to be tipped off when you compile your application if any unintended automatic conversions are happening. Getting your application running might take a little more time, but when it is running, you'll be more certain that everything is going the way you planned.

Using the Strict option helps you to force yourself to use conversion functions for narrowing conversions.

Chapter 17

My, What Big Namespaces You Have, Mr. Framework

*T*he .NET Framework is more than just a set of languages and an environment for creating Windows and Web applications. It's also a vast library of useful code for your daily work. In fact, the .NET Framework Class Library implements many of the tedious aspects of common programming tasks and virtually hands them to you on a silver platter to use from any page in your application.

In this chapter, I show you how to use this vast library, and I provide just a glimpse into its many possibilities. I also demonstrate an exciting feature of VB 2005 which uses the My keyword to provide you quick access to common .NET Framework features.

The Great Organizer: Namespaces

In .NET, the word *namespaces* refers to a way of organizing all the objects that Microsoft has created for you to use. With so many objects, you need a very specific organization scheme. Fortunately, the organization scheme itself isn't that complicated.

Namespaces are organized as a hierarchy, where one namespace can contain other namespaces, which can, in turn, contain additional namespaces. Think of them like you think of folders on your hard drive. A folder typically holds files, but a folder also can have subfolders inside it. Those subfolders, in turn, have their own files and subfolders. There's no limit to the number of levels deep the subfolders can go.

Likewise, a namespace typically holds objects, but a namespace can also hold other namespaces. Again, there's no limit to the number of levels deep namespaces can go.

Sending E-Mail from Your ASP.NET 2.0 Page

In this section, I show you how to access classes in a namespace, and I give you a pretty handy technique in the process — sending e-mail from your ASP.NET 2.0 page. Listing 17-1 shows how to specify a sender, a subject, and a message body before firing off your message.

Listing 17-1:   Sending E-Mail in ASP.NET 2.0

```
<%@ Page Explicit="True" Language="VB" Debug="True" %>
<html>
<body>
<%
    Dim EMailFrom As String = "bill@edgequest.com"
    Dim EMailTo As String = "billhatfield@edgequest.com"
    Dim EMailSubject As String = "Important message!"
    Dim EMailBody As String = "Thanks for reading this" & _
        "message but I must admit, I lied. There's " & _
        "nothing important about this message at all."

    Dim MySmtpClient As New _
        System.Net.Mail.SmtpClient("localhost")

    MySmtpClient.Send(EMailFrom, EMailTo, _
        EMailSubject, EMailBody)
%>
</body>
</html>
```

The SmtpClient class is all you need to send e-mail. Its Send method accepts four strings: the from address, the to address, the subject, and the e-mail body. In addition, when you instantiate the SmtpClient class, you must pass the name of the SMTP server you want to use to send your e-mail.

But notice that you can't simply instantiate the SmtpClient class. The SmtpClient class is in the Mail namespace. In turn, the Mail namespace is in the Net namespace, which is in the System namespace. All this together, as it is in the preceding code, is called the *fully qualified name:*

```
Dim MySmtpClient As New _
    System.Net.Mail.SmtpClient("localhost")
```

It's just like when you want to refer to a file on your hard drive. The path often includes several folder and subfolder names so that you can identify exactly where the file exists on the hard drive.

But specifying a namespace can be even easier. Add this line at the top of your file, right after the @ Page directive line:

```
<%@ Import Namespace="System.Net.Mail" %>
```

The @ Import directive is a quick and easy way to say, at the start of your page, "Look, I'm going to be using stuff inside this namespace, so make it immediately available to me everywhere on this page." You can import as many namespaces on a page as you like, but you have to use a separate @ Import directive line for each.

I'll extend the analogy a bit for those of you who are ancient enough to remember the days of dinosaurs and DOS. Using the @ Import directive is a little like putting a folder in the Path statement of your Autoexec.bat file. Doing so made all the files in that folder available to you no matter what folder you were in. Whew! I'm showing my age.

Now you can change the instantiation line of your ASP.NET 2.0 code to look like this:

```
Dim MySmtpClient As New SmtpClient("localhost")
```

In most cases, when you're going to use any classes from a namespace, simply importing the namespace at the top of the page is easier than using the fully qualified object name. However, the choice is yours!

Finding Your Way through the Forest of Namespaces

If you're hankering for a big list or diagram showing you all the available namespaces and the classes and objects they offer, I'm sorry to disappoint, but you won't see it here. Why? Two reasons:

- ✔ So many namespaces are available and so many objects exist within each namespace that I would need a book twice this size to provide even brief descriptions for them all.

- ✔ Many of the namespaces (and objects within them) are used by the ASP.NET 2.0 system itself. All the commands of the Visual Basic 2005 language, for example, have their places, as does all the functionality that compiles and runs ASP.NET 2.0 pages. So, many namespaces wouldn't be of much help or direct use to you in your everyday programming because they're designed to work behind the scenes.

So what do I do instead? Well, I tell you where you can go. (Ahem!)

The .NET Framework Microsoft Developer Network (MSDN) documentation provides a pretty complete list of all the namespaces and classes/objects that are available. You find the *Class Library Reference* section under *.NET Framework SDK,* which is, in turn, under *.NET Development* in the Contents. That's your exhaustive list.

A great online resource for the .NET Framework 2.0 Class Libraries can be found at `http://beta.asp.net/QUICKSTART/util/classbrowser.aspx`.

The .NET Framework MSDN documentation is much easier to navigate than a diagram or a giant list. But beware — it's not as friendly as this book! And keep your eye out for examples. The documentation has lots of them, and some are even helpful.

Classes? Objects? Automatically instantiated? Static classes? Help, I'm going mad!

Throughout this chapter, I often refer to the things inside the namespaces as *objects.* For those purists out there (you know who you are), I must admit that they aren't actually objects — they are *classes* (thus the name *Class Libraries*).

In Chapter 8, I explain that you need to instantiate classes before you can use them. You often do this with the `New` keyword. After you instantiate a class, it is an object that you can use directly. However, some objects, such as the `Request` and `Response` objects (which I describe in Chapter 9), are created for you automatically ahead of time so that you always have them available to use.

When you start using the stuff in these namespaces, you'll find classes you can use to create

your own objects. You'll also find things that *look* like already-created objects, but which are actually *static classes.* Static classes are special classes that you can use without the need to ever instantiate them first!

Whether an object is created for you ahead of time or it is, in fact, a static class really ends up making very little difference to you. Either way, you can use them without instantiating them yourself.

To keep things simple, I refer to things you have to instantiate before you can use them as *classes* and things that are ready to use as *objects.*

ASP.NET 2.0 — It's in There!

The @ Import directive is very handy. But you can actually access many of the .NET Framework libraries from your ASP.NET 2.0 page without ever using it. Why? Because every ASP.NET 2.0 page *automatically* includes these namespaces:

- System
- System.Collections
- System.Collections.Specialized
- System.Configuration
- System.IO
- System.Text
- System.Text.RegularExpressions
- System.Web
- System.Web.Caching
- System.Web.Security
- System.Web.SessionState
- System.Web.UI
- System.Web.UI.HTMLControls
- System.Web.UI.WebControls

These namespaces provide a whole host of capabilities — some of which you already know how to use. The System.Web.UI.WebControls namespace, for example, contains all the server controls I describe in Chapters 10 through 15. And the ArrayList class I describe in Chapter 9 is made available thanks to System.Collections.

My Keyword! You Can't Have Any . . .

VB 2005 provides an easy shortcut to some of the common .NET Framework Class Library features. It's the My keyword. The My keyword allows you to use objects within the various namespaces without the need for a long fully qualified name or an Import statement. In the following section, I show you an example of using the My keyword to access objects that allow you to work with files on your Web server's hard drive. Then I show you how to manipulate the files.

For a more complete example of the features in this section, I include a Guestbook application and a complete description of how it works (see Bonus Chapter 3 on the CD). The application demonstrates how to create a text file, update it with information, retrieve and display the contents of the file on a page, and save copies of the file as backups and then later restore them.

Creating and deleting files

Listing 17-2 shows you how to create a file on the hard drive and then delete it.

Listing 17-2: Creating and Deleting a File

```
<%@ Page Explicit="True" Language="VB" Debug="True" %>
<html>
<script runat="server">
Dim Path As String = "c:\inetpub\wwwroot\filefun\"

Sub Create_Click(Sender As Object, E As EventArgs)
My.Computer.FileSystem.WriteAllText(Path & "Greet.txt", _
    "Hello", False)
End Sub

Sub Delete_Click(Sender As Object, E As EventArgs)
My.Computer.FileSystem.DeleteFile(Path & "Greet.txt")
End Sub
</script>
<body>
<h1>File Fun</h1>
<form runat="server">
<asp:linkbutton id="Create" runat="server"
onclick="Create_Click">
Create File</asp:linkbutton><br>
<asp:linkbutton id="Delete" runat="server"
onclick="Delete_Click">
Delete File</asp:linkbutton><br>
</form>
</body>
</html>
```

Adjust the path in the Path variable as appropriate for your setup.

The body of the page is little more than a couple link buttons. When you try this page, be sure to open the folder referred to in the Path variable on the server's hard drive. When you click the Create link, a file named Greet.txt should appear in the folder. If you double-click the file, Notepad opens. You see that it contains the word "Hello." After you close Notepad, click the Delete link, and the file disappears.

You can try out these examples (and the Guestbook example on the CD-ROM) only if you have the permissions required to create files in the folder where your page is located.

If you get a permissions error when you try to access the server's hard drive with `My.Computer.FileSystem`, it's because the ASP.NET process doesn't have access to modify files in the folder you specified. To change this, access the folder Windows Explorer, right-click the folder, and choose Properties. Click the Security tab. (If you don't see the Security tab, go to `http://weblogs.asp.net/kencox/archive/2005/01/24/359695.aspx` to find out how to solve that problem.) Now select the ASPNET user (you might have to add it if it's not there already) and set the appropriate permissions.

The `My` keyword gives you direct access to the `FileSystem` object that has the `WriteAllText` and `DeleteFile` methods (along with a boatload of other useful methods).

The `WriteAllText` method accepts three arguments:

- ✔ A path and filename of the file to write to
- ✔ A string to write to the file
- ✔ A Boolean (`True` or `False`) value indicating whether the text should be appended to the end of the file (if a file on the hard drive already has that name) or whether this text should overwrite what's there

The first time you run the code in Listing 17-2, no file out there has this name, so a new one is created. If you click the Create link several times without clicking the Delete link, the file's "Hello" text is overwritten with the new "Hello" text each time because the last argument is `False` — meaning *don't append*.

Deleting the file is just as easy:

```
My.Computer.FileSystem.DeleteFile(Path & "Greet.txt")
```

Clicking the Delete link causes the code to be executed. The code sends the path and filename to the `DeleteFile` method, and it does the dirty work.

Copying and moving files

To copy and move files, you use the `Copy` and `Move` methods. (Please try to contain your shock.)

Using the code from Listing 17-2, add a link button to your page with the text `Copy File` and set its `onclick` attribute to call the `Copy_Click` subroutine. Then add this subroutine to the `<script>` section at the top of your page:

```
Sub Copy_Click(ByVal Sender As Object, ByVal E As
        EventArgs)
  My.Computer.FileSystem.CopyFile(Path & "Greet.txt", _
    Path & "Greet2.txt")
End Sub
```

Now when you try the page, check to see whether the `Greet.txt` file exists in the folder. If it doesn't, use the Create File link to create it. Then click the Copy File link. A new file should appear in the folder: `Greet2.txt`.

The `CopyFile` method accepts two arguments: the path and filename of the file you want to copy and the new path and name to be used by the copy. In this case, you're copying it to the folder where `Greet.txt` is, but you're giving it the new name `Greet2.txt`.

In Listing 17-2, create a link button with the text `Move File` and set its `onclick` attribute to call the `Move_Click` subroutine. Add these lines to the `<script>` section of your page:

```
Sub Move_Click(ByVal Sender As Object, ByVal E As
        EventArgs)
  My.Computer.FileSystem.MoveFile(Path & "Greet.txt", _
    Path & "Greet2.txt")
End Sub
```

Before you try the page, open the folder you're working in and delete the `Greet.txt` and `Greet2.txt` files. Then bring up the page. Click the Create File link button. The `Greet.txt` file appears. Now click the Move File link button. The `Greet.txt` file disappears, and the `Greet2.txt` file appears.

The `Move` method accepts the same arguments and works just like `Copy`. The only difference is that it deletes the original after the copy is made. (Basically, `Move` works just like moving a file in Windows Explorer.)

Chapter 18

Real-World Web Application Issues

· ·

In This Chapter

▶ Understanding and identifying Web applications

▶ Using the `global.asax` file to respond to events and import namespaces

▶ Configuring your application with `web.config`

· ·

As you begin to develop more complex Web applications, they stop being a collection of pages and start to take on a coherent life of their own. When you browse books at Amazon or search for bargains on eBay, you don't have the perception that you're simply jumping from one page to the next. It feels more like you're in a data-rich, interactive environment. That's the experience you want to present to your users.

However, on the road to creating an interactive Web application, you will inevitably begin to run into questions and problems that you didn't have when you were just creating a few simple pages. To answer these questions and provide mechanisms for creating larger, more flexible Web applications, Microsoft has created ways to identify your jumble of pages as an independent application with its own identity and support. These ways include virtual folders, the `global.asax` file, and the `web.config` file. This chapter explains how each of these works and shows you how to use them to accomplish your application goals.

What's a Web Application?

Earlier in the book, I describe a *Web application* as a group of pages that work together to create an experience for the user that is not unlike working with a normal Windows application. But when you begin to work on larger projects, you need something more concrete than that. Through IIS and its Internet Information Services manager, you can identify a specific folder as the root of a Web application. All the files and subfolders within that folder are then considered part of that application.

Clearly, that isn't necessary. The ASP.NET 2.0 pages and examples in this book work together quite well without identifying the application folder in any special way. What benefits do you gain by identifying your folder as an application? Actually, I can name several:

✔ **Process separation:** All the pages that are part of a Web application run in their own process (their own separate memory) on the Web server. If one Web application locks up, it doesn't bring down all the other Web applications because they're all running as separate processes on the machine.

✔ `global.asax`: An identified Web application can have its own `global.asax` file. This file always appears in the root folder of a Web application. It provides a place where you can put code that is executed when the application starts up or when a new user first begins to use an application, for instance. It also enables you to import namespaces for your application globally so you don't need to do it on each and every page.

✔ `web.config`: A Web application can have a `web.config` file. This file appears in the root folder of a Web application. It contains all the configuration settings that you want to specify for this application.

I use this chapter to introduce you to the `global.asax` file and the `web.config` file and give you a glimpse of what they can do for you. But before I do that, I show you the steps that are involved in identifying a folder as the root folder for a Web application.

If you're using Visual Web Developer 2005 Express, you don't have to worry about the process of identifying your Web application by creating a virtual folder. Express does that for you automatically.

Creating a Virtual Folder for Your Web Application

To follow the steps that I describe in this section, you need to have direct access to the Web server and be sitting in front of it. You also need permissions that allow you to create a new Web application in IIS. If you don't have access to your Web server or you don't have the security privileges to make these changes, contact your system administrator or your Web hosting service to see what options are available for creating ASP.NET 2.0 Web applications (also referred to as creating a *virtual folder*).

The good news is that after you mark a folder as the root for a Web application, you don't have to bother your system administrator or have much interaction with the server configuration software anymore. Between the `global.asax` and the `web.config` files, you'll have all the control you need over your application.

To create a new Web application, follow these steps:

1. **Create a new root folder for your new Web application under `c:\inetpub\wwwroot`. Name it anything you like.**

2. **Launch the Internet Information Services manager by choosing Start➪Control Panel➪Administrative Tools➪Internet Information Services.**

   The Internet Information Services window that appears looks similar to Figure 18-1.

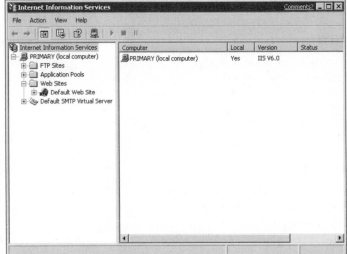

Figure 18-1:
The Internet
Information
Services
manager.

If you've worked with the Internet Information Server (IIS) much, you might be familiar with the Internet Information Services manager. This application gives you access to the features and configuration settings of IIS.

Along the left side, you see a hierarchy of items. Under the top-level Internet Information Services icon is an icon that represents your server. Under that, you see one or more entries. Among them should be one titled Default Web Site.

If you don't see Default Web Site but you do see Web Sites, open that and Default Web Site should be inside. (These differences depend on the operating system you're using.)

3. **Open Default Web Site.**

   Here you see a list of all the virtual folders and other folders that appear under `c:\inetpub\wwwroot`.

4. **Find the folder you created in Step 1. (It has a plain-looking folder icon.) Right-click it and choose Properties from the contextual menu.**

   You see a *Web Folder* Properties dialog box appear, looking like Figure 18-2. (The figure shows a dialog for a folder named classy.)

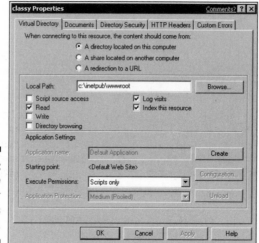

Figure 18-2:
The *Web Folder* Properties dialog box.

The bottom half of the dialog box is labeled Application Settings. The Application Name text box is disabled, and beside it is a Create button.

5. **Click the Create button.**

   The text box becomes enabled and is automatically filled in with the name of the folder.

6. **Click OK.**

7. **Close the Internet Information Services manager.**

After you complete these steps, you may begin creating your Web application in this folder and its subfolders. You may create a `\bin` folder under the root, and you can create `global.asax` and `web.config` files there, too.

The Global.asax File

The `global.asax` file never gets opened directly. Instead, it contains code that applies to the entire application.

Application and Session object events

In Chapter 9, I describe the `Application` and `Session` objects. These objects enable you to create variables that hold information at the application and session levels, respectively. The application begins when the first person accesses one of the application pages for the first time. The application ends when the server is shut down. It is a truly global scope.

On the other hand, a new session begins every time a new user opens a page in your application. The session continues until that person goes away and the session times out (20 minutes after the last page request made by that person, by default).

Chapter 9 shows you how to use the `Application` and `Session` objects to create application- and session-level variables. But there's more to those objects than simply a place to create variables.

The `global.asax` file provides a place where you can write code to respond to `Application` object events and `Session` object events. Just as the page has a `Page_Load` event that happens every time the page is retrieved, so the `Session` object has a `Session_OnStart` event that happens every time a new user begins working with your application. In fact, here are several of the more common events for which you can write code in the `global.asax` file:

- ✔ `Session_OnStart`: Happens whenever a new user accesses a page that's part of your application. You can use it to initialize session variables and session-level objects.

- ✔ `Session_OnEnd`: Happens when a session times out. You can use it to do any final cleanup of session variables and session-level objects. You can also use it to save any important session variables that have been created while the user has been accessing the site.

- ✔ `Application_OnStart`: Happens once — when the first user accesses a page in this application for the first time. You can use it to retrieve or initialize information that will be used across all the sessions in the application. It is often used to cache commonly used data.

- ✔ `Application_OnEnd`: Happens once when the server is shut down. You can use it to clean up any application-level variables, objects, or cached data.

- ✔ `Application_OnBeginRequest`: Happens every time a page in the application is requested, before the request is serviced.

- ✔ `Application_OnEndRequest`: Happens after each request is serviced. This is the last event that can have an effect on the response.

Listing 18-1 shows an example of a `global.asax` file that uses several of the preceding events. The file initializes and tracks two application variables that provide interesting statistics that any page in the application can display.

Listing 18-1:   The global.asax File Tracks Sessions

```
<%@ Application Language="VB" %>
<script runat="server">
Sub Application_OnStart(Sender As Object, E As EventArgs)
Application("TotalSessions") = 0
Application("CurrentSessions") = 0
End Sub

Sub Session_OnStart(Sender As Object, E As EventArgs)
Application.Lock
Application("TotalSessions") = _
    CInt(Application("TotalSessions")) + 1

Application("CurrentSessions") = _
    CInt(Application("CurrentSessions")) + 1
Application.Unlock
End Sub

Sub Session_OnEnd(Sender As Object, E As EventArgs)
Application.Lock
Application("CurrentSessions") = _
    CInt(Application("CurrentSessions")) - 1
Application.Unlock
End Sub
</script>
```

The first thing to notice about this file is that it doesn't begin with the @ Page directive like ASP.NET 2.0 pages do. It has an @ Application directive instead. This, like the @ Page directive, isn't strictly necessary, but including it is a good idea.

Also notice that the file has no HTML. It is never displayed, so you should never need to include HTML in the global.asax file.

What does this file do? TotalSessions is an application variable that tracks the number of sessions for this application over the application's lifetime. CurrentSessions tracks the number of people who currently have active sessions with this application. When the application first starts up, both numbers are set to 0 (zero). Every time a new session starts, both numbers are increased by one. When a session ends, the CurrentSessions variable is reduced by one.

Use Application.Lock and Application.Unlock whenever you change the value of an Application variable; otherwise, several sessions could access the same variable at once. If this happens, you can end up with a corrupted value in the variable. Using Lock and Unlock ensures that all the changes happen one after the other, as they should. However, you don't need to use `Lock` and `Unlock` in the `Application_OnStart` or `Application_OnEnd` events because both are triggered only once, and you can be sure nothing else will be going on in this application when they are. For more information on `Application` and `Session` variables or the `Lock` and `Unlock` methods, see Chapter 9.

Global directives: @ Import

You can include directives in the `global.asax` file. Probably the most important directive you can include is the `@ Import` directive. In Chapter 17, I discuss using the `@ Import` directive in your ASP.NET 2.0 pages. Doing so makes all the objects in a particular namespace available to the page. Using the `@ Import` directive in the `global.asax` file does the same for the *entire application*. For example, if you want to make the `System.Net.Mail` namespace available to every page in your application (without needing to put an `@ Import` at the top of each page), you simply include the following line at the top of the `global.asax` file:

```
<%@ Import Namespace="System.Net.Mail" %>
```

The Configuration File

ASP.NET 2.0 makes configuring your application as easy as editing a text file thanks to the `web.config` file. No complex Web server configuration applications, no registry settings, and no system administrator privileges are required.

The machine.config versus web.config

After you install the .NET Framework on a Web server, all ASP.NET 2.0 applications draw their configuration information from one file: `machine.config`. This file is stored deep within the folders of the .NET Framework installation:

```
[Windows]\Microsoft.NET\Framework\[Ver]\Config\machine.con
         fig
```

In this path, replace *[Windows]* with the Web server's primary Windows folder. Replace *[ver]* with the version number of the .NET Framework.

The `machine.config` file is a long XML file. (Don't worry — you don't need to know much about XML to use these files. I show you everything you need to know to get started.) Feel free to take a look at it, if you like, but don't make any changes right now.

When it comes to the specific configuration settings for your ASP.NET 2.0 application, the `machine.config` file doesn't have the final say. You can create another file called `web.config` and put it in the root folder of your application. Your application will use all the configuration settings specified in `machine.config` *except* for those you specify in your application's `web.config`. That is, your `web.config` file takes precedence and overrides the settings in the `machine.config`.

You don't have to restate all the configuration information from the `machine.config` file in the `web.config` file. You include only the things you want to change. If you want to change only one setting, your `web.config` file will be very short.

If you'd rather not muck around with an XML file to change your configuration settings, and you just happen to be using Visual Web Developer 2005 Express, you're in luck. Open your Web application in Express and choose Website⇨ASP.NET Configuration from the menus. This opens a browser and gives you a slick Web interface that allows you to change the settings of the `web.config` file without ever touching an XML tag.

How does XML work?

The `web.config` file, like the `machine.config` file, is formatted using XML (eXtensible Markup Language). XML isn't difficult to understand. It's simply a way of laying out a text file that uses tags, much like HTML does.

Just as with HTML, you can nest XML tags inside other XML tags, and some tags have attributes. The following simple XML file demonstrates both of these concepts:

```
<configuration>
   <system.web>
      <httpRuntime executionTimeout="90"
         maxRequestLength="6144" />
   </system.web>
</configuration>
```

In this code, the `<system.web>` tag is nested inside the `<configuration>` tag. Not because the `<system.web>` tag is indented (that just makes it easier to notice), but because the `<system.web>` start tag and end tag are both within the `<configuration>` tag. The `<httpRuntime>` tag is, in turn, nested inside the `<system.web>` tag. (Just as with server controls, a tag that ends in `/>` represents both the start and the end tag.)

In addition, the `<httpRuntime>` tag has two attributes: `executionTimeout`, with the value `"90"` assigned to it, and `maxRequestLength`, with the value `"6144"` assigned to it.

XML is a lot pickier than HTML about capitalization — it is case-sensitive. It's also picky about other details. For example, the values assigned to the attributes must be in quotes. In HTML, that's usually optional. In XML, it isn't. Another important rule to remember is that every opening tag must have a corresponding closing tag. No ifs, ands, or buts! (Of course the `/>` at the end of the opening tag counts as a closing tag, too.)

In XML, you aren't bound to using the tags that are defined for HTML. In fact, different applications can define their *own* sets of tags to mean whatever they want the tags to mean. And they can define *how* their tags work together. For example, they can say the `<tagA>` always surrounds the entire file, and it can have `<tagB>` and `<tagC>` nested inside it, and `<tagB>` can have three attributes, and so on. The `web.config` file uses XML and defines its own set of tags and rules about how they are used.

The web.config file

In this section, I show you the important tags and rules for the `web.config` file and how to change many of the standard settings for your Web application.

First, everything in a `web.config` file is surrounded by the `<configuration>` tags. You can think of this as you would the `<html>` tag in a Web page:

```
<configuration>
    . . .
</configuration>
```

In web.config files, you typically see two tags nested between the `<configuration>` tags: `<appSettings>` and `<system.web>`. For example:

```
<configuration>
    <appSettings>
     . . .
    </appSettings>
    <system.web>
     . . .
    </system.web>
</configuration>
```

The `<appSettings>` section is used to allow you to store your own application-specific information. I discuss this tag and its contents later in this chapter in a section titled "Your application settings in the web.config file." For now, you can feel free to leave it out.

The `<system.web>` section specifies system configuration settings for your Web application, and I discuss this in the next few sections.

Although you don't usually have to worry about how you capitalize things in HTML, with the ASP.NET 2.0 server controls, or in VB 2005 code, the `web.config` file is a big exception! Make sure you capitalize all the tags exactly as you see them here, or they won't work. Typically, the `web.config` file uses what is called *camel notation*. In that style, if a tag is actually multiple words run together, it starts lowercase, but the first letter of each word after that is capitalized, like this: `<exampleOfCamelNotation>`. It's called camel notation because it has humps in the middle. (Insert your own joke here.)

Changing general settings

You might want to change a couple general settings in the `web.config` file:

- ✔ `executionTimeout`: Determines how long a request — for a page or a graphic — is allowed to process before the system gives up on it and returns an error. The default for this setting is 90 seconds, but if your pages are doing work that you think might regularly take longer than that to complete, like large database queries, you might want to increase this number.

- ✔ `maxRequestLength`: Specifies a limit to how many kilobytes of information can be sent *to the server* from your users. Typically, if you're doing nothing more than accepting input from forms and the like, the default of 4096 (4MB) should be more than adequate. However, if you give your users the ability to upload images, MP3 files, or other large files, you might want to increase this limit.

In your `web.config` file, you change these general settings by using a tag named `<httpRuntime>`. You specify `executeTimeout` and `maxRequest Length` as attributes of that tag. The following code sets the `execution Timeout` to 90 seconds and the `maxRequestLength` to 6144, or 6MB:

```
<configuration>
   <system.web>
      <httpRuntime executionTimeout="90"
         maxRequestLength="6144" />
   </system.web>
</configuration>
```

I specify both `executionTimeout` and `maxRequestLength` attributes in this code, but if I want to specify only one, I can leave out the other. If I don't want to specify either, I can leave out the `<httpRuntime>` tag altogether, as I've left out the `<appSettings>` tag. In fact, that's true of all the elements I describe in the configuration file. Remember, if a tag or attribute isn't specified here, the default specified in the `machine.config` is the value used for the setting.

Using page settings

The following settings directly affect the pages in your Web application:

- ✔ enableSessionState: Normally, ASP.NET 2.0 tracks sessions and provides the Session object where you can store session-level variables (see Chapter 9). It also kicks off the Session_OnStart and Session_OnEnd events in the global.asax file (see "Application and Session object events," earlier in this chapter). These features can be handy, but if you don't need them, you can save significant resources on the server by turning off this capability. You do this by assigning false to this attribute. It's true by default.

- ✔ enableViewState: The server controls on a form keep track of their contents from one server round-trip to the next. This is handled by an ASP.NET feature called ViewState. In fact, you can save your own variables in ViewState to be remembered on the next round-trip to the server (as I explain in Chapter 11). You can increase performance a little by turning off this capability. You do that by setting this attribute to false. It's true by default. It's usually a good idea to leave this one alone.

A tag called <pages> provides the page settings. The following example web.config sets the value for both enableSessionState and enableViewState to false. It also sets the maximum request length to 6144, which is 6MB (see the preceding section in this chapter):

```
<configuration>
   <system.web>
      <httpRuntime maxRequestLength="6144" />
      <pages enableSessionState="false"
         enableViewState="false" />
   </system.web>
</configuration>
```

Adjusting session settings

When you save information in a Session variable, where is it actually stored? Well, by default, ASP.NET 2.0 takes that value and stores it in memory along with your running Web application. This works fine in most cases.

But if your Web site begins to receive lots of traffic, you might buy additional Web servers to help keep up with the demand. This setup is referred to as a *Web farm*. If you ask for a page from a site with a Web farm, Server A might answer your request this time, but later when you request another page, Server B might answer your request. As long as each machine has the identical Web pages, that should work just fine — except for the Session variables. If some ASP.NET 2.0 Session variables were created on Server A, how would Server B know about them? It wouldn't. That's a problem.

So Microsoft created two other ways of storing `Session` information. One is called a *Session State server* (`StateServer`). This is a program that runs on a single server in the Web farm. Whenever one of the Web servers needs to create a `Session` variable, it does so using the Session State server. Whenever a Web server needs to access a previously created `Session` variable, it goes back to the Session State server. That way, no matter how many servers are in the Web farm and regardless of which one processes your request, they all go to the same place to get your `Session` information.

But what if that Session State server crashes? Then all the `Session` variable information instantly disappears! Microsoft offers another option that addresses this problem: `SQLServer`. With this option, a single machine running SQL Server is used to maintain the `Session` variables — and they are all stored in a SQL Server database. This is perhaps the safest way to do it, but also the slowest.

The session settings in the configuration file enable you to choose how you want to keep track of your `Session` variables:

✔ mode: Set the `mode` variable to one of three values: `InProc`, `StateServer`, or `SQLServer`. `InProc` is the default; it simply stores the session information in memory with your application. `StateServer` and `SQLServer` are as I describe them earlier in this section.

✔ stateConnectionString: Used only in `StateServer` mode. It provides the address of the machine that will take the role of the State Server.

✔ sqlConnectionString: Used only in `SQLServer` mode. It provides the connection string necessary to connect to the database where the session information will be stored.

✔ cookieless: Specifies whether ASP.NET 2.0 should use cookies to handle sessions. Usually, the server tracks sessions by putting a unique ID in the user's cookie file. When the user comes back, the server recognizes the ID. If the user has a browser that doesn't support cookies, or the user has turned off cookie support, this method doesn't work. ASP.NET 2.0 has an alternate method that it can use, but it requires a little more overhead. This attribute is usually set to `false`, meaning that ASP.NET 2.0 uses cookies to handle sessions. Setting this attribute to `true` causes ASP.NET 2.0 to use its alternative method. Very few users have browsers that don't support cookies. Unless you have reason to believe that a larger-than-usual number of your users' browsers won't support cookies, you're probably better off leaving this setting alone.

✔ timeout: Indicates how long ASP.NET 2.0 waits between requests from a user before ending a session. A session goes from the time a user first retrieves a page from the site until the user goes away (either to another site or off the Web entirely). How long do you wait for another request before you decide that the user has gone for good and end the session? By default, 20 minutes. You can change that by assigning a different value to this attribute.

The session settings use a tag called `<sessionState>`. The following code sets the session mode to use SQL Server and then provides a connection string to access the database. In addition, it sets `cookieless` to `true` and `timeout` to 30 minutes:

```
<configuration>
   <system.web>
      <sessionState mode="SQLServer"
         sqlConnectionString=
            "data source=DBServer; uid=usr1; pwd=xyz"
         cookieless="true"
         timeout="30" />
   </system.web>
</configuration>
```

Note that when you need to divide a line in two in the `web.config` file, you don't use the _ as you do in VB 2005. You can divide lines anywhere you like in the configuration file, and the file will work fine. The only thing you have to be careful to do is to leave attribute values (within quotes) all on one line.

Another way to change your configuration

If you have direct access to your Web server and administrative access to IIS, you can use a tabbed dialog interface instead of directly editing the `web.config` file. To access this interface, follow these steps:

1. **Launch the Internet Information Services manager by choosing Start➪Control Panel➪Administrative Tools➪Internet Information Services.**

   The window looks similar to Figure 18-1, shown earlier in this chapter.

   Along the left side, you see a hierarchy of items. Under the top-level Internet Information Services icon is an icon that represents your server. Under that, you see one or more entries. Among them should be one titled Default Web Site.

   If you don't see Default Web Site, but you do see Web Sites, open that and Default Web Site should be inside. (These differences depend on the operating system you're using.)

2. **Open Default Web Site. Here you see a list of all the folders that appear under c:\inetpub\wwwroot.**

3. **Find the folder that contains your application (the one whose configuration you want to edit). Right-click the folder and choose Properties from the contextual menu.**

   A *Web Folder* Properties dialog box appears, and it looks like Figure 18-2, shown earlier in this chapter.

4. **Click the ASP.NET tab.**

   On this tab, you see some basic information about your Web application.

5. **Click the Edit Configuration button near the bottom of the dialog box.**

   If this button is disabled, it means that this folder isn't configured as an ASP.NET 2.0 application or that it is configured for an earlier version of ASP.NET.

   If you want to upgrade this folder to the newest version of ASP.NET, simply select the appropriate version from the ASP.NET Version drop-down list at the top of this dialog box, and then click Apply. The Edit Configuration button should become enabled.

   The ASP.NET Configuration Settings dialog appears.

6. **Select the appropriate tab and make the desired changes to the Web application settings.**

7. **Click OK when you're finished.**

Storing your application settings in the web.config file

In addition to setting up ASP.NET 2.0 to work the way you want it to, the `web.config` file has another handy use: It gives you a place to store your own application settings.

Storing connection strings

Suppose you want to store the connection string you use to access the database. There's a section of the `web.config` file just for that purpose. It's called `<connectionStrings>` and it looks like this:

```
<configuration>
   <connectionStrings>
      <add name="pubsConnection"
         connectionString=
"Server=Aron1;Database=pubs;Trusted_Connection=True;"
         providerName="System.Data.SqlClient" />
   </connectionStrings>
   <system.web>
      <httpRuntime maxRequestLength="6144" />
      <pages enableSessionState="true"
         enableViewState="true" />
   </system.web>
</configuration>
```

You can include as many <add> tags between the <connectionStrings> tags as you like, each with name and connectionString attributes specified.

Now, in your application, you can access the information quickly and easily:

```
Dim cs As ConnectionStringSettings
cs = ConfigurationManager.ConnectionStrings( _
    "pubsConnection")
Dim cn As New SqlConnection(cs.ConnectionString)
```

With this approach, all your pages can pull the information from the same source, and if you ever need to change it, you make your changes in only one place: the configuration file.

For more information on connecting to a database, see Chapter 19.

Storing application-specific settings

You can store your own application-specific settings in the web.config file by using the <appSettings> section. Here's an example:

```
<configuration>
    <appSettings>
        <add key="ServerName"
            value="Aristotle" />
    </appSettings>
    <system.web>
        <httpRuntime maxRequestLength="6144" />
        <pages enableSessionState="true"
            enableViewState="true" />
    </system.web>
</configuration>
```

You can have as many <add> tags as you like to store as many different settings as you like. And to access these settings from your code, enter the following:

```
Dim ServerName As String
ConnectString = System.Configuration. _
    ConfigurationSettings.AppSettings("ServerName")
```

Part VII
Tapping the Database

The 5th Wave   By Rich Tennant

"I'll be with you as soon as I execute a few more commands."

In this part . . .

What do people look for on the Web? Information! And where can you find the deepest, meatiest information? In databases. But how do you get at the information in those databases? Aren't databases big and complex, and don't they require advanced degrees just to understand? Absolutely not.

Databases are actually pretty simple after you get the hang of them. And they provide powerful capabilities for storing, indexing, sorting, and retrieving exactly what you want. In this part of the book, you discover how to use the new ASP.NET 2.0 database access controls to retrieve data from a database and display it in a pleasant way on your Web page. You also find out how to store your own data.

If you're completely new to databases, you might want to make a quick stop at Bonus Chapter 7 (on the CD) before you dive into this part of the book. Bonus Chapter 7 provides a quick but informative introduction to all the stuff most database books think you already know.

Chapter 19

Accessing a Database with Simple Queries

● ●

In This Chapter

▶ Understanding the libraries and controls used for database access

▶ Connecting to a database and retrieving data with the `SqlDataSource` server control

▶ Using the `GridView` server control to display, sort, and page through query results

● ●

A Web page can be flashy. It can even be smart. But without a way to store and retrieve important information, it's just a novelty — not a critical resource. That's why database access and retrieval is critical for virtually all Web development projects today. The Web enables you to take important database information and make it available any time, anywhere.

In this chapter, you discover the technologies that ASP.NET 2.0 provides to access databases. All the controls and techniques that I describe in this chapter are new to ASP.NET 2.0, and they make it easier than ever to develop information-rich applications for the Web.

If you're new to databases, take a quick detour through Bonus Chapter 7 on the CD. It's not long, and it gives you the essentials you need to make the most out of this chapter and the next.

Building Classy Classifieds 1.0: AllAds.aspx

Classy Classifieds (Classy, for short) is an ASP.NET 2.0 application that I've included with this book. It presents visitors with classified ads that are organized into different categories for browsing. It also enables visitors to place their own ads for others to see.

In this chapter and the next, I demonstrate the database access techniques I describe in the text by showing you how to create version 1.0 of Classy Classifieds. You can find the pages created for this chapter on the CD in this folder: \Author\Chapter19. I describe the final version, Classy Classifieds 2.0, in Bonus Chapter 2. It adds the use of Master Pages and is just a little more polished. You can find Classy Classifieds 2.0 on the CD in this folder: \Author\Classy2.

In this chapter, you create the Classy1 folder and prepare it to be used as a home for your application. You also create a page called AllAds.aspx that accesses the Microsoft Access database I created for use with Classy. AllAds. aspx simply retrieves and displays all the rows in the Ads table. This page isn't part of the final Classy application, but it helps you to get a firm handle on the basics of retrieving and displaying database data. When you've got the basics down in this chapter, you can move to Chapter 20 and focus all your energies on creating the various pages that are a part of Classy Classifieds 1.0.

To get a better idea of what Classy Classifieds does, you might want to run the application on the CD before you proceed with this chapter and the next.

The Import of Database Access Libraries

The .NET Framework provides the ability to access a variety of different DBMSs (Database Management Systems) including Microsoft Access, Microsoft SQL Server, Oracle, and others. So that your pages access each DBMS quickly and efficiently, Microsoft has created separate libraries of code for each database. These libraries are referred to as *.NET data providers*. You use the same techniques to access a database no matter what DBMS it is. The .NET data provider is the piece that does the magic of translating your request into a request that the DBMS can understand.

You need to add two Import statements to the top of every page that accesses the database. (For information on namespaces and @ Import, see Chapter 17.) The first one is always the System.Data namespace. That has essential classes in it that you need no matter what database you're accessing:

```
<%@ Import Namespace="System.Data" %>
```

The second namespace is determined by the .NET data provider you want to use.

▶ **For Microsoft SQL Server**, you use the .NET data provider library called System.Data.SqlClient:

```
<%@ Import Namespace="System.Data.SqlClient" %>
```

✔ **For Oracle,** you use the .NET data provider library called `System.Data.OracleClient`:

```
<%@ Import Namespace="System.Data.OracleClient" %>
```

✔ **For Microsoft Access,** you use the .NET data provider library called `System.Data.OleDb`:

```
<%@ Import Namespace="System.Data.OleDb" %>
```

The OLE DB data provider is a fall-back position when you don't have a specific .NET data provider available for your database. The OLE DB data provider gives you access to any database that has an OLE DB driver available for it. OLE DB is an older technology, and although it isn't as efficient as a .NET data provider, OLE DB drivers are available for almost all the major DBMSs. Because Microsoft Access doesn't have a specific .NET data provider written for it, you use the OLE DB provider to access it.

Cool Database-Access Server Controls

The preceding sections explain which .NET data provider library you need to access the database, and here I tell you about a few server controls you can use to access databases from ASP.NET 2.0:

✔ `SqlDataSource`: Provides the means of access. It retrieves and updates data based on a SQL query. It's designed to be used as a source for data-bound controls such as `GridView` and `DetailsView`.

✔ `GridView`: Presents multiple database table rows in the form of a spreadsheet-style grid. You can use the `GridView` to display data or edit it directly.

✔ `DetailsView`: Presents a single row of data from a table in the form of labeled text boxes. You can use this server control to display data or edit it directly.

Who comes up with these names?

What does OLE DB mean? DB is probably database, right? But OLE? Is it Spanish?

The term *OLE* has been around Microsoft for a long time. It used to mean Object Linking and Embedding. Along with the term COM (which stands for Component Object Model, if you must know), it now refers to Microsoft's technologies that enable different applications or components to talk to each other. OLE DB is a technology that works behind the scenes, enabling your pages to talk to DBMSs from various vendors.

It works like this: You drop a `SqlDataSource` control on your page and set its properties. It has all kinds of properties — everything you need to get connected to the database and retrieve some data.

Then you add a `GridView` or a `DetailsView` control to your page, depending on how you want to present the data. Then you set the `Grid` or `DetailsView` control's `DataSourceID` property to the `SqlDataSource`. That connection is all the `Grid` or `DetailsView` needs to display the data. From there, finishing up is just a matter of tweaking properties to make sure you're showing the right data and to make it look beautiful.

Getting Ready to Access the Database

You need to take a few steps to prepare to work with the examples in this chapter and the next one. The following sections describe those steps.

Getting the database

Before you begin creating a database-access application, you need a database! I provide one on the CD in the back of this book. The database is called `classydb.mdb`, and you can find it in the `\Author\Chapter19` folder on the CD. If you know anything about Microsoft Access, feel free to double-click the `classydb.mdb` file and take a look at the database in Access. There's no magic. If you don't know much about Access, I describe the table and its columns next.

This database holds only one table, called Ads. It has the following columns:

- **AdNum:** The primary key of the table. Access calls it an `AutoNumber`, which means that when you create a new record, Access automatically generates a unique value for this field. This is a *surrogate key,* which means the field doesn't hold any important data itself and won't be entered or viewed by the users. It just uniquely identifies each row. (See Bonus Chapter 7 on the CD for more on primary keys and surrogate keys.)

- **Title:** The name of the item, like "Michael Jordan Rookie Playing Card."

- **Category:** A `string` holding the name of the category with which this item is associated. The Category column in each row holds one of five categories: Vehicles, Computers and Software, Real Estate, Collectibles, and General Merchandise.

- **Description:** The actual classified ad itself. This information is held in a *memo* field — a type of field that's designed to hold a *lot* of text.

- **Price:** The amount the user wants to get for the item.

✔ **Phone:** The user's phone number, including the area code.

✔ **Email:** The user's e-mail address.

✔ **State:** The state the user lives in (for geographical searches).

✔ **Posted:** The date the ad was posted.

✔ **Password:** A user-created secret word, which she enters when she creates the ad. Passwords enable users to identify themselves later to edit or delete their ads.

The database included on the CD-ROM has quite a few rows of test data for you to work with — several ads for each category.

Creating a home for your application

Create a folder under your `wwwroot` and call it Classy1. Identify this folder as a Web application by making the folder into a virtual folder. Be sure to visit the ASP.NET tab of the properties dialog box to change the *ASP.NET version* to 2.0. (For information on how to do this, see Chapter 18.)

Copy the `classydb.mdb` file to the Classy1 folder.

Web.config and the connectionStrings

One more file you need in the Classy1 folder is a `web.config` file. I describe the `web.config` file in Chapter 18. What I don't mention there is a section of the `web.config` file called `connectionStrings`. You use the `connectionStrings` section of the `web.config` file to hold the information your application needs to connect to your database. Your pages read this information as needed. This arrangement is better than hard-coding the information in your page. This way, if the connection information ever changes, you have to change only the `web.config` file — not every page of your application!

Here's what your `web.config` file should look like:

```
<configuration >
   <connectionStrings>
      <add name="classydbConnectString"
connectionString="Provider=Microsoft.Jet.OLEDB.4.0;
Data Source=C:\Inetpub\wwwroot\Classy1\classydb.mdb"
         providerName="System.Data.OleDb" />
   </connectionStrings>
</configuration>
```

This configuration file contains one entry in the `connectionString` section. The name for the entry is `classydbConnectString`, and by using that name, your application can access the connection string and the provider name.

The `connectionString` contains several values assigned to the appropriate names, each separated from each other with a semicolon (`;`). For Microsoft Access, the provider (an indication of what DBMS is being used) is assigned to `Provider`, and the filename of the database is assigned to `Data Source`.

If you connect to a different DBMS, the information you need to provide in the connection string will be different. For example, if you're using the SQL Server, you need to provide more information in the connection string:

- ✔ A server name (the name of the machine on the network that runs the DBMS)
- ✔ A database name
- ✔ A user name and password to log on

Depending on your configuration, you might need to provide other information, as well. Here's an example of a SQL Server connection string:

```
connectionString="UID=sa;PWD=pass;Data Source=myServer;
Initial Catalog=Northwind;"
```

Here, `Data Source` refers to the server where the DBMS is running, and `Initial Catalog` refers to the database you want to access on that server. `UID` and `PWD` refer to the user ID and password used to log on.

If you're using Oracle, DB2, or another DBMS, check your DBMS documentation for details on what information it requires you to place in the connection string.

Retrieving and Displaying Data

Now I show you how to create a simple page that retrieves all the ads from the database table and displays them to the user. Such a long list isn't terribly useful to a visitor to your site, so you don't see this one in the final application. But it provides a good springboard for exploring the database server controls.

Create a page named `AllAds.aspx`. It should look like Listing 19-1.

Listing 19-1:   Retrieving and Displaying the Ads

```
<%@ Page Explicit="True" Language="VB" Debug="True" %>
<%@ Import Namespace="System.Data" %>
<%@ Import Namespace="System.Data.OleDb" %>
<html>
<body vlink="red">
<h1>Classy Classifieds</h1>

<h2>All Ads</h2>
<form runat="server">
<asp:GridView ID="GridView1" runat="server"
DataKeyNames="AdNum" DataSourceID="SqlDataSource1" >
</asp:GridView>

<asp:SqlDataSource ID="SqlDataSource1" runat="server"
ConnectionString=
"<%$ ConnectionStrings:classydbConnectString %>"
ProviderName=
"<%$ ConnectionStrings:classydbConnectString.ProviderName
          %>"
SelectCommand="SELECT * FROM Ads">
</asp:SqlDataSource>
</form>
</body>
</html>
```

Save the page, launch a browser, and navigate to the page. Your browser should show a page that looks a lot like Figure 19-1.

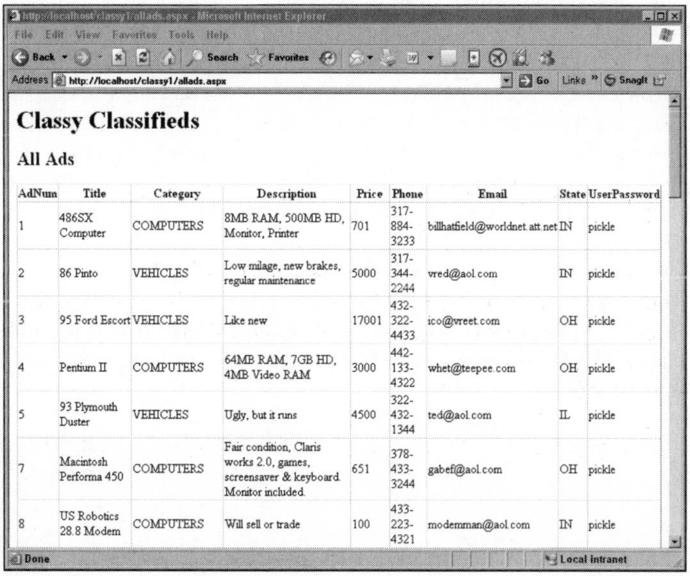

Figure 19-1:
The AllAds
page.

In the following sections, I walk through this page piece by piece because all the other examples in this chapter and the next build on this one.

The SqlDataSource control and its properties

At the bottom of Listing 19-1 is the `SqlDataSource` control:

```
<asp:SqlDataSource ID="SqlDataSource1" runat="server"
ConnectionString=
"<%$ ConnectionStrings:classydbConnectString %>"
ProviderName=
"<%$ ConnectionStrings:classydbConnectString.ProviderName
        %>"
SelectCommand="SELECT * FROM Ads">
</asp:SqlDataSource>
```

This control does a whole lot of heavy lifting for you. It's responsible for making the connection to the database, for executing a SQL query, and for receiving the results back and making them available to display on the page. All this is made possible by setting just a few properties.

You must fill in the `ConnectionString` property with an appropriate connection string that connects the application to the database. The `ProviderName` property expects a value indicating which .NET data provider you want to use to access the database. The value you would assign to `ProviderName` is a string containing the name of the library holding the .NET data provider, like `System.Data.OleDb` or `System.Data.SqlClient`.

The `ConnectionString` and `ProviderName` properties are assigned a value inside quotes that looks very strange. It uses <% and %> (the delimiters), which mean that some sort of server-side processing is going to happen. But then both begin with a dollar sign ($). This special syntax makes it easy for you to refer to information in the `web.config` file's `connectionStrings` section. Both the connection string and the provider are retrieved from the `web.config` file and assigned to the appropriate property.

The `SelectCommand` property is the only other important property, and its use is probably obvious — this is the SQL query that will be executed on the database to retrieve the rows.

The connection and retrieval occur when the `GridView` control attempts to bind to the `SqlDataSource`. And that happens when the page is loaded.

The GridView control and its properties

The GridView control has only a few properties to discuss:

```
<asp:GridView ID="GridView1" runat="server"
DataKeyNames="AdNum" DataSourceID="SqlDataSource1" >
</asp:GridView>
```

The DataSourceID property ties the GridView to the SqlDataSource and associates the grid to the data retrieved.

This process of associating a visual control with data retrieved is called *data binding*. I use it here to display data, but as you see in Chapter 22, data binding is a two-way street. The user can change data that is bound to a server control and then send the changes back to the database.

The DataKeyNames property isn't technically necessary on this page, but it is a good idea to always specify it. As you might guess, it just identifies the name of the column that is the key. This information can be used by the GridView for a variety of purposes and makes GridView features available to your application that would otherwise be impossible.

Identifying the columns to display

The simple example in the preceding section uses a feature of the GridView called AutoGenerateColumns. By default, this feature is *on,* so you don't have to specify the property to get it to work. This feature automatically creates a column in the GridView for every column returned in the result set.

But perhaps you don't want to display every column. Suppose, for example, that you want to display only the title, price, and state. You could, of course, just change the SELECT statement in the SelectCommand of the SqlDataSource. That would work, but you might actually want to retrieve all the columns, even if you want to show only a few of them in this grid.

Fortunately, changing the grid so that you can control the columns displayed is pretty easy. Change the GridView tag so that it looks like this (changes are in bold):

```
<asp:GridView ID="GridView1" runat="server"
AutoGenerateColumns="False"
DataKeyNames="AdNum" DataSourceID="SqlDataSource1" >
    <Columns>
        <asp:BoundField DataField="Title"
```

```
          HeaderText="Title" />
       <asp:BoundField DataField="Price"
       HeaderText="Price" />
       <asp:BoundField DataField="State"
       HeaderText="State" />
   </Columns>
</asp:GridView>
```

That cleans up the table a lot, as you can see in Figure 19-2.

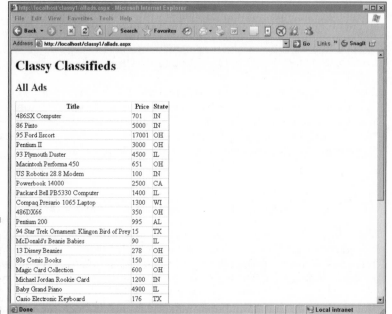

Figure 19-2:
The AllAds
page with
fewer
columns.

Because the default value of the AutoGenerateColumns property is true, I
had to specifically set it to false so that I could control the columns displayed.

Then I use the <Columns> tag to identify what columns are to be displayed
and what they should look like. There's one <asp:BoundField> tag for each
column I want to display. I identify the column name from the query in the
DataField. And I even have the option to provide a more human-readable
header with HeaderText.

Notice that <Columns> doesn't have the asp: prefix. Why? Who knows!
Sometimes when you put tags within server control tags like this, you're
supposed to use the asp: prefix, and sometimes you're not. You just have
to pay close attention to the online help.

Using GridView beautification properties

Do you want to turn that drab, boring `GridView` into something you'd be proud to show your friends and neighbors? It only takes setting a few properties to really make it shine! Or at least make it a little less ugly. . . .

Change the `GridView` tag so it looks like this (the new stuff is in bold):

```
<asp:GridView ID="GridView1" runat="server"
AutoGenerateColumns="False"
BackColor="#FFFF99" BorderColor="Black"
          BorderStyle="Solid"
BorderWidth="1px" Width="100%"
DataKeyNames="AdNum" DataSourceID="SqlDataSource1" >
<HeaderStyle HorizontalAlign="Left" />
  <Columns>
    <asp:BoundField DataField="Title"
      HeaderText="Title" />
    <asp:BoundField DataField="Price"
      DataFormatString="{0:c}"
      HeaderText="Price" />
    <asp:BoundField DataField="State"
      HeaderText="State" />
  </Columns>
</asp:GridView>
```

The result is quite attractive, as you can see in Figure 19-3.

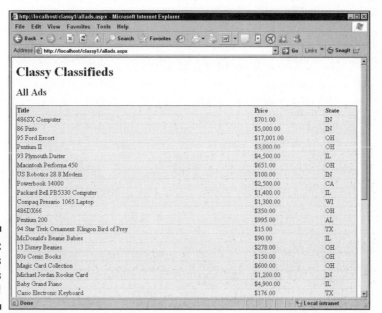

Figure 19-3: The AllAds page is beautified!

`BackColor` specifies the background color of the grid. The rest of the properties added to the `GridView` control are mostly self-explanatory. And they are the same kinds of display properties you'd see on other server controls.

Notice that a new tag is added between the `GridView` tags. In addition to `<Columns>`, you see `<HeaderStyle>`. This allows you to control how the column headers look. I use it to align the headers along the left instead of the default which is to center them.

The one property that's really different is `DataFormatString`. This property allows you to apply formatting to a specific column so that the data displayed in that column looks the way you want it to. In this case, the value is a number, and you want it to be displayed as a price.

The string you use to indicate what formatting should be used in the `DataFormatString` property is a little odd. It's always surrounded by curly braces, and it always begins with `0:`. The only thing that changes is what comes after the colon. For a column with numbers, the `c` character, for currency, is probably the most useful. It adds a dollar sign and ensures that two decimal places appear. You can also use `d` for decimal format, `e` for scientific (exponential) format, and when you want to impress your geeky friends, `x` for hexadecimal format.

Sorting out the grid

Site visitors often welcome the opportunity to sort and filter the information shown in a grid. Fortunately, adding these features is very easy. I begin with sorting. The first step is to add one simple property to the `GridView`:

```
AllowSorting="True"
```

Setting this property makes the column headers in your grid turn into links. When the user clicks those links, the `GridView` tries to sort the information in the grid based on the column header clicked. But to do the sorting, the `GridView` needs one more piece of information: the data column it should use to do the sorting.

You might think this is obvious. If the user clicks the column header for State, the grid should sort itself based on the states. But in more complex grids, you don't always have a one-to-one relationship between what's displayed and what was retrieved from the database. Because of this, you have to specify the name of the column by which to sort for each bound column in your grid. Fortunately, it's no big deal.

Change your `Columns` section to look like this (the new properties are in bold):

```
<asp:GridView ID="GridView1" runat="server"
AutoGenerateColumns="False"
BackColor="#FFFF99" BorderColor="Black"
          BorderStyle="Solid"
BorderWidth="1px" Width="100%"
DataKeyNames="AdNum" DataSourceID="SqlDataSource1"
AllowSorting="True" >
<HeaderStyle HorizontalAlign="Left" />
  <Columns>
    <asp:BoundField DataField="Title"
      HeaderText="Title"
      SortExpression="Title"/>
    <asp:BoundField DataField="Price"
      DataFormatString="{0:c}"
      HeaderText="Price"
      SortExpression="Price" />
    <asp:BoundField DataField="State"
      HeaderText="State"
      SortExpression="State" />
  </Columns>
</asp:GridView>
```

As you can see, for simple `BoundField` columns, the `SortExpression` property is often the same as the `DataField` property.

That's all you have to do to provide sorting. When you try your page (see Figure 19-4), you can click a header to sort by that column and then click the header again to get a sort in the reverse order on that same column. Pretty handy!

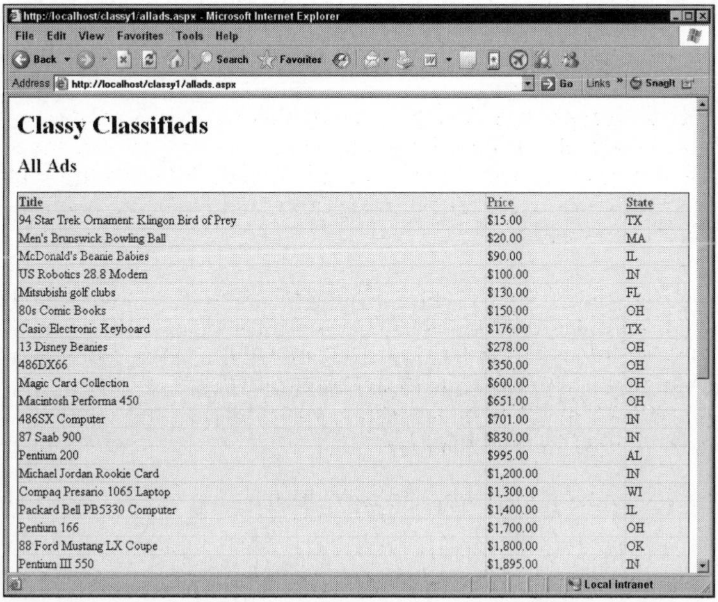

Figure 19-4:
Sorting the AllAds page with the column header links.

Paging Dr. GridView . . .

When you have a long list of items in a grid, the user often prefers to page through the list, looking at only a few entries at a time, rather than scrolling up and down a giant list. Adding paging to your grid is just as easy as adding sorting.

Add this property to the `GridView`:

```
AllowPaging="True"
```

That's all you need to do to add the default paging! Try it out. Your page should look like Figure 19-5.

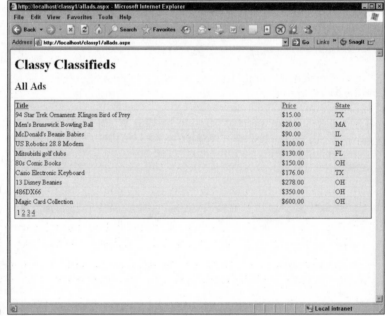

Figure 19-5:
Applying the default paging features to the AllAds page.

Of course, if you want to customize the paging features, you can use quite a few properties to do that. They all appear inside a new tag called `<PagerSettings>`. For example, suppose you want to use next and previous links instead of the page numbers. And suppose you want the next and previous links to be labeled Previous Page and Next Page. Simply change your `GridView` to look like this:

```
<asp:GridView ID="GridView1" runat="server"
AllowSorting="True" AllowPaging="True"
AutoGenerateColumns="False"
BackColor="#FFFF99" BorderColor="Black"
            BorderStyle="Solid"
BorderWidth="1px" Width="100%"
DataKeyNames="AdNum" DataSourceID="SqlDataSource1" >
  <HeaderStyle HorizontalAlign="Left" />
  <Columns>
    <asp:BoundField DataField="Title"
      HeaderText="Title"
      SortExpression="Title"/>
    <asp:BoundField DataField="Price"
      DataFormatString="{0:c}"
      HeaderText="Price"
      SortExpression="Price" />
    <asp:BoundField DataField="State"
      HeaderText="State"
      SortExpression="State" />
  </Columns>
  <PagerSettings Mode="NextPrevious"
    NextPageText="Next Page"
    PreviousPageText="Previous Page" />
</asp:GridView>
```

Notice that `<PagerSettings>` appears between the `<asp:GridView>` tags, but outside of the `<Columns>` tags, just like the `<HeaderStyle>`.

The `PagerSettings Mode` property can have any of the following values:

- ✔ `Numeric`: The default. A list of page numbers, each appearing as a link that the user can click to jump directly to the page.

- ✔ `NumericFirstLast`: Same as numeric, but additional links appear, allowing the user to jump directly to the first or last page of the list.

- ✔ `NextPrevious`: Provides a next page link and a previous page link so the user can walk through the pages consecutively, one by one.

- ✔ `NextPreviousFirstLast`: Adds first page and last page links as well as the next and previous links.

In addition, you can set a number of other properties of the `<PagerSettings>` property. Here are a few of them:

- ✔ `FirstPageText`/`FirstPageImageUrl`: Set the text or image that will appear as a link that allows the user to jump to the first page.

- ✔ `LastPageText`/`LastPageImageUrl`, `NextPageText`/`NextPageUrl`, `PreviousPageText`/`PreviousPageUrl`: Set the text or image that will appear as a link that allows the user to jump to the last page, previous page, or next page.

✔ `Position`: Indicates the position where the paging links appear on the grid. Possible values are `Bottom` (the default), `Top`, and `TopAndBottom`.

✔ `PageButtonCount`: When the mode is `Numeric` or `NumericFirstLast`, this property determines how many page links appear (at most).

Chapter 20

Using Sophisticated Queries and Updating the Database

In This Chapter

▶ Narrowing your database searches with selection criteria

▶ Using the `DetailsView` control to display all the columns for a single row

▶ Adding, updating, and deleting rows

*I*n the preceding chapter, you find out how to connect your page to the database, retrieve data, and bind the data to a `GridView` to display it on a page. You also create the `Classy1` folder, add a simple `web.config` file, and create the `allads.aspx` page, which retrieves and displays all the rows from a database table.

In this chapter, you create pages that perform more sophisticated queries — responding to information sent to the page as a query string or selection criteria entered by the user. In addition, you discover the `DetailsView` control and how to insert, update, and delete data in the database. With this basic knowledge, you can begin tackling your own database projects.

All of the controls and techniques that I describe in this chapter are new to ASP.NET 2.0.

In Chapter 19, you begin creating the Classy Classifieds 1.0 application. In this chapter, you complete it. You can find the pages created for this chapter on the CD in the `\Author\Chapter20` folder. I describe the final version, Classy Classifieds 2.0, in Bonus Chapter 2. It uses the Master Pages feature and is just a little slicker and more polished. You can find Classy Classifieds 2.0 on the CD in the `\Author\Classy2` folder.

Using Select Parameters to Narrow Your Query

Now it's time to begin creating the `category.aspx` page. This page provides a list of all the ads for a specific category. The user selects the category on the `default.aspx` page by clicking a link. One link exists for each category, but all the links point to the same page: `category.aspx`.

So how does the Category page know which category to display? Each link also passes a value on the URL line as a query string. (For more information on passing values with query strings, see Chapter 9.)

The cool thing is that the `SqlDataSource` control has the ability to pluck the value right out of the query string and plug it into your SQL `SELECT` statement without you writing a line of code. That's what I show you how to do in the following sections.

There's no place like home

To begin, you need to create two pages: `default.aspx` and `category.aspx`. The `default.aspx` page is pretty simple. Listing 20-1 shows . (You create the `category.aspx` page in the next section.)

Listing 20-1:   The default.aspx Page for Classy 1.0

```
<%@ Page Explicit="True" Language="VB" Debug="True" %>
<html>
<body vlink="red">
<h1>Classy Classifieds</h1>
<p>Welcome to Classy Classifieds. We make it easy to turn
your stuff into cash and to get other people's stuff
cheap.</p>
<asp:label ID="Label1" runat="server" font-size="18 pt"
font-names="Arial" font-bold="true"
text="The Categories:" /><br><br>
<table width=100% cellpadding="10">
<tr><td>
<asp:hyperlink id="VehiclesLink" runat="server"
navigateurl="category.aspx?Category=VEHICLES"
font-names="Arial" font-size="16 pt">
Vehicles</asp:hyperlink>
</td><td>
<asp:hyperlink id="ComputersLink" runat="server"
navigateurl="category.aspx?Category=COMPUTERS"
font-names="Arial" font-size="16 pt">
```

```
Computers and Software</asp:hyperlink>
</td></tr><tr><td>
<asp:hyperlink id="RealEstateLink" runat="server"
navigateurl="category.aspx?Category=REALESTATE"
font-names="Arial" font-size="16 pt">
Real Estate</asp:hyperlink>
</td><td>
<asp:hyperlink id="CollectiblesLink" runat="server"
navigateurl="category.aspx?Category=COLLECTIBLES"
font-names="Arial" font-size="16 pt">
Collectibles</asp:hyperlink>
</td></tr><tr><td>
<asp:hyperlink id="GeneralLink" runat="server"
navigateurl="category.aspx?Category=GENERAL"
font-names="Arial" font-size="16 pt">
General Merchandise</asp:hyperlink>
</td><td>
<asp:hyperlink id="SearchLink" runat="server"
navigateurl="search.aspx"
font-names="Arial" font-size="16 pt">
Search</asp:hyperlink>
</td></tr><tr><td>
<asp:hyperlink id="PlaceAdLink" runat="server"
navigateurl="placead.aspx"
font-names="Arial" font-size="16 pt">
Place A New Ad</asp:hyperlink>
</td><td>
</table>
</body>
</html>
```

This page provides a link for each category, as you can see in Figure 20-1.

The links, created with HyperLink server controls, all point to the same page: category.aspx. But the Category page needs to know which category the user wants to see. So that information is sent after the question mark on the URL line as a QueryString.

Using the QueryStringParameter

In Chapter 9, I introduce the idea of passing variables from one page to another on the URL line and accessing the value with the Request.QueryString property. In Classy, I use this same technique in the links on the default page to pass the category selected to the category page. The SQLDataSource is a very powerful and flexible control. It allows you to specify a parameter value from the QueryString sent to a page without the need to even write a line of code to retrieve the value using the Request.QueryString property. You can just add a QueryStringParameter tag to the SQLDataSource control and it happens automatically.

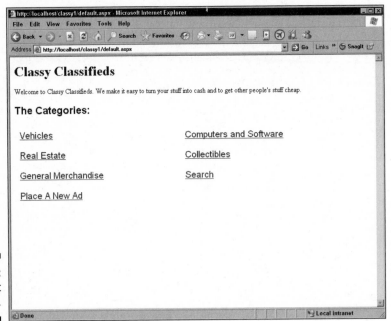

Figure 20-1:
The default
page.

The `category.aspx` page should look like Listing 20-2. The parts of the code that demonstrate new concepts are highlighted in bold.

Listing 20-2: The category.aspx Page

```
<%@ Page Explicit="True" Language="VB" Debug="True" %>
<%@ Import Namespace="System.Data" %>
<%@ Import Namespace="System.Data.OleDb" %>
<html>
<body vlink="red">
<h1>Classy Classifieds</h1>
<form runat="server">
<h2>Category: <%=Request.QueryString("Category")%></h2>

<asp:GridView ID="GridView1" runat="server"
AllowPaging="True" AllowSorting="True"
AutoGenerateColumns="False" BackColor="#FFFF99"
BorderColor="Black" BorderStyle="Solid"
BorderWidth="1px" DataKeyNames="AdNum"
DataSourceID="SqlDataSource1" Width="100%">

<HeaderStyle HorizontalAlign="Left" />

<Columns>
    <asp:BoundField DataField="Title" HeaderText="Title"
    SortExpression="Title" />
```

```
    <asp:BoundField DataField="Price"
    DataFormatString="{0:c}" HeaderText="Price"
    SortExpression="Price" />
    <asp:BoundField DataField="State" HeaderText="State"
    SortExpression="State" />
</Columns>

</asp:GridView>

<asp:SqlDataSource ID="SqlDataSource1" runat="server"
ConnectionString=
"<%$ ConnectionStrings:classydbConnectString %>"
ProviderName=
"<%$ ConnectionStrings:classydbConnectString.ProviderName
        %>"
SelectCommand="SELECT * FROM Ads WHERE (Category = ?)">

<SelectParameters>
    <asp:QueryStringParameter Name="Category"
    QueryStringField="CATEGORY" Type="String" />
</SelectParameters>

</asp:SqlDataSource>

</form>
</body>
</html>
```

When you click one of the links on the default page, the `category.aspx` page appears, showing the appropriate ads, as you can see in Figure 20-2.

This page is similar to the example I present in Chapter 19. I add only two pieces of code to make use of the query string to change the SQL SELECT statement. First, the SELECT statement itself has a new WHERE clause:

```
SelectCommand="SELECT * FROM Ads WHERE (Category = ?)">
```

The question mark acts as a placeholder for the information I want to plug in there. To tell ASP.NET *what* I want to plug in, I use a new tag — this one is within the `<asp:SqlDataSource>` control.

```
<SelectParameters>
    <asp:QueryStringParameter Name="Category"
    QueryStringField="CATEGORY" Type="String" />
</SelectParameters>
```

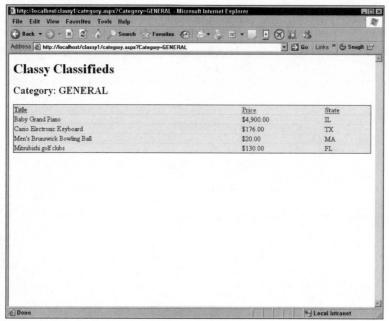

If you had multiple question marks in the query, you'd see multiple tags between the `<SelectParameters>` tags. As it is, there's only one — an `<asp:QueryStringParameter>`. As the name implies, it retrieves its information from the query string. You specify the `QueryStringField` name and the data type. That's all the information the `SqlDataSource` control needs to grab the information, stuff it into the SQL Select's `WHERE` clause and execute the query.

You can put other tags between the `<SelectParameters>` tags to get information from various sources. These useful tags include:

- ✔ `<asp:ControlParameter>`: Uses the value from a property of a server control on your page, like the `Text` property of a `TextBox` control or the `SelectedValue` property of a `DropDownList` control.

- ✔ `<asp:SessionParameter>`: Uses the value from a specified `Session` variable.

- ✔ `<asp:CookieParameter>`: Uses the value from a specified cookie.

- ✔ `<asp:ProfileParameter>`: Uses the value from any property exposed by the ASP.NET Profile object.

These tags give you a lot of options for automatically filling in selection criteria for your SQL queries. In the next section, I demonstrate the use of `<asp:ControlParameter>` in the `search.aspx` page of the Classy Classifieds application to retrieve information from the controls on the page.

Using the ControlParameter tag

What information should you retrieve? Why not let the user decide? Just provide server controls where users can enter their search criteria. Then use the `SqlDataSource` control's `ControlParameter` tags to retrieve the information from the controls and stuff them into your SQL `SELECT` statement.

Create the page in Listing 20-3, and save it as `search.aspx`.

Listing 20-3:   The search.aspx Page

```
<%@ Page Explicit="True" Language="VB" Debug="True" %>
<%@ Import Namespace="System.Data" %>
<%@ Import Namespace="System.Data.OleDb" %>
<html>
<body vlink="red">
<h1>Classy Classifieds</h1>

<h2>Search</h2>
<form runat="server">

<script runat="server">
Sub Search_Click(ByVal Sender As Object, _
  ByVal E As EventArgs)
        ' No code is necessary here
        ' When there's a round trip to the server,
        ' the grid is updated automatically based
        ' on the selection criteria entered.
End Sub
</script>

Select the category you wish to search, enter your search
criteria and click the Search button to see the results.
<br />

<table>
<tr><td>Category:</td><td>
 
<asp:dropdownlist id="CategoryDropDown" runat="server" >
    <asp:listitem value="VEHICLES">Vehicles</asp:listitem>
    <asp:listitem
          value="COMPUTERS">Computers</asp:listitem>
    <asp:listitem value="REALESTATE">
    Real Estate</asp:listitem>
    <asp:listitem value="COLLECTIBLES">
    Collectibles</asp:listitem>
    <asp:listitem value="GENERAL">
    General Merchandise</asp:listitem>
</asp:dropdownlist>
```

(continued)

Listing 20-3 *(continued)*

```
</td></tr>
<tr><td>Title:</td><td>
 
<asp:textbox id="TitleText" runat="server"
columns="30"/></td></tr>
<tr><td>Description:</td><td>
 
<asp:textbox id="DescriptionText" runat="server"
columns="30"/></td></tr>
<tr><td>State:</td><td>
<asp:textbox id="StateText" runat="server"
columns="2"/>
</td></tr>
<tr><td>Price:</td>
<td>From:
<asp:textbox id="PriceFromText" runat="server"
columns="10"/>
To:
<asp:textbox id="PriceToText" runat="server"
columns="10"/>
</tr>
<tr><td>
<asp:button id="Search" runat="server"
text="Search" onclick="Search_Click" />
</td></tr>
</table>

<br />

<asp:GridView ID="GridView1" runat="server"
AllowPaging="True" AllowSorting="True"
AutoGenerateColumns="False" BackColor="#FFFF99"
BorderColor="Black" BorderStyle="Solid"
BorderWidth="1px" DataKeyNames="AdNum"
DataSourceID="SqlDataSource1" Width="100%">

    <Columns>
        <asp:HyperLinkField DataNavigateUrlFields="AdNum"

          DataNavigateUrlFormatString="detail.aspx?AdNum=
          {0}"
        DataTextField="Title" HeaderText="Title"
        SortExpression="Title" />

        <asp:BoundField DataField="Price"
           HeaderText="Price"
        SortExpression="Price" />
        <asp:BoundField DataField="State"
           HeaderText="State"
        SortExpression="State" />
```

```
    </Columns>

    <HeaderStyle HorizontalAlign="Left" />
</asp:GridView>

<br>

<asp:SqlDataSource ID="SqlDataSource1" runat="server"
ConnectionString=
"<%$ ConnectionStrings:classydbConnectString %>"
ProviderName=
"<%$ ConnectionStrings:classydbConnectString.ProviderName
       %>"
SelectCommand="SELECT Title, Price, State, Category,
Description, AdNum FROM Ads WHERE ((Price >= ?) AND
(Price <= ?) AND (Category = ?) AND
(State LIKE '%' + ? + '%') AND (Title LIKE '%' + ? + '%')
       AND
(Description LIKE '%' + ? + '%'))">

    <SelectParameters>
        <asp:ControlParameter ControlID="PriceFromText"
        DefaultValue="0" Name="Price" PropertyName="Text"
        Type="Decimal" />
        <asp:ControlParameter ControlID="PriceToText"
        DefaultValue="9999999" Name="Price2"
        PropertyName="Text" Type="Decimal" />
        <asp:ControlParameter ControlID="CategoryDropDown"
        Name="Category" PropertyName="SelectedValue"
        Type="String" />
        <asp:ControlParameter ControlID="StateText"
        DefaultValue="%%" Name="State2"
           PropertyName="Text"
        Type="String" />
        <asp:ControlParameter ControlID="TitleText"
        DefaultValue="%%" Name="Title" PropertyName="Text"
        Type="String" />
        <asp:ControlParameter ControlID="DescriptionText"
        DefaultValue="%%" Name="Description"
        PropertyName="Text" Type="String" />
    </SelectParameters>
</asp:SqlDataSource>


</form>
</body>
</html>
```

The default page has a link to this Search page, too. When you open it in your browser, it looks like Figure 20-3.

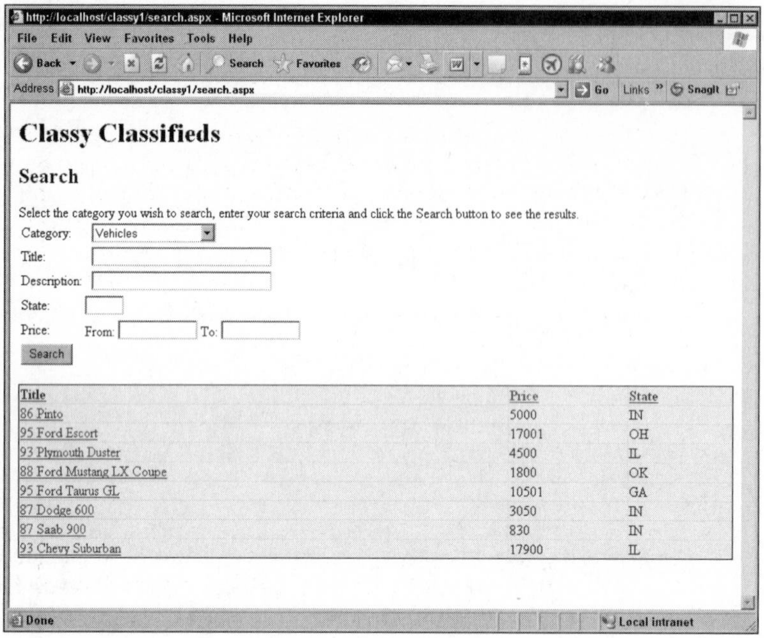

Figure 20-3:
The Search
page.

The `<asp:ControlParameter>` is used to fill in query parameters with the value of properties from server controls on the page. Typically, this is used to retrieve information the user has entered as selection criteria in text boxes and drop-down lists. That's what I've done in Listing 20-3. The `<asp:ControlParameter>` has two properties that make this possible. `ControlID` and `PropertyName` hold the name of the control and its property that should be used as the value for this parameter. The first parameter, for example, uses `PriceFromText.Text` for its value. Likewise, the second parameter uses `PriceToText.Text` for its value. The third parameter is a little different — it uses `CategoryDropDown.SelectedValue` for its value.

`DefaultValue` provides a very handy feature. If no value is provided for a given parameter, its `DefaultValue` is used. For most of the controls on this page, I use `"%%"` as the default value. This is a *wildcard,* which means "match on anything." In other words, if the criterion isn't filled in, it doesn't constrain the search — which is exactly what I want here.

Notice that for the price, I add two text boxes so that the user can enter a range of values. The default values I use there are 0 and 9999999 — a value larger than I expect any product will be!

In addition, I wanted to make sure that the user could type in just a part of the name or just a word or two of the description and the search would still pull back the matching information. Because of this, I often use the LIKE keyword in the WHERE clause and surround the entered value with % signs. So if the user types *babies* for the title, that part of the WHERE clause will actually look like this: ... AND (Title LIKE %babies%).... This causes a match on Beanie babies as well as All the babies of the world.

The DropDownList control in Listing 20-3 always has a valid category selected, so when the page is first displayed, it lists all the ads in the selected category. The user can change the category and/or add any other selection criteria he wants in any of the text boxes. When he clicks the Search button, the page returns to the server, but no code exists in the button's click event. All the work — evaluating the entered information, plugging it into the SELECT statement, executing the query, and then displaying the results on the page — is handled by the SqlDataSource and the GridView.

Using DetailsView

The detail.aspx page is used to display all the information for a single ad. This is where the user goes when she wants to read an ad and potentially respond to it. In this page, I use a DetailsView server control. I also use a SqlDataSource control with a QueryStringParameter tag much as I did in the Category page.

Create the detail.aspx page, which you see in Listing 20-4.

Listing 20-4:   The detail.aspx Page

```
<%@ Page Explicit="True" Language="VB" Debug="True" %>
<%@ Import Namespace="System.Data" %>
<%@ Import Namespace="System.Data.OleDb" %>

<script runat="server">
Sub Page_Load(ByVal Sender As Object, ByVal E As
            EventArgs)
   EditLink.NavigateUrl = "confirm.aspx?AdNum=" & _
      Request.QueryString("AdNum")
End Sub
</script>

<html>
<body vlink="red">
<h1>Classy Classifieds</h1>
<form runat="server">
<h2>Ad Detail</h2>

<asp:DetailsView ID="DetailsView1" runat="server"
    AutoGenerateRows="False" CellPadding="4"
    DataKeyNames="AdNum" DataSourceID="SqlDataSource1"
```

(continued)

Listing 20-4 *(continued)*

```
      ForeColor="#333333" GridLines="None" Height="65px"
      Width="100%">

      <FieldHeaderStyle BackColor="#FFFF99" Font-Bold="True"
             />
      <RowStyle BackColor="#FFFBD6" ForeColor="#333333" />

      <Fields>
          <asp:BoundField DataField="Title"
             HeaderText="Title"
          SortExpression="Title" />
          <asp:BoundField DataField="Category"
          HeaderText="Category" SortExpression="Category" />
          <asp:BoundField DataField="Description"
          HeaderText="Description"
          SortExpression="Description" />
          <asp:BoundField DataField="Price"
             HeaderText="Price"
          SortExpression="Price" />
          <asp:BoundField DataField="Phone"
             HeaderText="Phone"
          SortExpression="Phone" />
          <asp:BoundField DataField="Email"
             HeaderText="Email"
          SortExpression="Email" />
          <asp:BoundField DataField="State"
             HeaderText="State"
          SortExpression="State" />
      </Fields>
</asp:DetailsView>

<p><i>To respond to this ad, just click the email address
above to send the poster a message.</i></p>
If you created this ad, you can
<asp:hyperlink id="EditLink" runat="server" >
edit or delete it.</asp:hyperlink> <br>

<asp:SqlDataSource ID="SqlDataSource1" runat="server"
 ConnectionString=
"<%$ ConnectionStrings:classydbConnectString %>"
ProviderName=
"<%$ ConnectionStrings:classydbConnectString.ProviderName
          %>"
SelectCommand="SELECT * FROM Ads WHERE (AdNum = ?)">

    <SelectParameters>
        <asp:QueryStringParameter Name="AdNum"
        QueryStringField="AdNum" Type="Int32" />
    </SelectParameters>
```

```
</asp:SqlDataSource>

</form>
</body>
</html>
```

As you can see, the `DetailsView` in Figure 20-4 provides a different look at your data than the `GridView` does in Figure 20-3.

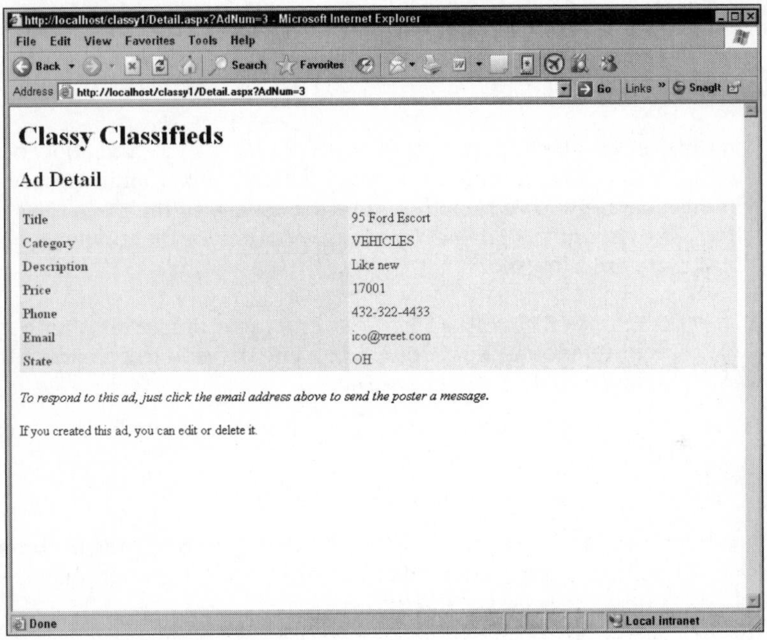

Figure 20-4:
The
`Details
View` in
action on
the Ad
Detail page.

The `DetailsView` server control has many properties that are identical to those of the `GridView`. Most of them are associated with the control's look and feel. Within the tag are two additional tags that allow you to set more look-and-feel properties for specific parts of the `DetailsView` — the field header and the row style.

The `<Fields>` tag corresponds to the `GridView` control's `<Columns>` tag. Between the `<Fields>` tags is a set of bound column definitions where the retrieved data is displayed. All the bound field properties work in the same way as the bound field properties of the `GridView`.

The `SqlDataSource` doesn't hold many surprises either. I've got a single select parameter. This time it's the AdNum column of the ad that I want to display. And again, it's passed as a query string.

At the bottom of the page, a link is provided. The link allows the user to edit or delete the ad if she is the person who created it. She can accomplish this with a `HyperLink` control, but no `NavigateUrl` property is specified in the tag. Instead, the `Page_Load` event fills in this property so that the `AdNum` `QueryString` that was sent to this page can be passed along to `confirm.aspx`. For more information on `confirm.aspx`, see the section "Retrieving and Working with Data from Code," later in this chapter.

Binding in New Ways: Alternatives to BoundField

In Chapter 19, I demonstrate the `<asp:BoundField>` and show how it is used with the `GridView` control to identify the columns from the query to display. In this chapter you've seen this same tag used with the `DetailsView` control. But `<asp:BoundField>` isn't your only option for identifying columns to display. Here are a few more:

- ✔ `<asp:HyperLinkField>`: Creates a hyperlink to another page on your site or to another site. Bound data can be used to construct the link or can be passed as a query string.

- ✔ `<asp:CheckBoxField>`: Displays Boolean (`true/false`) information in the form of a check box.

- ✔ `<asp:ImageField>`: Displays an image.

- ✔ `<asp:CommandField>`, `<asp:ButtonField>`: Adds buttons or links that can trigger commands to be executed on the server.

- ✔ `<asp:TemplateField>`: Can create a template that gives you more flexibility in exactly how you want to display the information.

You can use each of these display data from the database in different ways. As an example, I can use the `<asp:HyperLinkField>` in both the Category page and the Ad Detail page.

On the Category page, I list all the ads for the selected category. I want to change the page so that the user can then click a specific ad to see its details. To accomplish this, I replace `<asp:BoundColumn>` for the `Title` column with a `<asp:HyperLinkField>`, which displays the same information, but appears as a link that the user can click to view the Ad Detail page.

To accomplish this, change the `category.aspx` page — add the lines in bold:

```
<Columns>

    <asp:HyperLinkField DataNavigateUrlFields="AdNum"
    DataNavigateUrlFormatString="detail.aspx?AdNum={0}"
    DataTextField="Title" HeaderText="Title"
    SortExpression="Title" />

    <asp:BoundField DataField="Price"
    DataFormatString="{0:c}" HeaderText="Price"
    SortExpression="Price" />
    <asp:BoundField DataField="State" HeaderText="State"
    SortExpression="State" />
</Columns>
```

Now each title appears as a link, as you can see in Figure 20-5.

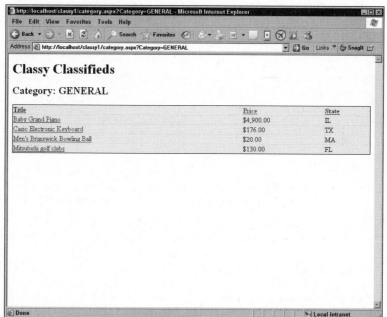

Figure 20-5:
The
Category
page with
links.

I discuss `HeaderText` and `SortExpression` in Chapter 19, so I focus on the other properties here.

`DataTextField` determines what information will be displayed for this column. It is similar to the `DataField` property in the `<asp:BoundField>` tag.

The `DataNavigateUrlFields` and `DataNavigateUrlFormatString` work together. Because this is a link, you have to specify the URL you want to link to. You do that with the `DataNavigateUrlFormatString`. However, the format string has a wildcard in it: `{0}`. That wildcard is filled in with the value specified in the `DataNavigateUrlFields`. In this case, for each row displayed, the link points to the `detail.aspx` page and passes the `AdNum` of the current row as the query string.

Here's an example. If the `Title` column is `"87 Saab 900"` and the `AdNum` is 27, this column would display "87 Saab 900" as a hyperlink. If the user clicks the hyperlink, this page is displayed:

```
detail.aspx?AdNum=27
```

I also use the `<asp:HyperLinkField>` in the detail page, but for a different reason—to create an e-mail link.

Replace the e-mail address `<asp:BoundColumn>` in `detail.aspx` with the lines in bold:

```
<Fields>

    ...

    <asp:BoundField DataField="Phone"
        HeaderText="Phone"
    SortExpression="Phone" />

    <asp:HyperLinkField DataNavigateUrlFields="Email"
    DataNavigateUrlFormatString="mailto:{0}"
    DataTextField="Email" HeaderText="Email" />

    <asp:BoundField DataField="State"
        HeaderText="State"
    SortExpression="State" />
</Fields>
```

Here, I don't want to link to a particular page or to pass a query string. I just want to make the e-mail address a link, so that when the visitor clicks it, her e-mail package is invoked. So I simply create a `mailto:` link and drop in the same e-mail address that the page is displaying. The resulting HTML generated by this server control would end up looking something like this:

```
<a href="mailto:bill@edgequest.com">bill@edgequest.com</a>
```

Retrieving and Working with Data from Code

Throughout the examples in this chapter, I show you all the amazing things you can do to retrieve and display data without writing any VB 2005 code at all.

But inevitably you will run in to circumstances where you will need to access and update data from your code. In this section, I show you an example of one approach to doing that. Remember, there are always two-dozen ways to shave a cat in .NET!

The `confirm.aspx` page of the Classy Classifieds application appears when a user who created a particular ad now wants to edit or delete that ad. To confirm that the user is who he says he is, the `confirm.aspx` page asks him to enter a secret password that he chose when he first created the ad. After he enters the password, the page retrieves the ad from the database and compares it with the password the user typed. If these passwords are a match, the user is sent on to the `editad.aspx` page (which you create later in this chapter). Otherwise, the user can try again.

First you have to create the `confirm.aspx` page. Listing 20-5 shows you the way.

Listing 20-5: The confirm.aspx Page

```
<%@ Page Explicit="True" Language="VB" Debug="True" %>
<%@ Import Namespace="System.Data" %>
<%@ Import Namespace="System.Data.OleDb" %>
<html>
<body vlink="red">
<h1>Classy Classifieds</h1>

<h2>All Ads</h2>
<form runat="server">


<script runat="server">
    Sub Page_Load(ByVal Sender As Object, _
      ByVal E As EventArgs)

        If Not IsPostBack Then
            If Trim(Request.QueryString("AdNum")) = ""
          Then
                Response.Redirect("default.aspx")
             End If
        End If
    End Sub
```

(continued)

Listing 20-5 *(continued)*

```
    Sub EnterPassword_Click(ByVal Sender As Object, _
      ByVal E As EventArgs)

        Dim passwordDV As DataView
        Dim arg As New DataSourceSelectArguments
        passwordDV = SqlDataSource1.Select(arg)

        If passwordDV(0)("UserPassword") = _
          PasswordText.Text Then
            Response.Redirect("editad.aspx?AdNum=" & _
              Request.QueryString("AdNum"))
        Else
            Message.Text = "Invalid Password - Try Again"
        End If


    End Sub
</script>

<p>Please enter the password you used when you
created your ad.</p>
<table>
<tr><td>Password:</td><td>
<asp:textbox id="PasswordText" runat="server"
textmode="password" columns="50"/>
</td></tr><tr><td>
<asp:button id="EnterPassword" runat="server"
text="Enter Password"
onclick="EnterPassword_Click" />
</td></tr>
</table>
<br>
<asp:label id="Message" runat="server" />

<asp:SqlDataSource ID="SqlDataSource1" runat="server"
ConnectionString=
"<%$ ConnectionStrings:classydbConnectString %>"
ProviderName=
"<%$ ConnectionStrings:classydbConnectString.ProviderName
          %>"
SelectCommand=
"SELECT UserPassword FROM Ads WHERE (AdNum = ?)">

    <SelectParameters>
        <asp:QueryStringParameter Name="AdNum"
        QueryStringField="AdNum" Type="Int32" />
    </SelectParameters>
</asp:SqlDataSource>


</form>
</body>
</html>
```

This page simply asks the user for a password, as you can see in Figure 20-6.

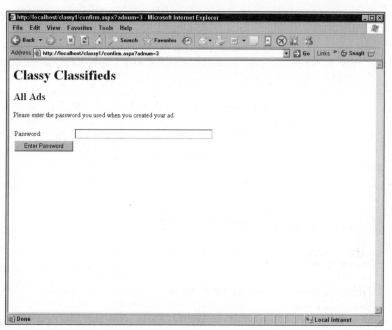

Figure 20-6:
The Confirm
page.

This page contains a `SqlDataSource` control that retrieves the `UserPassword` column from the ad specified in the query string. It's very similar to other `SqlDataSource` controls you've seen.

What's different about this page is that it has no `GridView` or `DetailsView`. So the `SqlDataSource` control doesn't end up being bound to a server control. And because there's no control to bind to, the `SqlDataSource` doesn't automatically run its query when the page loads. You have to initiate that from code.

The interesting code for this page is in the `click` event of the `EnterPassword` button:

```
Dim passwordDV As DataView
Dim arg As New DataSourceSelectArguments
passwordDV = SqlDataSource1.Select(arg)

If passwordDV(0)("UserPassword") = _
  PasswordText.Text Then
    Response.Redirect("editad.aspx?AdNum=" & _
      Request.QueryString("AdNum"))
Else
    Message.Text = "Invalid Password - Try Again"
End If
```

The `SqlDataSource` control has a method called `Select`. This method triggers the `SelectCommand` query and executes it in the database.

An argument of type `DataSourceSelectArguments` is required for the `Select` method. With it you can specify additional steps you want taken with the result set (sorting, for example). In this case, I don't want to do anything except retrieve the data, but because the argument is required, I instantiate the object and pass it.

The `Select` method returns a `DataView` object. With a `DataView`, you can access the information returned using an index number for the row and a column name for the column, as I've done here in the `If...Then` statement. The code compares the value returned with what the user typed into the text box and then redirect to `editad.aspx` if they match.

Allowing the User to Update the Database

All the database activity I describe in Chapter 19 and earlier in this chapter has been focused on getting data and showing it to the user, in one way or another. This activity is probably the most common one you'll do in your Web applications.

However, there usually comes a time when the user wants to add new data and/or maintain the existing data in the database. So in the following sections, I show you how to take advantage of the `DetailsView`'s insert, update, and delete capabilities.

With the `DetailsView`, you can allow the user to scroll forward and backward through the rows of a result set and insert, update, and delete from a single page, if you like.

In the Classy Classifieds application, it makes sense to restrict the `DetailsView` to working only with the selected row. It is also convenient to divide the tasks of displaying, inserting, and updating/deleting into three different pages. In your own applications, you have to decide what would make the most sense to your users.

The `GridView` offers the ability to allow users to insert, update, and delete rows, too. And the process is very similar to the process I describe here for the `DetailsView`.

Letting the User Insert a New Row

The GridView and the SqlDataSource work together to make it possible for the user to insert new rows in a database table, once again, with no code necessary. You can do this because the GridView control has the ability to work in different *modes*. By default, the GridView is in ReadOnly mode. This allows you to view the data but not modify it. When it is placed into Insert mode or Edit mode, however, text boxes appear, and the user can add new information or edit the existing information. This automatic feature makes creating pages to add or edit data a snap.

Use the code in Listing 20-6 to create the placead.aspx page.

Listing 20-6: The placead.aspx Page

```
<%@ Page Explicit="True" Language="VB" Debug="True" %>
<%@ Import Namespace="System.Data" %>
<%@ Import Namespace="System.Data.OleDb" %>
<html>
<body vlink="red">
<h1>Classy Classifieds</h1>

<form runat="server">

<h2>Place A New Ad</h2>

<script runat="server">
Protected Sub Page_Load(ByVal sender As Object, _
  ByVal e As System.EventArgs)

    DetailsView1.ChangeMode(DetailsViewMode.Insert)
End Sub

Protected Sub DetailsView1_ItemInserted( _
  ByVal sender As Object, ByVal e As _
  System.Web.UI.WebControls.DetailsViewInsertedEventArgs)

    Response.Redirect("default.aspx")
End Sub

Protected Sub DetailsView1_ItemCommand( _
  ByVal sender As Object, ByVal e As _
  System.Web.UI.WebControls.DetailsViewCommandEventArgs)

    If e.CommandName = "Cancel" Then
        Response.Redirect("default.aspx")
    End If
End Sub
```

(continued)

Listing 20-6 *(continued)*

```
</script>

Enter your new ad and then click Insert.
If you change your mind, press Cancel to
return to the home page.<br />
<br />

<asp:DetailsView ID="DetailsView1" runat="server"
Height="50px" Width="100%" AutoGenerateRows="False"
DataKeyNames="AdNum" DataSourceID="SqlDataSource1"
CellPadding="4" ForeColor="#333333" GridLines="None"
OnItemInserted="DetailsView1_ItemInserted"
OnItemCommand="DetailsView1_ItemCommand">

    <Fields>
        <asp:BoundField DataField="Title"
            HeaderText="Title"
             SortExpression="Title" />
        <asp:BoundField DataField="Category"
             HeaderText="Category"
             SortExpression="Category" />
        <asp:BoundField DataField="Description"
             HeaderText="Description"
             SortExpression="Description" />
        <asp:BoundField DataField="Price"
            HeaderText="Price"
             SortExpression="Price" />
        <asp:BoundField DataField="Phone"
            HeaderText="Phone"
             SortExpression="Phone" />
        <asp:BoundField DataField="Email"
            HeaderText="Email"
             SortExpression="Email" />
        <asp:BoundField DataField="State"
            HeaderText="State"
             SortExpression="State" />
        <asp:BoundField DataField="UserPassword"
             HeaderText="UserPassword"
             SortExpression="UserPassword" />
        <asp:CommandField ButtonType="Button"
             ShowInsertButton="True" />
    </Fields>

    <RowStyle BackColor="#FFFBD6" ForeColor="#333333" />

    <FieldHeaderStyle BackColor="#FFFF99" Font-Bold="True"
         />
```

```
</asp:DetailsView>

 

<asp:SqlDataSource ID="SqlDataSource1" runat="server"
ConflictDetection="CompareAllValues"
ConnectionString=
"<%$ ConnectionStrings:classydbConnectString %>"
InsertCommand="INSERT INTO Ads (Title, Category,
           Description,
Price, Phone, Email, State, UserPassword) VALUES (?, ?, ?,
           ?,
?, ?, ?, ?)"
ProviderName=
"<%$ ConnectionStrings:classydbConnectString.ProviderName
           %>"
SelectCommand="SELECT Title, Category, Description, Price,
Phone, Email, State, UserPassword, AdNum FROM Ads" >

    <InsertParameters>
        <asp:Parameter Name="Title" Type="String" />
        <asp:Parameter Name="Category" Type="String" />
        <asp:Parameter Name="Description" Type="String" />
        <asp:Parameter Name="Price" Type="Decimal" />
        <asp:Parameter Name="Phone" Type="String" />
        <asp:Parameter Name="Email" Type="String" />
        <asp:Parameter Name="State" Type="String" />
        <asp:Parameter Name="UserPassword" Type="String"
           />
        <asp:Parameter Name="AdNum" Type="Int32" />
    </InsertParameters>
</asp:SqlDataSource>

</form>
</body>
</html>
```

The `placead.aspx` page looks like Figure 20-7.

I begin by looking at the `SqlDataSource` control. In it, a new command is defined: `InsertCommand`. This command contains a SQL `INSERT` statement that contains all the columns of the Ads table. There's a question mark for each column in the `VALUES` clause. These question marks correspond to the `<asp:Parameter>` tags in the `<InsertParameters>` tag.

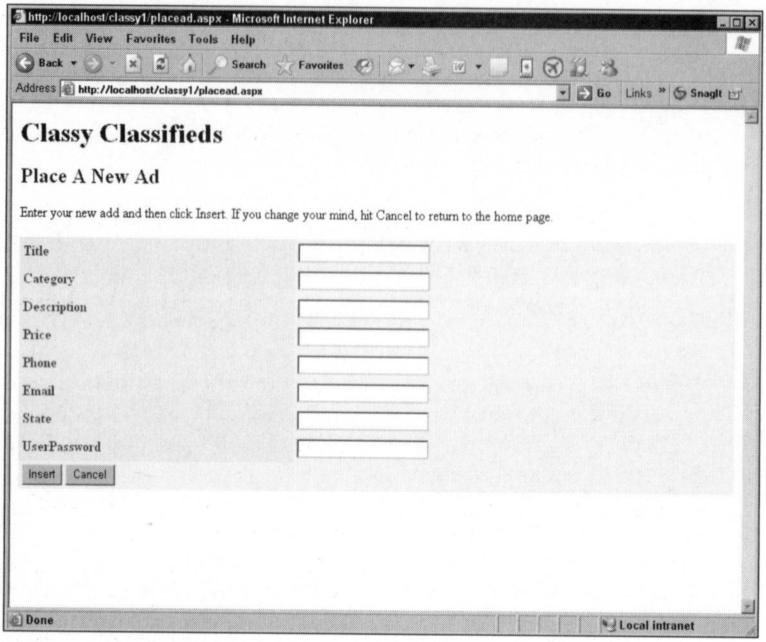

Figure 20-7:
The Place A
New Ad
page.

Now look at the `DetailsView` control:

```
<asp:DetailsView ID="DetailsView1" runat="server"
...
OnItemInserted="DetailsView1_ItemInserted"
OnItemCommand="DetailsView1_ItemCommand">

    <Fields>

        ...

        <asp:BoundField DataField="UserPassword"
            HeaderText="UserPassword"
            SortExpression="UserPassword" />
        <asp:CommandField ButtonType="Button"
            ShowInsertButton="True" />
    </Fields>

        ...

</asp:DetailsView>
```

A new field is added to the `DetailsView` — an `<asp:CommandField>`. This displays buttons allowing information to be inserted. Typically, this means that when the control is in View mode, a New button shows on the page, and when it's in Insert mode, the user sees an Insert button and a Cancel button.

Two events are associated with the `DetailsView` in Listing 20-6 —
`OnItemInserted` and `OnItemCommand`. These events are triggered when
the user clicks the buttons.

Now take a look at the code on this page. When the page is first retrieved, the
`Page_Load` event is triggered:

```
Protected Sub Page_Load(ByVal sender As Object, _
   ByVal e As System.EventArgs)

    DetailsView1.ChangeMode(DetailsViewMode.Insert)
End Sub
```

The user has to come to the `placead.aspx` page because she clicked a
Place Ad link. So it makes sense to go ahead and put the control in Insert
mode right away. That way, the user doesn't have to go through the additional step of clicking the New button when she arrives at the page. The only
code besides the `Page_Load` event that's required is the `ItemInserted` and
the `ItemCommand` events for the `DetailsView` control:

```
Protected Sub DetailsView1_ItemInserted( _
   ByVal sender As Object, ByVal e As _
   System.Web.UI.WebControls.DetailsViewInsertedEventArgs)

    Response.Redirect("default.aspx")
End Sub

Protected Sub DetailsView1_ItemCommand( _
   ByVal sender As Object, ByVal e As _
   System.Web.UI.WebControls.DetailsViewCommandEventArgs)

    If e.CommandName = "Cancel" Then
        Response.Redirect("default.aspx")
    End If
End Sub
```

The insert itself is automatically handled between the `DetailsView` and
`SqlDataSource` controls, so you don't have to do anything to make that
happen. The only reason I wrote code for these events is so that I could redirect the browser to the `default.aspx` page whether the user clicks Insert
or Cancel.

If you get an error when trying to update the database from your ASP.NET 2.0
application, it might be because the ASP.NET process doesn't have the appropriate rights to modify the Access database file. For more information on this
problem and how to solve it, see `http://support.microsoft.com/`
`default.aspx?scid=kb;en-us;316675`.

Allowing the User to Edit or Delete a Selected Row

The DetailsView control is very flexible, allowing you to view, insert, update, and delete depending on its mode. In this application, it made sense to place the insert capabilities on a separate page (as I discuss in the preceding section). But you can update and delete from the same page.

Create the editad.aspx page, which you can see in Listing 20-7.

Listing 20-7:   The editad.aspx Page

```
<%@ Page Explicit="True" Language="VB" Debug="True" %>
<%@ Import Namespace="System.Data" %>
<%@ Import Namespace="System.Data.OleDb" %>
<html>
<body vlink="red">
<h1>Classy Classifieds</h1>

<form runat="server">

<h2>Edit Ad</h2>

<script runat="server">

Protected Sub DetailsView1_ItemUpdated( _
  ByVal sender As Object, ByVal e As _
  System.Web.UI.WebControls.DetailsViewUpdatedEventArgs)

    Response.Redirect("default.aspx")
End Sub

Protected Sub DetailsView1_ItemDeleted( _
  ByVal sender As Object, ByVal e As _
  System.Web.UI.WebControls.DetailsViewDeletedEventArgs)

    Response.Redirect("default.aspx")
End Sub

Protected Sub DetailsView1_ItemCommand( _
  ByVal sender As Object, ByVal e As _
  System.Web.UI.WebControls.DetailsViewCommandEventArgs)
    If e.CommandName = "Cancel" Then
        Response.Redirect("default.aspx")
    End If
End Sub

</script>
```

```
To make changes, click Edit, make your changes,
then click Update. To delete this ad, just click the
          Delete
button.
<br />
<br />

<asp:DetailsView ID="DetailsView1" runat="server"
Height="50px" Width="100%" AutoGenerateRows="False"
DataKeyNames="AdNum" DataSourceID="SqlDataSource1"
CellPadding="4" ForeColor="#333333" GridLines="None"
OnItemUpdated="DetailsView1_ItemUpdated"
OnItemDeleted="DetailsView1_ItemDeleted"
OnItemCommand="DetailsView1_ItemCommand">

    <Fields>
        <asp:BoundField DataField="Title"
          HeaderText="Title"
        SortExpression="Title" />
        <asp:BoundField DataField="Category"
        HeaderText="Category" SortExpression="Category" />
        <asp:BoundField DataField="Description"
        HeaderText="Description"
        SortExpression="Description" />
        <asp:BoundField DataField="Price"
          HeaderText="Price"
        SortExpression="Price" />
        <asp:BoundField DataField="Phone"
          HeaderText="Phone"
        SortExpression="Phone" />
        <asp:BoundField DataField="Email"
          HeaderText="Email"
        SortExpression="Email" />
        <asp:BoundField DataField="State"
          HeaderText="State"
        SortExpression="State" />
        <asp:BoundField DataField="UserPassword"
        HeaderText="UserPassword"
        SortExpression="UserPassword" />

        <asp:CommandField ButtonType="Button"
          ShowDeleteButton="True"
ShowEditButton="True" />

    </Fields>

    <RowStyle BackColor="#FFFBD6" />
    <FieldHeaderStyle BackColor="#FFFF99" Font-Bold="True"
          />
</asp:DetailsView>
```

(continued)

Listing 20-7 *(continued)*

```
 

<asp:SqlDataSource ID="SqlDataSource1" runat="server"
ConflictDetection="CompareAllValues"
ConnectionString=
"<%$ ConnectionStrings:classydbConnectString %>"
ProviderName=
"<%$ ConnectionStrings:classydbConnectString.ProviderName
        %>"
SelectCommand="SELECT AdNum, Title, Category, Description,
Price, Phone, Email, State, UserPassword FROM Ads
WHERE (AdNum = ?)"
DeleteCommand=
"DELETE FROM Ads WHERE AdNum = ? AND Title = ? AND
Category = ? AND Description = ? AND Price = ? AND
Phone = ? AND Email = ? AND State = ? AND
UserPassword = ?"
UpdateCommand="UPDATE Ads SET Title = ?, Category = ?,
Description = ?, Price = ?, Phone = ?, Email = ?, State =
        ?,
UserPassword = ? WHERE AdNum = ? AND Title = ? AND
Category = ? AND Description = ? AND Price = ? AND
Phone = ? AND Email = ? AND State = ? AND UserPassword =
        ?" >

    <SelectParameters>
        <asp:QueryStringParameter Name="AdNum"
        QueryStringField="AdNum" Type="Int32" />
    </SelectParameters>

    <DeleteParameters>
        <asp:Parameter Name="original_AdNum"
        Type="Int32" />
        <asp:Parameter Name="original_Title"
        Type="String" />
        <asp:Parameter Name="original_Category"
        Type="String" />
        <asp:Parameter Name="original_Description"
        Type="String" />
        <asp:Parameter Name="original_Price"
        Type="Decimal" />
        <asp:Parameter Name="original_Phone"
        Type="String" />
        <asp:Parameter Name="original_Email"
        Type="String" />
        <asp:Parameter Name="original_State"
        Type="String" />
        <asp:Parameter Name="original_UserPassword"
        Type="String" />
    </DeleteParameters>

    <UpdateParameters>
```

```
                <asp:Parameter Name="Title" Type="String" />
                <asp:Parameter Name="Category" Type="String" />
                <asp:Parameter Name="Description" Type="String" />
                <asp:Parameter Name="Price" Type="Decimal" />
                <asp:Parameter Name="Phone" Type="String" />
                <asp:Parameter Name="Email" Type="String" />
                <asp:Parameter Name="State" Type="String" />
                <asp:Parameter Name="UserPassword" Type="String"
                    />
                <asp:Parameter Name="original_AdNum" Type="Int32"
                    />
                <asp:Parameter Name="original_Title" Type="String"
                    />
                <asp:Parameter Name="original_Category"
                Type="String" />
                <asp:Parameter Name="original_Description"
                Type="String" />
                <asp:Parameter Name="original_Price"
                Type="Decimal" />
                <asp:Parameter Name="original_Phone" Type="String"
                    />
                <asp:Parameter Name="original_Email" Type="String"
                    />
                <asp:Parameter Name="original_State" Type="String"
                    />
                <asp:Parameter Name="original_UserPassword"
                Type="String" />
        </UpdateParameters>

</asp:SqlDataSource>

</form>
</body>
</html>
```

The editad.aspx page looks like Figure 20-8 when it first appears.

The user arrives at the editad.aspx page by clicking the link at the bottom of detail.aspx to indicate that she wants to edit or delete the displayed ad. After being verified as the original creator of the ad in confirm.aspx, she is redirected here to make the changes. The AdNum QueryString is passed from the detail.aspx page, to the confirm.aspx page and finally to this one.

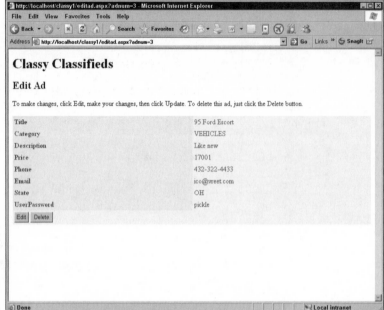

Figure 20-8:
The Edit Ad
page.

If the discussion in the preceding section on inserting a row makes sense to
you, this page is probably not too difficult to figure out. The same process is
used for all database operations. For example, two commands are specified
for the `editad.aspx` page:

```
DeleteCommand=
"DELETE FROM Ads WHERE AdNum = ? AND Title = ? AND
Category = ? AND Description = ? AND Price = ? AND
Phone = ? AND Email = ? AND State = ? AND
UserPassword = ?"
UpdateCommand="UPDATE Ads SET Title = ?, Category = ?,
Description = ?, Price = ?, Phone = ?, Email = ?, State =
        ?,
UserPassword = ? WHERE AdNum = ? AND Title = ? AND
Category = ? AND Description = ? AND Price = ? AND
Phone = ? AND Email = ? AND State = ? AND UserPassword =
        ?" >
```

All the question marks correspond to parameters specified in the
`SqlDataSource` control's `<DeleteParameters>` and
`<UpdateParameters>` tags.

The DetailsView shows buttons for deleting and editing:

```
<asp:CommandField ButtonType="Button"
    ShowDeleteButton="True"
    ShowEditButton="True" />
```

There's no Page_Load event to set the mode of the DetailsView on this page when it begins. Instead, the user sees the default ReadOnly mode. This offers the user the ability to immediately click the Delete or Edit buttons depending on what she wants to do.

The rest of the events work the same as they did for the placedad.aspx page — returning the user to default.aspx after she's done with this row.

Part VIII
Exploring New ASP.NET 2.0 Features

The 5th Wave · By Rich Tennant

"I have to say I'm really impressed with the interactivity on this car wash Web site."

In this part . . .

This part provides introductions to a number of important features that are new in ASP.NET 2.0. The Master Pages feature allows you to create a common format and common elements—such as a header and footer—and then apply those to all the pages in your site. It's easy to use and makes updating your site a breeze.

You discover how to implement ASP.NET 2.0 security by using a group of new server controls that make creating login and registration pages as easy as dragging and dropping controls.

Themes and skins allow you to apply look-and-feel properties throughout your site by making changes in one place. This handy feature will have your site looking fine in no time.

Finally, Web Parts allow you to begin creating portal applications. Portals are designed specifically to allow the user the ultimate in customization capabilities. Find out how you can leverage these exciting capabilities!

Chapter 21

Mastering Master Pages

. . . .

. . . .

A welcome new feature added in ASP.NET 2.0 is Master Pages. With Master Pages, you can create a *master page* (sometimes called a *parent page*) that contains elements common to most or all of the pages on your site — a header, a footer, a menu, a series of links, whatever. You then use this master page as a template (which is like a virtual cookie-cutter) for the rest of your pages.

A page that uses a master page is referred to as a *content* page. The content page automatically gets all the features of its master page. In addition, the content page can add specific content unique to it, based on what the page is supposed to do.

In this chapter, I demonstrate how to create a master page and then how to create content pages that use the master. For a more complete example, see the Classy Classifieds application, which I describe in Bonus Chapter 2. You can find the Classy Classifieds application on the CD.

Getting to Know Master Pages and Content Pages

The master page looks just like any .aspx page. It can include server controls, HTML, and code that responds to page and server control events. However, be aware of the following differences between master pages and regular .aspx pages:

✔ The master page has a `.master` extension, not an `.aspx` extension.

✔ The master page has a `@ Master` directive at the top instead of a `@ Page` directive.

✔ The master page has one or more named `<asp:contentplaceholder>` tags within it that act as placeholders. These identify where the content pages can fill in their page-specific content.

After you create the master page, you can begin to create content pages. Content pages *do* have an `.aspx` extension. However, they look different from usual `.aspx` pages in a few important ways:

✔ The content page has a `@ Page` directive at the top with a new property: `MasterPageFile`. This property is assigned the master page's filename. The `MasterPageFile` property associates the content page with the master.

✔ The content page doesn't have an `<html>` tag, a `<body>` tag, or a `<form runat="server">` tag. It inherits all these from the master page.

✔ The content page has one or more `<asp:content>` tags within it. These tags contain the server controls and HTML that fill in the placeholders in the master. Typically, you have one content tag in the content page for every placeholder in the master.

Suppose you have a master page with a header, a footer, and a menu along the left side. It also has two content placeholders: one for the page header and one for the main body of the page. The master might look like Figure 21-1.

Figure 21-1:
The master
page.

A content page that uses this master page would get the header, footer, and menu automatically. It would just fill in the content placeholders with the content tags. One content page using this master might look like Figure 21-2. Another page, using the same master, might look like Figure 21-3.

Figure 21-2:
The first
content
page.

Figure 21-3:
The second
content
page.

A master page accomplishes two important goals. First, it makes the task of creating a page easier because you have to worry only about things that are specific to your page. You don't have to provide site navigation, headers, and all the rest. Those things are inherited automatically from the master page.

Second, it encourages consistency. When someone begins the process of creating a new page, she doesn't have to worry about what font to use in the header or which color to use for the menus. Every page looks and works the same, because, again, they all inherit from the same master.

Making Your Master Page

So how do you create a master page? Actually, it's easy. In the steps below I'll walk you through the process of creating a master page and point out specifically what it should contain.

1. **Create a new page, but give it the extension `.master` instead of `.aspx`.**

2. **Instead of a `@ Page` directive, begin with a `@ Master` directive. It should look something like this:**

   ```
   <%@ Master Explicit="True" Language="VB" %>
   ```

3. **Create the page using HTML, server controls, and anything else you'd normally use in an `.aspx` page, including code to respond to events.**

   You can create a header, a menu, a footer, banner ads, or whatever you like. Just remember that whatever you include will appear on every page that uses this master.

4. **In the places where you want the content pages to put their stuff, use a `<asp:contentplaceholder>` tag. It should look something like this:**

   ```
   <asp:contentplaceholder id="PageBody"
       runat="server">
   </asp:contentplaceholder>
   ```

5. **You can include as few as one content placeholder or as many as you like.**

   Name each one something appropriate by changing the value of its `ID` property. Possible names might include `PageHeader`, `PageBody`, `RightSideTowerAd`, and so on.

6. **Save the page — you're done!**

To create a master page in Visual Web Developer 2005 Express, all you have to do is choose Website➪Add New Item. Then select Master Page in the Add New Item dialog, give it a name, and click Add. The `@ Master` directive and all the standard HTML tags are created for you. In addition, one placeholder tag is automatically created in the body of the page to get you started.

The Content Page: Jack of All Trades, Master of None

Creating a content page is easy:

1. **Create a new page with an `.aspx` extension.**

   Don't put anything but a `@ Page` directive in it — no `<html>` tag, no `<head>` tag, no `<body>` tag and no `<form runat="server">` tag.

2. **Add a `MasterPageFile` property to the `@ Page` directive. Set the `MasterPageFile` property equal to the filename of the master page inside quotes. It might look like this:**

```
<%@ Page Explicit="True" Language="VB"
    MasterPageFile="MasterPage.master" %>
```

3. **Add `<asp:content>` tags for each placeholder specified in the master.**

   Each `<asp:content>` tag should have a `ContentPlaceholderID` property that is assigned a value that corresponds to the ID of a `<asp:contentplaceholder>` tag in the master. This is how the content tags are matched up with the appropriate placeholders on the master. A `<asp:content>` tag might look like this:

```
<asp:Content ID="BlogList"
        ContentPlaceHolderID="PageBody"
    Runat="Server">
</asp:Content>
```

4. **Within each content tag, add the HTML, server controls, and other content for this page.**

   All the content in your content pages must be inside the `<asp:content>` tags.

5. **Save the page — you're done!**

 To create a content page in Visual Web Developer 2005 Express, all you have to do is add a page as you normally would and be sure that the Select Master Page check box in the Add New Item dialog is selected. When you click Add, the Select a Master Page dialog appears, allowing you to identify which page should be the master of this content page. When the content page is created, it has a content tag for each placeholder in the master.

Running and Testing Your Pages

When you test your pages, you enter the name of the *content* page into the browser's Address line. You can never retrieve a master page directly.

Then when the server receives the request, it recognizes that the content page is associated with a master page when it sees the `MasterPageFile` property in the `@ Page` directive. The server then retrieves the master page and combines it together with the content page. The resulting HTML output is then sent to the browser.

No Content Page Can Serve Two Masters . . .

I've collected several important facts about master pages and assembled them into the following list:

- ✔ A content page can have one and only one master page.

- ✔ Any number of content pages can use the same master page.

- ✔ You can never retrieve a master page directly. The server renders the master page's content only when you request a content page that uses it.

- ✔ A content page typically includes a `<asp:content>` tag for every place-holder in the master. But this isn't required. If a placeholder isn't filled in, that part of the page simply remains empty.

- ✔ A master page *can* include default content within a `<asp:contentplaceholder>` tag. This content appears on a page only if the content page doesn't provide a `<asp:content>` tag for that placeholder.

- ✔ You can have more than one master page in a Web site. Some pages can use one master while other pages use a different master. This might be useful, for example, if you want to have a significantly different look in different sections of the same site.

- ✔ The master page and content page don't have to use the same language. That is, if someone else created a master page with events coded in C# and you want to use that master page, it's okay for you to code the events in your content page with VB 2005.

Chapter 22

Security: The Basics

● ●

In This Chapter

▶ Configuring authentication and authorization in `web.config`

▶ Creating a registration page

▶ Creating a login page

● ●

*T*he Internet has made the world a smaller place. With it, you can easily reach out to family and friends all over the world. It can help you do business with suppliers, partners, and customers. Unfortunately, the same technology has made it easier for a small but dangerous group of criminals to steal, vandalize, and destroy other people's property. And that's why security dominates the headlines of computer journals today.

Security is a very large topic, and some people devote their careers to understanding all its subtleties. However, you don't have to be a security expert to begin implementing secure Web applications in ASP.NET. In fact, with ASP.NET 2.0, Microsoft has dramatically simplified the creation of secure sites with new classes and server controls that automatically do all the common grunt work for you.

In this chapter, I walk you through the creation of a simple application that implements ASP.NET 2.0 forms-based security by using the new ASP.NET 2.0 `Login` controls.

All the controls and techniques I describe in this chapter are new to ASP.NET 2.0.

ASP.NET TipVault: For Registered Users Only!

The simple application I create in this chapter is called the ASP.NET TipVault because it offers exclusive tips and tricks for ASP.NET programmers — but only to registered users. It has a public welcome page that links to a registration page and a login page. On the registration page, new users can enter their essential information to join the site. On the login page, users can type their user ID and password. After they do, they are taken to the members-only section where they can browse all they like. However, if a user tries to access the members-only section without logging in (even if he happens to have a Favorite set up to take him there), he's kicked back to the login page automatically.

This is a very common scenario for public Web sites, and it allows you to easily create both public pages and private pages that only registered users can access.

Creating the Folder, Application, and web.config

First you need to create a folder under your wwwroot and call it ASPNETVault (no dot between ASP and NET). Identify this folder as a Web application by making the folder into a virtual folder. Be sure to visit the ASP.NET tab of the properties dialog box to change the *ASP.NET version* to 2.0. (For information on how to do this, see the section on identifying your Web application in Chapter 18.)

Next, under the ASPNETVault folder, create another folder called MembersOnly. Do *not* identify this second folder as a Web application (virtual folder). It is simply a subfolder of the ASPNETVault application.

The next step is to create a web.config file. I describe the web.config file in the section on the configuration file in Chapter 18. In the web.config file, you can tell ASP.NET what kind of security approach you want to use (how you'll authenticate or verify users) and how you want to use that security to protect your site.

Create a web.config file for your application that looks like Listing 22-1.

Listing 22-1: The web.config for ASP.NET TipVault

```
<configuration>
    <system.web>
        <authentication mode="Forms">
            <forms loginUrl="login.aspx"/>
        </authentication>
```

```
        </system.web>

        <location path="MembersOnly">
            <system.web>
                <authorization>
                    <deny users="?"/>
                </authorization>
            </system.web>
        </location>
    </configuration>
```

This simple configuration file does two things:

✔ It identifies the kind of authentication you want to use — in this case, forms authentication.

✔ It specifies that users that aren't logged in are not allowed to access anything in the `MembersOnly` folder. (It doesn't restrict access to any other files/folders in this application.)

Using a Web interface to set your authentication and authorization settings

Visual Web Developer Express simplifies editing your `web.config` file. You don't need to touch the XML at all. I introduce the VWDE Web interface to `web.config` in Chapter 18. This interface is called the ASP.NET Web Site Administration Tool. It is especially helpful when setting your security authentication and authorization settings. To do so, just follow these steps:

1. **Choose Website⇨ASP.NET Configuration from the VWDE menus.**

   A browser is launched displaying the ASP.NET Web Site Administration Tool.

2. **Click the Security tab.**

3. **Under Users, click the Select Authentication Type link.**

   A page is displayed asking how users will access your site.

4. **To choose forms-based authentication, select the From the Internet radio button. Click Done.**

   You are returned to the Security page.

5. **Under Access Rules, click the Create Access Rules link.**

   A page is displayed allowing you to add new access rules.

6. **Select the MembersOnly folder on the left side of the page.**

7. **Select the Anonymous Users radio button.**

8. **Select Deny under Permission.**

9. **Click OK in the lower-right corner of the page.**

   You are returned to the Security page

Authentication

Look at the first part of the `web.config` file:

```
<authentication mode="Forms">
    <forms loginUrl="login.aspx"/>
</authentication>
```

Authentication simply means proving that you are who you say you are. For Web site access, this is typically done with user accounts and passwords. But the question is, who keeps track of the list of valid users — and how?

ASP.NET 2.0 has built-in support for three different authentication approaches. The one you choose appears in the `mode` attribute of the `<authentication>` tag.

- **Windows:** If the users in your company typically log in when they turn on their computers in the morning, they already have an account on the Windows domain server. You can use those accounts to provide access to your Web application. This might be handy if your site is only for people in your office. However, you can't easily create a registration page that adds a new user to the domain server. Besides, even if you could, doing so could create security problems for your internal network. So if your application is for a broader audience than just those people within your company, Windows authentication is probably not the best option.

- **Passport:** Microsoft has a service that companies can pay to use called Microsoft Passport. The idea of Passport is that it provides a single user ID and password for a whole bunch of different sites. So when a Passport user logs into one site in the morning, he doesn't have to repeatedly log into all the other sites that he uses if all those sites use Microsoft Passport authentication. This can be handy for the user if he visits a lot of Passport-enabled sites. However, this authentication service hasn't been quite as widely accepted as Microsoft would have liked and so most of the sites that use Passport are Microsoft-owned sites. The fee that Microsoft charges for the use of Passport isn't trivial, and most companies opt to use another, less expensive option.

- **Forms:** Forms security is the most flexible option available for Web developers. You can store the login information wherever you want to maintain as much control as you like. But in ASP.NET 2.0, forms security has been enhanced so that you don't have to do all the work yourself if you don't want to. In fact, by default, forms security takes very little work to get set up and working.

If you decide on forms authentication, you can use a `<forms>` tag between the `<authentication>` tags to specify a number of options. In this configuration file, I've chosen to specify only one: the login page. This is the page that the user is redirected to if he tries to access a page that he isn't authorized for.

Authorization

After you know who someone is, you need to specify what she is authorized *(allowed)* to do. In ASP.NET 2.0 forms, you do this in the `web.config` file with the `<authorization>` tag, as shown in the following:

```
<location path="MembersOnly">
    <system.web>
        <authorization>
            <deny users="?"/>
        </authorization>
    </system.web>
</location>
```

The `<location>` tag identifies a specific file or a folder. That file or folder is affected by all the tags within the `<location>` tag. In this case, I specify an `<authorization>` tag to deny certain users access to the MembersOnly folder. The question mark is a symbol that refers to all unauthenticated users (any user who hasn't logged in yet).

Knowing that, you can probably figure out that the user can get into the `MembersOnly` folder only if she logs in.

The automatically created authorization database

If you create the TipVault application as I describe it in this chapter, going largely with the default options each step of the way, ASP.NET automatically creates an authorization database for you. A Microsoft SQL Express database (an `.mdf` file) is generated within an automatically created subfolder of your application called `App_Data`, and the database tracks users that have registered and ASP.NET 2.0 validates login information against that database automatically.

Creating the Public Welcome Page

The first page that user views simply welcomes her to the site. If the user is already registered, she can simply click the Log In link. If not, she can click the Register link to create a new account.

Create a new page in the ASPNETVault folder and name it default.aspx. It should look something like Listing 22-2.

Listing 22-2:   The ASP.NET TipVault default.aspx Page

```
<%@ Page Language="VB" %>
<html >
<head >
    <title>ASP.NET TipVault</title>
</head>
<body>
    <form id="form1" runat="server">
    <div>
    <h1>ASP.NET TipVault</h1>
    Welcome to the ASP.NET TipVault. Here you'll find lots
    of cool tips and tricks you can use in your ASP.NET
    projects. But before you check out the goodies, I need
    for you to register. I won't sell your name to anyone
    else and I won't send you spam. I'll only send you
    occasional emails to inform you of events and site
    updates.<br />
    <br />
    <a href=register.aspx>Register now</a>!
    <br />
    <br />
    I'm registered. I want to <a href=login.aspx>Log
         in</a>!
    <br />

    </div>
    </form>
</body>
</html>
```

The result looks like Figure 22-1.

This is just a public page for the user to begin from — one that any user can access, whether or not he's logged in. If he isn't registered, he clicks the Register Now link. If he is, he clicks the Log In link.

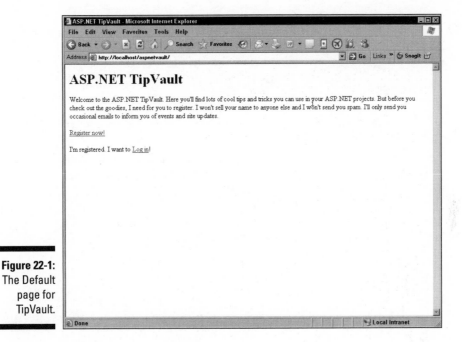

Figure 22-1:
The Default
page for
TipVault.

Registration, Please!

To restrict access to a site or portions of a site, you have to provide a way to add new users to the list of those allowed access. This can be an administrator-only task or, for more informal sites like this one, it can happen automatically after the user provides the requested information. If you want to provide a simple registration page where the user requests a user ID and password while providing an e-mail address — you're in luck! Microsoft has created a server control that automatically does all that for you: CreateUserWizard.

Create a new page named register.aspx in the same folder and give it the content you see in Listing 22-3. This page consists of little more than the CreateUserWizard control.

Listing 22-3:   The register.aspx Page

```
<%@ Page Language="VB" %>
<html >
<head >
    <title>ASP.NET TipVault Registration</title>
</heFad>
```

(continued)

Listing 22-3 *(continued)*

```
<body>
    <form id="form1" runat="server">
    <div>
        <h1>ASP.NET TipVault Registration</h1>
        <asp:CreateUserWizard ID="CreateUserWizard1"
        runat="server"
        ContinueDestinationPageUrl="default.aspx" >
            <WizardSteps>
                <asp:CreateUserWizardStep runat="server">
                </asp:CreateUserWizardStep>
                <asp:CompleteWizardStep runat="server">
                </asp:CompleteWizardStep>
            </WizardSteps>
        </asp:CreateUserWizard>

    </div>
    </form>
</body>
</html>
```

You can see the result in Figure 22-2.

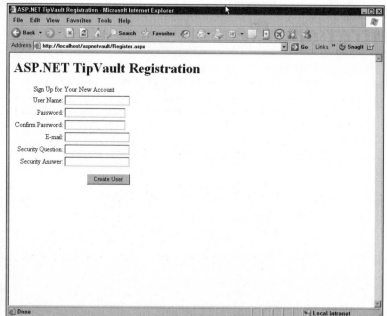

Figure 22-2:
The
Registration
page for
TipVault.

The `CreateUserWizard` control is called a wizard because it technically has two steps or pages that it presents to the user. (Any process with two or more pages or steps can be called a wizard.) The first page asks for all the information: the user ID, the password, an e-mail address, and a security question and answer (used to verify who the user is if he looses his password). The second page simply informs the user that the registration process was successful. That it isn't much of a wizard, but the idea is that you can add steps to the process and gather additional information if you like. This is actually a very flexible control that you can use for virtually any registration process, no matter how complex it is.

The only property I've set on this control is the `ContinueDestination PageUrl`. This is the page that is opened when the user clicks the Continue button that appears on the process-completed step. In this application, I simply want the user to be returned to the page `default.aspx`. There, he can click the Log In link.

Whooo Are You? Whooo, Whooo

The login page is the gatekeeper for your secured site. And, once again, ASP.NET makes creating the Login page easy with a server control!

Create a page called `login.aspx`. This time, the control's name is `Login`, and Listing 22-4 shows you what `Login` can do.

Listing 22-4:   The ASP.NET TipVault login.aspx Page

```
<%@ Page Language="VB" %>
<html >
<head >
    <title>ASP.NET TipVault Login</title>
</head>
<body>
    <form id="form1" runat="server">
    <div>
        <h1>ASP.NET TipVault Login</h1>
        <asp:Login ID="Login1" runat="server"

          DestinationPageUrl="~/MembersOnly/aspnettips.as
          px">
        </asp:Login>

    </div>
    </form>
</body>
</html>
```

The result looks like Figure 22-3.

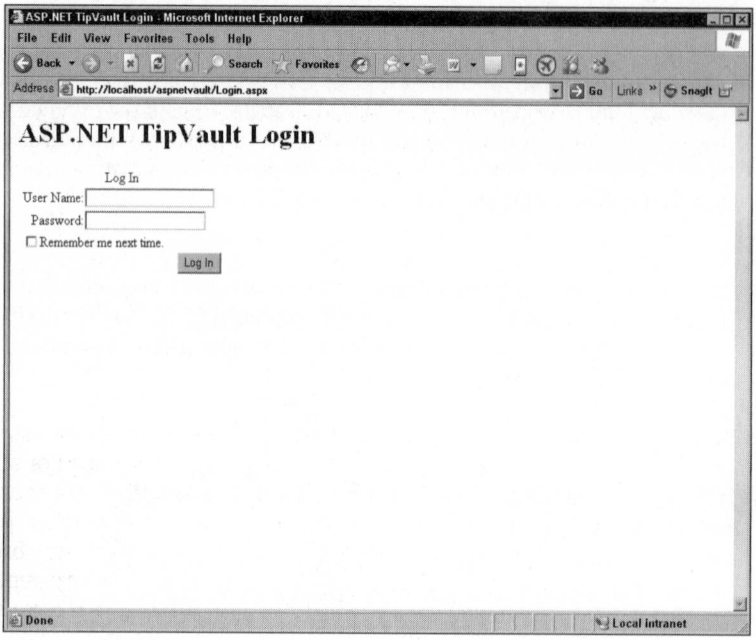

Figure 22-3:
The Login
page for
TipVault.

Users simply enter their credentials and click the button. I set the `DestinationPageUrl` on this page to take the user to the `aspnettips.aspx` page in the `MembersOnly` folder upon successful login.

Enforcing Security on Private Content

When you have the `web.config` file authorization specified and the server controls in place, what do you have to do on the actual content pages (such as `aspnettips.aspx` in the example in this chapter) to assure that they are protected? Absolutely nothing! ASP.NET 2.0 handles this for you. Even if the user has a direct link to a protected page, she won't be able to open the page until she logs in. The content pages don't need any special code or settings to make that happen.

Putting a Sniffer's Nose out of Joint with SSL

One of the simplest and most effective snooping tools a hacker can use on the Internet is a *sniffer*. A sniffer allows a hacker to intercept messages as they fly through cyberspace. Smart sniffers look for information in certain patterns — patterns that look like credit card numbers, for example, or ones that look like usernames and passwords.

If you use the TipVault application as it is presented in this chapter and take no further measures to secure it, it will provide a moderate level of security for your site. However, a sniffer could defeat it. That's because the username and password are sent over the Internet in plain text — easily readable by anyone who can intercept them.

To protect your site from sniffers, consider making use of secure-sockets layer (or SSL) encryption. SSL is a standard approach for *encrypting* (or scrambling) information sent over the Internet from the browser to the server and from the server back to the browser. Whenever you're on an SSL-encrypted page, you can see a small lock icon appear in the lower-right corner of your browser. SSL-encrypted information is very difficult for a hacker to make any sense of, so it protects username and password information from being stolen and misused.

More — MUCH More

This chapter provides an effective, easy-to-use security approach for your ASP.NET Web applications. However, when you begin writing more complex applications, you'll likely need more flexibility and more capabilities. Don't worry — ASP.NET 2.0 is up to the task.

In this chapter, I showed you only the default settings for the server controls presented. You can configure each server control by using its properties and tags to provide the look and functionality that you need in your application. In addition, several other security-related server controls are available to you, including:

- ✔ LoginView: Allows you to display different content based on whether the user is logged in and, if he is, what *roles* (security groups) he belongs to.

- ✔ PasswordRecovery: Provides a wizard-like control that asks for the user's username, asks him to answer his security question. Then, if he answers the question correctly, it resets his password and e-mails him the new one.

✔ LoginStatus: Allows you to easily provide a visual cue indicating whether the user is logged in. You can use text or graphics and, optionally, provide a link to the login page when the user is not logged in, and a link to log out if the user is logged in.

✔ LoginName: A simple label that is automatically filled in with the logged-in user's username.

✔ ChangePassword: Provides a user interface for the user to enter his old password and a new password and then makes the change.

For more information on the server controls used in this chapter or the ones listed in this section, simply search the .NET Framework 2.0 online help for the server control's name. You can find a summary description for each control, examples of how to use the controls, and a list of all their properties and methods.

Chapter 23

Themes and Skins

· ·

· ·

As a developer, you probably spend most of your time just trying to make your Web application work, devoting little attention to how pretty your pages look. But an ugly Web site is often a lonely Web site. Surfers have become spoiled with an abundance of beautiful graphics, colors, and designs, and they expect your site to measure up.

Fortunately, ASP.NET 2.0 has new features that make dressing up your site (and changing its clothes) much easier than it's ever been before. In this chapter, you discover what those features are, how they work, and how you can use them to give your site a facelift.

Do You See a Theme Here?

A *theme* is a look that you can apply to your Web site. It can consist of graphics, Cascading Style Sheets (CSS files), skin files (which I discuss later in this chapter), and anything else you might need to dress up your pages. Physically, a theme is a just a folder that contains all the files that make up the theme. For example, suppose you want to create a theme called MintGreen. You create a theme folder with the name MintGreen. Then, inside the folder, you create a CSS file that sets the background color of the page, the style of the headers and other HTML-related settings. In addition, you add a skin file which defines how buttons, labels, text boxes and other server controls in your application should look, by default. Then when you apply the MintGreen theme to your site, the CSS file and the skin are automatically applied to all your pages.

The term *skin* is commonly used with Windows applications to refer to a look and feel that you can apply to applications, like Windows Media Player. However the use of the term in ASP.NET 2.0 is a little different. ASP.NET 2.0 themes are not designed to be applied by the user. Instead they are a method of allowing site designers to apply and maintain their designs more easily at a site-wide level.

Creating a theme

To create a theme for your Web application, you begin by creating a folder with the name App_Themes under your application's root folder. Then inside the App_Themes folder, you create another folder to hold your theme. You can create as many theme folders as you like under the App_Themes folder for use in your application. The name you give the folder is the name of the theme.

After you create a theme folder, then what? You begin putting files in that folder that you want to be a part of the theme.

Suppose you want to create a theme named MellowYellow that simply makes all the pages of the site yellow. First, you create the App_Themes folder. Then you create the MellowYellow folder under App_Themes. Inside the MellowYellow folder, you create a CSS file that looks like this:

```
body
{
    font-family: Arial;
    list-style-type: square;
    background-color: yellow;
}
PLAINTEXT
{
    font-size: medium;
}
H1
{
    font-weight: bold;
    font-size: xx-large;
}
H2
{
    font-weight: bold;
    font-size: x-large;
}
```

This simple CSS file does the following things:

- ✔ Sets the font used throughout the page to Arial.
- ✔ Sets the bullet used in bulleted lists to the square bullet.
- ✔ Sets the background color of the page to yellow.
- ✔ Sets the size of plain text (text where no style tags have been applied) to medium.
- ✔ Sets the header 1 and header 2 tags to an xx-large and x-large size, respectively. Both are bold.

CSS allows you to identify virtually any HTML tag and define how that tag should change the display of its associated text. It's a powerful tool.

The CSS file can have any name at all — it doesn't matter. The only thing that matters is that it's located in the MellowYellow folder.

In VWDE, you can add a theme to your site by right-clicking on the site in Solution Explorer and choosing Add Folder⇨Theme Folder. An App_Themes folder is created with a second folder inside it, and after you name that folder, you can right-click the theme folder and choose Add New Item to add style sheets or skin files. VWDE also makes creating style sheets easy, even if you don't know anything about CSS. Just create a new style sheet and then, with the style sheet open, click the CSS Outline tab along the left side of the window, in the same place where the Toolbox normally is. (If the CSS Outline tab does not appear, select View ⇨ Other Windows ⇨ Document Outline from the menus to display it.) Here you can create new elements and define styles for those elements by right-clicking the various folders or items and choosing menu options. Dialog boxes provide you with access to all the common style features.

If you want to create several themes, one for each of the major sections of your Web site, for example, the easiest way to do that is to divide up the application into different folders — one folder for each section, with all the pages for each section in its appropriate folder. You can then include a web.config file in each folder, identifying the appropriate theme for that section.

Using a theme

When you have one or more themes created, you can make use of them in your pages. Doing so is as easy as adding an attribute to your page directive:

```
<%@ Page Language="VB" Theme="MellowYellow" %>
```

Now when you request that page, the server applies all the files in the specified theme folder to the page before it sends it out. The result for my MellowYellow example? A yellow page!

Of course, if you have 100 pages on your site, you might not want to open each one of them to modify their page directive. There is another way — you can apply a theme globally to an application by adding a setting to the web.config file. Inside the <system.web> section, simply add this tag:

```
<pages theme="MellowYellow" />
```

This applies the theme to all the pages on the site.

You can actually set the theme for a page in the Properties window, which is handy if you prefer to work in Design mode as much as possible. Click an empty place anywhere on your page and then select DOCUMENT from the drop-down list at the top of the Properties window. Now scroll down; you should find a Theme property. VWDE even provides a drop-down list so that you can select the theme's name. Be aware that no matter how you associate a theme with a page, the theme's effects aren't visible in Design mode. You see the skins and style sheets applied to the page only when you run your application.

If you want a theme to be applied for most of the pages in your site but you want a different look on just one page or a few pages, you can set the theme in the web.config file and then simply specify a different theme in the page directives of the pages that are different. When both a web.config setting and a page directive are specified, the page directive takes priority.

To change your application so that no theme is applied to it, all you have to do is remove the pages tag (or at least the theme attribute) from the web.config file. However, there is no way to apply a theme at a global level and apply no theme at a page level.

Beauty Really Is Skin Deep

You might be thinking that themes seem like just another way to apply style sheets to your Web pages. That isn't so. The real power of themes comes when you use them in combination with skins.

CSS files allow you to apply a specific look to your HTML tags. However, in an ASP.NET 2.0 page, although you use HTML, your primary user interface is typically made up of server controls. Skins provide a way to apply a specific look to your server controls.

A skin is a file with the .skin extension. When you create a skin file, you place it in a theme folder. Within the skin file are server control declarations. These declarations include properties which are set to specific values that define how you want your controls to look.

So, for example, if you want all the text boxes on your site to have a yellow background color, you could include this declaration in your skin file:

```
<asp:TextBox runat="server" BackColor="Yellow" />
```

Then when the skin's theme is applied to a page, the property settings specified in the skin (BackColor="Yellow") are applied to the controls on that page. That is, by default, all the text boxes on the page will now have a default BackColor value of Yellow.

Creating skins

Create a file named YellowControls.skin. In it, enter the code you see in Listing 23-1.

Listing 23-1:   The Yellowcontrols.skin File

```
<asp:TextBox runat="server" backcolor="yellow"
font-names="Comic Sans MS" borderstyle="solid"
bordercolor="red" borderwidth="3"
forecolor="blue"></asp:TextBox>

<asp:Button runat="server" backcolor="yellow"
font-names="Comic Sans MS" borderstyle="solid" />

<asp:Label runat="server" backcolor="yellow"
font-names="Comic Sans MS" font-size="large" >
</asp:Label>
```

Be sure to notice two important details about this page:

✔ It has no @Page declaration and no <html>, <body>, or <form> tags — only server control declarations.

✔ The server control declarations may specify many different properties, but none of them specify an id property. In fact, if you do specify an id property, an error is generated.

Using skins

Now suppose you're ready to apply the MellowYellow theme with its CSS file and skin file to a page, like the one in Listing 23-2.

Listing 23-2: The dogage.aspx File

```
<%@ Page Language="VB" Theme="MellowYellow" %>
<html>
<head runat="server"></head>
<body>
    <form id="form1" runat="server">
        <asp:Label ID="Label1" runat="server"
        Text="Enter Your Age:"></asp:Label>
        <br />
        <asp:TextBox ID="TextBox1"
        runat="server"></asp:TextBox>
        <br />
        <asp:Button ID="Button1" runat="server" Text="OK"
            />
        <br />
        <asp:Label ID="Label2" runat="server"></asp:Label>
    </form>
</body>
</html>
```

No special colors or look are defined within the page. However, when you retrieve it in the browser (see Figure 23-1), the look is more striking.

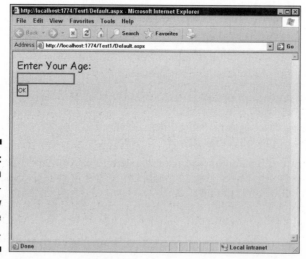

Figure 23-1:
A page with the Mellow-Yellow theme applied.

The only additional requirement of the pages that use themes is that you specify a `<head>` tag with the `runat="server"` attribute.

You can have multiple skin files in a single theme folder. When you do this, all the skin file declarations are combined together as if they were in one file and used for that theme. However, if any duplicate default declarations exist (that is, two declarations for the same control where neither specified a `skinid`), an error is generated when you compile your application.

Although VWDE provides no direct support for Design mode when creating and editing a skin file, an easy — and more visual — way of creating skin files is available through a simple trick. First, create a page and drop all the controls you want to declare in your skin file on that page. Then use the Properties window to set all the properties so that the controls look exactly as you want them to. Then switch over to Source view for the page, select and copy the controls, and paste them into the skin page.

Don't forget to go through each control and remove its `id` property after you copy and paste the controls into the skin file. VWDE will always insert them for you on a normal page, but they will trigger an error in the skin file.

Providing alternate skin definitions

Suppose you have a couple different looks that you want to provide for the same control in your theme. For example, you might want all labels that are used as headers to use one look, and you want other labels use a different look. Fortunately, the `skinid` property allows you to do exactly that.

Modify the `YellowControls.skin` file to provide a second skin definition for the label. In Listing 23-3, you see the changes in bold.

Listing 23-3:   The Modified YellowControls.skin File

```
<asp:TextBox runat="server" backcolor="Yellow"
font-names="Comic Sans MS" borderstyle="Solid"
bordercolor="Red" borderwidth="3"
forecolor="blue"></asp:TextBox>

<asp:Button runat="server" backcolor="Yellow"
font-names="Comic Sans MS" borderstyle="Solid" />

<asp:Label runat="server" backcolor="Yellow"
font-names="Comic Sans MS" font-size="Large" >
```

(continued)

Listing 23-3 *(continued)*

```
</asp:Label>

<asp:Label runat="server" backcolor="Yellow"
font-names="Comic Sans MS" font-size="XX-Large"
skinid="HeaderLabel">
</asp:Label>
```

Notice the two declarations for `<asp:Label>`. The first has no `skinid` specified (like the declarations that come before it), but the second does. The one without the `skinid` property is the default skin for all `Label` controls. The second (and any additional label declarations) must have a `skinid` specified and act as alternative label control skins. (Although I'm using the `Label` control as an example here, you can provide alternate skins for any control — they always work the same way.)

Now that you have defined an alternate skin, how do you use it in your pages? You just specify the `skinid` in the page on the control(s) where you want to use it.

Update the page you created in Listing 23-2, adding a header at the top. Listing 23-4 shows the updated page, and the changes are all in bold.

Listing 23-4:   The Modified dogage.aspx File

```
<%@ Page Language="VB" Theme="MellowYellow" %>
<html>
<head runat="server"></head>
<body>
    <form id="form1" runat="server">
        <asp:Label ID="Label3" runat="server"
        skinid="HeaderLabel"
        Text="Dog Age Calculator"></asp:Label>
        <br />
        <asp:Label ID="Label1" runat="server"
        Text="Enter Your Age:"></asp:Label>
        <br />
        <asp:TextBox ID="TextBox1"
        runat="server"></asp:TextBox>
        <br />
        <asp:Button ID="Button1" runat="server" Text="OK"
            />
        <br />
        <asp:Label ID="Label2" runat="server"></asp:Label>
    </form>
</body>
</html>
```

Notice that neither of the two label controls at the top of the page specify any `size` or `color` properties. However, the label used as a header does specify a `skinid`. The value assigned to `skinid` here is matched up with the appropriate `skinid` in the skin file, and the appropriate display properties are set, as you can see when this page appears in the browser (see Figure 23-2).

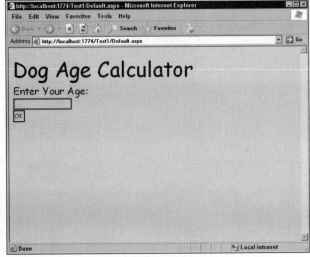

Figure 23-2:
Another
Mellow-
Yellow page
with two
kinds of
labels.

Applying Global Themes

The themes that I describe earlier in this chapter are referred to as *local* themes. That's because they can be used only within a single application — the one where their folders are located.

However, it's perfectly reasonable that you might want to create a theme that several different Web applications can use. That's what *global* themes are for.

A global theme is just like a local theme in that its folder name determines the name the theme is known by. Likewise, the names of the files within the folder don't matter. The only difference between the global and local themes is where they're located. Whereas local themes are located in the App_Themes folder of a specific application, global themes are always stored in the following folder:

```
Windows\Microsoft.NET\Framework\version\
    ASP.NETClientFiles\Themes\
```

Replace *version* with the exact version of the .NET Framework you're using. (You can look in the Framework folder to see what versions you have installed.) If the Themes folder doesn't exist on your computer, simply create it. Inside the Themes folder, you can place as many theme folders as you like.

You can create themes at both the global and local level. If you create a theme at the local level that has the same name as one at the global level, your page uses the one at the local level. This is usually a bad idea and can lead to a lot of confusion! Try to keep your theme names unique.

Chapter 24

Your Portal to Web Parts and Web Services

In This Chapter

▶ Creating a simple portal application

▶ Making the portal customizable

▶ Creating a Web part that calls a Web Service

*W*eb technology has grown dramatically in sophistication over the last ten years. It has moved from static pages to dynamic content to database-driven Web applications. Today users demand highly interactive and personalized sites that cater to their needs. To meet this demand, a new type of Web application has found popularity: the Web portal.

A Web portal is an application that presents its user interface in the form of small panels that can be added, removed or rearranged on a page by the user. This customization is then stored so that on future visits, the site continues to present the information the user prefers, organized as he wants to see it. Web portals first appeared on sites such as Yahoo! and MSN. These portals allow you to customize a page with the content you select, such as sports headlines or stock quotes, to create your own personalized home page. From there, the technology began to catch on in corporations for use in *intranets* — internal corporate Web sites designed to increase productivity and communication among employees.

In the past, to create portal applications, you had to buy specialized software, such as Microsoft SharePoint, that provided all the user interface capabilities and served up its content from a database. With ASP.NET 2.0, you now have the ability to create sophisticated Web portal interfaces for your own custom applications by using a feature called Web Parts.

The Web Parts feature of ASP.NET 2.0 is easy to use, but Microsoft has provided a lot of flexibility so that you can adapt it for use in virtually any kind of application. Of course, with that flexibility comes some complexity. In this chapter, my goal is to introduce you to the technology and show you how you can quickly get a simple portal interface running for your application.

In addition, later in this chapter, I show you how to call Web services over the Internet to retrieve information from other computers. This is an important feature for use in any Web application, but it becomes especially handy when you're creating new Web parts (those individual little panels) to make available in your portal application.

By the way, you'll notice that sometimes I refer to Web Parts and other times to Web parts. Web Parts (capitalized) is the name of the technology. A Web part, on the other hand, is the name Microsoft uses to refer to those little panels on the page.

In most of the chapters of this book, I present the features of ASP.NET 2.0 so that you can make use of them with any editor or development environment. However, the Web Parts server controls use a whole lot of tags and attributes, often one nested inside the other. This makes creating a Web Parts application in a simple editor such as Notepad a bewildering experience. Because of that, in this chapter, I assume that you're using Visual Web Developer 2005 Express (VWDE) or Visual Studio 2005 to create your Web Parts applications. All references to VWDE in these pages (and in the rest of the book) apply equally to Visual Studio 2005, unless otherwise noted.

Taking the MyNewsNow Portal Test Drive

To give you firsthand experience using an ASP.NET 2.0 portal application, I recommend that you crack open the CD that came with this book (if you haven't already) and install the MyNewsNow portal application. Open this application in VWDE and run it. A drop-down list box appears in the upper left of the page. This control determines the mode of the page. (I discuss modes later in this chapter.) The default is set to Browse. Select Design from the drop-down. This allows you to more clearly see the various parts of the page and how they are organized. Your page now looks like Figure 24-1. (I use Latin here as dummy text in a few places on this page to fill in where you'd normally see content.)

Figure 24-1:
The
MyNews-
Now portal
application.

Pay particular attention to the following details:

- ✔ The content of the page is divided into little panels, and each panel is a *Web part*.

- ✔ Each Web part has a title bar and a border. These elements are referred to as the *chrome*. (I'm not making this stuff up!)

- ✔ The Web parts on the page in Figure 24-1 are arranged into a main section to the left and a narrower sidebar along the right. These sections are referred to as *zones*. You can arrange zones as columns or rows of any width or height. Two zones are visible on this page, but you can create as many zones on a page as you like. The zone where a Web part is located determines the look of its chrome.

- ✔ You can see a drop-down list box in the top-left corner of the page. It indicates the mode of the page. The page opens in Browse mode. There are a fixed set of modes supported by Web Parts and they determine what parts are visible on the page and what you can do with them. (See "Getting in the Mode for Customization," later in this chapter.)

Now take a few minutes to play around with the user interface and try a few of the following actions:

- ✔ Click the down arrow on the right side of the title bar of one of the Web parts. A menu appears. Choose Minimize. The Web part collapses up into just a title bar. Click the down arrow to open the menu again. Choose Restore.

- ✔ Click another Web part's down arrow. Choose Close.

- ✔ Click the title of one of the Web parts and drag it from its zone to the other zone.

- ✔ Select Edit from the drop-down list box at the top of the page to switch into Edit mode. Nothing immediately changes. Click the down arrow on the right side of the title bar of one of the Web parts. Choose Edit from the menu. A new zone appears. It's called an EditorZone because it contains Web parts that allow you to edit the Web part's title, chrome type, and other properties. Enter a title, select a chrome type, and then click OK.

- ✔ Close the application and run it again. Notice that the page looks the same as it did when you closed it — the application retained the changes you made in Design mode and Edit mode.

By giving the user control over what Web parts are displayed and how they are arranged, as well as the ability to customize those parts, this technology provides a very powerful and flexible Web interface. It also provides powerful personalization features by remembering these customizations when the user returns.

The rest of this chapter is dedicated to showing you how you can begin to use this kind of interface in your own Web applications. And you'll discover these features by creating your own version of the MyNewsNow portal.

Building Your First Web Portal Application

In the following sections, you begin creating your MyNewsNow Web portal application. You start by building some simple user controls. Then you'll create a page, lay out the zones and then add the user controls to the page as Web parts.

If you have trouble at any point, you can always open the complete MyNewsNow portal application on the CD and take a look at how I did it there.

Making Web parts out of user controls

A slick portal begins life as a simple ASP.NET application. So use the ASP.NET Web Application template to create a new Web application. Name it MyNewsNow.

The magic is all in the server controls. The first step is to create a few simple Web parts that can plug into the cool portal architecture. To begin, I create some very simple Web parts to get rolling. You can go back later and make them more functional.

The most common way of creating Web parts is with user controls. All you have to do is choose Add New Item... from the Web site menu and select Web User Control. Then you can begin creating the user interface and writing the code as you normally would for a user control.

For the MyNewsNow portal, I created four user controls: News, Sports, Weather, and Links. In a production application, these user controls might retrieve information from a database, an RSS feed, or a Web service. But because my goal here is to show you how to create a Web portal user interface, I just created user controls that contain static HTML. You can create your own static user controls or you can simply copy the user controls I created from the CD and add them to your Web site. There's nothing special about them. They're just standard user controls like the ones I describe in Chapter 14.

Managing and zoning the portal page

When you have some Web parts in the form of user controls, you're ready to create a home for them on a *portal page*. A portal page is just a standard ASP.NET Web page with one important control added: the `WebPartManager`. Although this control is invisible to the user and you won't often work directly with it, the `WebPartManager` is essential. It sets up the page to work like a portal and creates a database for your application where it automatically keeps track of customizations that each user makes to the page, so that when they return to the site, the page looks just as they designed it. All this personalization and database work happens automatically, behind the scenes.

Using the MyNewsNow application you created in the last section, follow these steps to create the MyNewsNow portal page:

1. **Add a `WebPartManager` to your `default.aspx` page.**

2. **Open the HTML section of the Toolbox and drag and drop a table onto your page.**

A simple HTML table helps you organize your page into columns.

3. **Use the Properties window to set the table's `Width` property to 100%.**

4. **Delete one column and one row so that the table is two by two. (Use the Layout ⇨ Delete menu to do this.)**

   By default, the table has three columns and three rows. You'll use the table to create two columns on the page with a separate row at the top for additional controls used in Edit mode.

5. **Adjust the column width by hovering over the line between the two columns and dragging and dropping the line where you want it.**

   For this example, adjust the columns so that the left two cells are about two thirds the width of the page, leaving one third for the right two cells.

6. **Set the `VAlign` property to `top` for all the cells. Do this by clicking to place the cursor in a cell and then setting the property using the Properties window.**

7. **Open the Web Parts section of the Toolbox and drag and drop a `WebPartZone` into the lower-left cell of the table.**

8. **Set the `ID` property for the `WebPartZone` control to `MainContent` using the Properties window.**

9. **Add another `WebPartZone` to the lower-right cell of the table and set its `ID` property to `SideBar`.**

10. **Open the Standard section of the Toolbox and drag and drop a `DropDownList` to the upper-left cell of the table.**

The page, in Design view, should look like Figure 24-2.

The `WebPartZone` is the home for your Web parts. A zone can be set up to display its parts horizontally, in a row, or vertically, in a column, as I have done here. You can have as many zones on a page as you like and as many Web parts in a zone as you like.

Placing your parts

You add a user control to your portal page as a Web part by simply dragging the user control from Solution Explorer and dropping it in the `WebPartZone` where you want it to appear.

Drag the `News.ascx` user control from Solution Explorer and drop it inside the MainContent `WebPartZone`. (Be sure to drop it *inside* the MainContent zone, not just in the same table cell.) It should appear as a box with the contents of the user control inside.

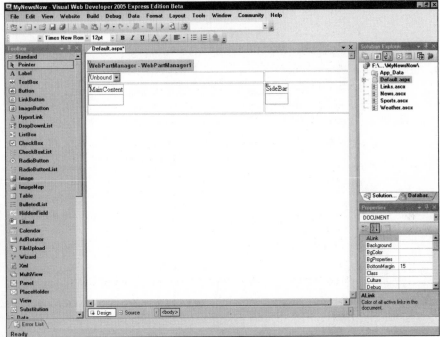

Figure 24-2:
The
MyNews
portal page
with the
table, two
zones and
a drop-
down list.

Drag the `Sports.ascx` user control from Solution Explorer and drop it
inside the MainContent `WebPartZone`, just under the News part.

Drag the `Weather.ascx` user control from Solution Explorer and drop it
inside the SideBar `WebPartZone`. Drag `Links.ascx` to the SideBar, beneath
Weather.

The page should look like Figure 24-3.

Although this page would work, it isn't very attractive. Fortunately, you can
dress it up easily.

Right-click the MainContent zone header (not the parts within it). From the
contextual menu, choose Auto Format. In the Auto Format dialog box, select
Classic from the list box. Click OK to apply it.

Right-click the SideBar zone header and choose Auto Format. This time,
select Professional in the list box and click OK.

The look of the chrome of the Web parts changes to reflect the format you
chose for each part, as shown in Figure 24-4.

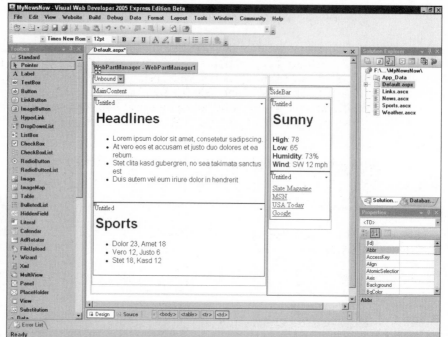

Figure 24-3:
The
Personal
Portal page
with Web
part user
controls
added.

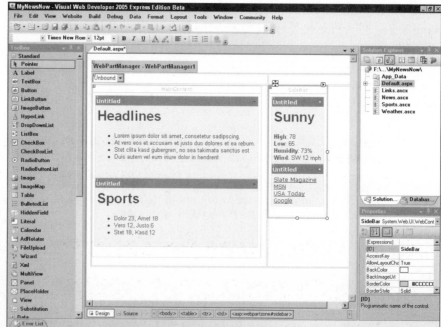

Figure 24-4:
Dressing
up the
Web parts
with the
zone's Auto
Format.

The first run done

You might be surprised to find out that you've just completed your first ASP.NET 2.0 portal application with Web Parts. That's all there is to it! Okay, that isn't all there is to it, I admit. Web parts have a whole lot more capabilities and features to discover and use. I demonstrate some of them later in this chapter. But you do have a functional portal application, so run it and see how it works. You should see a browser window that looks like Figure 24-5.

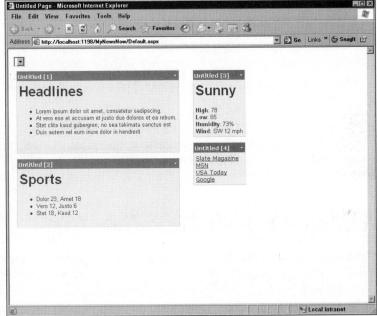

Figure 24-5:
Running
your portal
for the
first time.

Play around with it to see what you can do. You can minimize and close panels, but you can't move them around or change their titles. For that, you need to change the mode of the Web parts page. Adding that ability is the topic of the next section.

Getting in the Mode for Customization

The *mode* of a page determines what customization capabilities the user has available to them. Different modes allow for different kinds of customization. The application you create in previous sections of this chapter doesn't specify a mode for the page. So, by default, it uses the Browse mode. This is the typical mode of a page and it is perfect for viewing information.

However if you want to provide the user with more customization capabilities than Browse mode makes available, you must give the user a way to switch to a different mode. I'll show you how to do that in the next section. In this section, I introduce the modes that are available and show you what possibilities they open up for the user.

In addition to Browse, there are three other modes to choose from:

- **Design:** Allows the user to move Web parts around from one zone to another or to rearrange the parts within a zone so that the information appears in the order the user prefers.

- **Edit:** When the page is in Edit mode, an additional item (Edit) appears in the Web part menu (the down-arrow that appears on the right side of the Web part's title bar). Choosing the Edit option allows the user to change specific properties associated with the selected Web part.

- **Catalog:** Makes available a catalog of Web parts that can be added to the page.

In the next few sections, I demonstrate some of the techniques you can use to make your application more personalized. Specifically I'll demonstrate the Design mode and one of the key features Edit mode makes available to you. I leave the rest for you to explore.

Adding the mode drop-down list

The mode of a page is set by your code. So to give the user the ability to control it, you must provide a button, a link, or some other user-interface device. For this example, I use a simple drop-down list.

Click to select the drop-down list control. Select the Items property in the Properties window and click the ... button. In the ListItem Collection Editor dialog box, add three items and set their text as follows: Browse, Design, and Edit. Click OK.

Set the drop-down list control's AutoPostBack property to True.

Double-click the drop-down list control and add the following code in the default SelectedIndexChanged event:

```
Select Case DropDownList1.SelectedItem.Text
   Case "Browse"
      WebPartManager1.DisplayMode = _
         WebPartManager.BrowseDisplayMode
```

```
    Case "Design"
        WebPartManager1.DisplayMode = _
            WebPartManager.DesignDisplayMode
    Case "Edit"
        WebPartManager1.DisplayMode = _
            WebPartManager.EditDisplayMode
End Select
```

Setting the page's mode is as easy as setting the `WebPartManager` control's `DisplayMode` property.

Ready, set, run in Design mode!

The drop-down list you added in the last section changes the page's mode. To see what effect that has on your Web parts, run the application.

1. **Click the Start Debugging button on the toolbar to run your application.**

   The application opens in Browse mode, as usual.

2. **Select Design from the drop-down list to put the page in Design mode.**

   The zones now appear as boxes.

3. **Drag one of the panels by its title bar around the page.**

   The panel appears as a ghosted image of itself as you drag, and a bar appears between the other parts as you drag near them. The bar indicates where you'll drop the panel if you release the mouse button. You can drag it to a different location in the same zone or to a different zone.

4. **Drag one of the parts to a different zone.**

   You see that the title bar and background change color to match the other parts in that zone. As I mention earlier in this chapter, the title bar and background are referred to as chrome. The color and look of the chrome is defined by the zone, not the Web part itself.

   As you can see, Design mode makes it possible for the user to rearrange the Web parts on the page. The user can move a Web part to a different location within the same zone or drag it to a completely different zone. This kind of customization allows the user to organize the information in the way that makes the most sense to her and allows her to put important items near the top and less important items at the bottom of the page.

   Now, try using the drop-down list to change the page into Edit mode:

5. Click the drop-down list again. Select Edit to put the page in Edit mode.

You get an error indicating that the specified mode is not supported on this page. Why? There are a few steps you must take before you can get Edit mode working on your page.

Customizing parts with the EditorZone

Edit mode makes it possible for the user to modify settings associated with a specific Web part. So it requires a little more work on the developer's part than Design mode. The first step is to add a new zone to the page that appears only when the page is in Edit mode: the EditorZone. Like the WebPartZone, the EditorZone is an area where you can drop Web parts. (For more information on dropping Web parts in the WebPartZone, see the section titled "Managing and zoning the portal page," in this chapter.) But this zone is not for displaying information. Instead, you use it to display Web parts that are specifically designed to modify the settings of *other* Web parts.

Drag the `EditorZone` control from the WebParts section of the Toolbox to the upper-left cell of the table. Drop the control beside the drop-down list. The control ends up appearing below the drop-down list. Right-click the title of the `EditorZone` and choose Auto Format, select Simple, and click OK.

Now drag an `AppearanceEditorPart` control from the Toolbox and drop it inside the `EditorZone` control. Several controls appear, that allow the user to change aspects of the Web part's appearance:

✔ **Title:** The text that appears in the title bar of the Web part.

✔ **Chrome Type:** The type of title bar and border that should appear on the Web part. Options include: border only (no title bar), title bar and border, title bar only and no border or title bar.

✔ **Direction:** Indicates the direction and justification of the text within the Web part. Most languages display text from left-to-right, but right-to-left may be chosen for languages like Hebrew and Arabic.

✔ **Height and Width:** Used to set the dimensions of the control.

✔ **Hidden:** Can be used to hide the Web part, making it invisible.

Ready, set, run in Edit mode!

Now you're ready to run the application and see the Edit mode in action.

1. **Run the application again.**

2. **Select Edit from the drop-down.**

   No crash occurs this time. That's always a good sign. But not much change either.

3. **Click the arrow on the right of the title for one of the parts to display its menu. You should now see an Edit menu item. Choose it.**

   All of your content is pushed down to make way for the AppearanceEditorPart, as shown in Figure 24-6.

4. **Change the title to something appropriate and then click OK.**

   The AppearanceEditor goes away, and your part should have a new title.

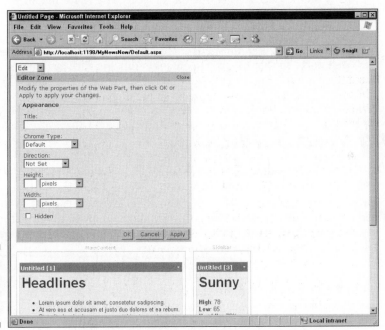

Figure 24-6:
Editing
a Web
part's title.

Exploring more editors, more zones

This chapter gives you a running start working with Web Parts, but more editors and zones are available for you to explore. To give you a taste of what's out there, here's a list of some of the other editors that you can add to the EditorZone:

✔ **LayoutEditor:** Allows users to modify layout properties — whether the Web part is minimized, what zone it's in, and so on.

✔ **PropertyGridEditor:** Allows the user to edit custom properties that you create in the Web part itself.

✔ **BehaviorEditor:** Allows users to control what other users can do with a Web part. For example, the user can decide if others should be able to close, move to another zone, or edit the Web part.

In addition to the WebPartsZone and the EditorZone, you can add two other kinds of zones to your portal page:

✔ **CatalogZone:** Allows users to display a list of Web parts that can be added to the page. You can display a list of all the parts that were originally on the page (to get one back if you close it, for instance), or you can display a static list of all the controls you want to offer the user. You can even import a catalog using XML.

✔ **ConnectionsZone:** Allows users to establish a connection between two Web parts so that the parts can communicate with each other and share information.

Calling Web Services

Web Services is another exciting technology provided by the .NET Framework. It isn't directly tied to Web Parts — you can call Web services from any Web (or Windows) application. However, when you create Web parts, Web services become particularly useful because they allow you to provide features and capabilities in your parts that you don't have to develop and implement yourself. You can build on the work others have done.

In the following sections, I briefly describe what a Web service is and how it works. I also show you where you can find publicly available Web services that you can call and use in your own application. Then I show you how to create a user control that calls a Web service, and explain how to add the user control to your portal page.

What's so exciting about Web services?

When you want to provide reusable functionality throughout your application, you create a class and write methods in that class that can be called from anywhere in your application when that class is instantiated. (For more on classes and instantiation, see Chapter 8.) A *Web service* is a class that is not a part of your own application — and probably not one that you wrote yourself. It may not even exist on your local network. A Web service is a class that can reside anywhere on the Internet. Your application, if it knows the service's address, can instantiate that class and make calls to its methods — and it's almost as easy as using a class that's defined in your own application.

Thousands of publicly available Web services are available to call from your application, and they provide all kinds of information and functionality. Here's just a taste of some of the things you can do with Web services:

- Provide Google searches, Amazon lookups, or mapping capabilities directly from your site, with your own interface.

- Retrieve global date/time information and perform virtually any kind of date/time calculations.

- Calculate the distance between any two points on earth.

- Perform various kinds of encryption and hashing and generate strong passwords.

- Convert virtually any weight, length, temperature, volume, or measurement from one unit to another.

- Retrieve Bible verses, quotes from famous people, the works of Shakespeare, and more.

- Convert data to or from XML, CSV, EDI, and other formats.

- Perform a search across multiple auction sites at once.

A wealth of information is out there, and all you have to do is make the call!

SOAP: Sliding into the next century with Web services

VWDE makes instantiating a Web service class and calling its methods almost as easy as using any class in the .NET Framework. But behind the scenes, a whole lot of work is going on.

A Web service can exist anywhere on the Internet. It doesn't have to be running on a Windows server, and it doesn't have to use the .NET Framework. That's because Microsoft, IBM, Sun and many other industry heavyweights have joined together to create standards describing how a Web service should work, and those standards have been implemented on all sorts of systems, from IBM mainframes to UNIX/Linux machines to Windows servers.

The pixie dust that makes all this possible is a specific flavor of XML called the Simple Object Access Protocol, or SOAP. (It provides cross-platform communication and keeps you squeaky clean in the process!) The process works like this:

1. **When you call a method, the .NET Framework takes that call and converts it into an XML SOAP request that is sent to the server.**

2. **The server that hosts the Web service receives the request, calls the method, and gets the result back.**

3. **The server bundles up the result as an XML SOAP response and sends it back to the .NET Framework, which unwraps it and sends the result to your application.**

Because all this conversion to XML and back happens behind the scenes you don't actually have to know anything about SOAP or XML in order to use Web services. All you have to do is find the Web service you want to use and add a Web Reference to your project — and you're in luck because I explain how to accomplish those tasks in the following sections.

Finding Web services

So where do you find Web services? Fortunately, various companies and individuals have created a whole lot of Web services and made them available to anyone who wants to use them — and many of them are free. Others cost a fee — some companies charge by the month, and others charge based on usage.

Catalogs that list Web Services are referred to by the acronym UDDI (Universal Description and Discovery and Integration). Fortunately, you don't have to know anything about UDDI to use a catalog. Most catalogs provide a simple Web interface that makes searching for a Web service almost as easy as searching for Web sites. Here are a few places where you can begin your search:

✔ **BindingPoint (`www.bindingpoint.com`):** Very slick interface allows Google-like searches or Yahoo-like category listings.

✔ **XMethods, Inc. (`www.xmethods.net`):** Not as snazzy as BindingPoint, but provides access to a whole lot of services.

✔ **Microsoft UDDI Business Registry Node (`http://uddi.microsoft.com`):** Requires registration. This site is tends to focus on business-to-business services.

When you find a Web service you want to use, you can read the documentation associated with it to find out what methods are provided, what arguments the methods accept and what they return. You can even try out the Web service yourself from the browser. To do this, just click the URL link associated with the service. You will see a Web interface, like the one in Figure 24-7, that allows you to make a call to the Web service, pass arguments, and see the result in your browser. This makes it easy to see how the service works (and to check that it's still available!) before you write code in your application to use it.

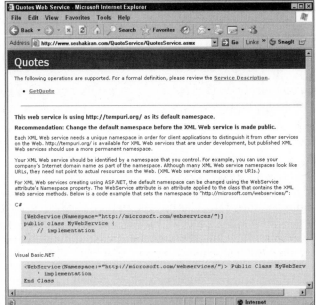

Figure 24-7:
Accessing a
Web service
from your
browser.

Adding a Web reference

After you find the Web service you want to use and you know what arguments it expects and what it returns, you are ready to use the Web service in your own application. To do that, you need to inform your application that you want to call a Web service. You do this by adding what VWDE calls a add a *Web reference* to your application. Once you define the Web reference by giving your application the appropriate Web service URL, VWDE can do all its behind-the-scenes work to set up your application to make the call and receive the results back.

Follow these steps to add a Web reference to your application:

1. **Find the Web service you want to use using one of the sites listed in the preceding section. Select and copy the URL for the service to your clipboard.**

2. **Return to your project in VWDE and right-click on your Web site in Solution Explorer and choose Add Web Reference from the contextual menu.**

   The Add Web Reference dialog box appears.

3. **Paste the URL into the text box at the top of the dialog and click the Go button.**

   The Web page for the service appears in the dialog box to let you know that you're in the right place.

4. **Type a name for the Web reference you're creating in the Web Reference Name text box.**

   If it's a ZIP code lookup service, for example, you might call the reference `ZipCodeLookupRef`.

5. **Click the Add Reference button.**

When you do this, VWDE goes out to the Internet, finds the Web service, and downloads a description of the classes and methods available for this service. It uses this information to create a *proxy,* an object on your machine that is a stand-in for the real class on the server. You instantiate and use this proxy with the Web reference name that you typed in when you created the Web reference. When you call a Web service method, the proxy, in turn, does all the work of translating your request to XML, calling the Web service, and giving you the results.

After you add a Web reference to a Web site, you can call the Web service from anywhere on the site. In the next section, I'll show you how you can call the Web service from a user control that will be pressed into service as a Web part in your portal page.

Creating the quote-of-the-day Web part

To demonstrate how you can use a Web service from your Web part user control and then integrate that Web part into your portal application, I make use of a simple, free public Web service that retrieves a famous-quote-of-the-day and then displays it.

1. **Right-click on your Web site and choose Add Web Reference from the contextual menu.**

2. **In the Add Web Reference dialog box, type the following URL into the URL text box:**

```
www.seshakiran.com/QuoteService/QuotesService.asmx
```

Due to the nature of public Web services, I can't guarantee that by the time you read this and try it for yourself that the Web service at this address will still be available. If it isn't, go to one of the sites listed in the "Finding Web Services" section and search for "quote of the day" or "famous quotes." You should be able to find a substitute.

3. **Click Go.**

You should see the Web site appear in the dialog box, as in Figure 24-8.

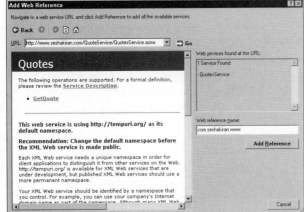

Figure 24-8:
Adding
a reference
to the
Quotes Web
service.

4. **Type** QuoteRef **in the Web Reference Name text box and click the Add Reference button.**

The Web Reference is added in Solution Explorer.

5. **Create a new Web User Control for this site named QuoteOfTheDay.ascx.**

6. **Add a single label to the user control. Set its ID to QuoteLabel.**

7. **In the Page_Load event of the user control, add this code:**

```
Dim QuoteProxy As New QuoteRef.Quotes
QuoteLabel.Text = QuoteProxy.GetQuote()
```

The first line above instantiates the proxy. The second simply calls the GetQuote() method and displays the string returned in the label.

8. Save `QuoteOfTheDay.ascx`, and open `Default.aspx`.

9. Drag `QuoteOfTheDay.ascx` from Solution Explorer onto the bottom part of the SideBar Web zone, under Links.

10. Run the application.

Your quote should appear at the bottom of the SideBar, as in Figure 24-9.

Figure 24-9:
The new
Personal
Portal
with the
QuoteOf
TheDay
Web part.

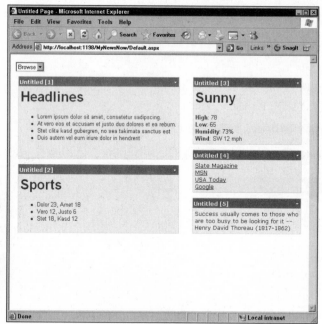

Part IX
The Part of Tens

The 5th Wave   By Rich Tennant

"Great goulash, Stan. That reminds me, are you still scripting your own Web page?"

In this part . . .

Where do you go for help when you have a problem with an ASP.NET page you are creating? What if you just want to find out more about a particular topic? What does it take to be an ASP.NET 2.0 guru? I answer all these questions and more in the Part of Tens.

Chapter 25

The Ten Best Places to Get ASP.NET 2.0 Answers

In This Chapter

▶ Using manuals and books

▶ Trekking through technical journals

▶ Checking out discussion forums and newsgroups

▶ Browsing blogs, Webcasts, and Web sites

▶ Getting the goods from geeks and user groups

▶ Cruising conferences

*Y*ou have a killer idea for a new Web application. You've designed your masterpiece and you've already started developing it. Then you hit a snag — a *big* one. You can't really go on until you get an answer to the problem that has tripped you up. Where do you turn? What do you do?

This chapter gives you ten answers to those questions. Only one of these answers has to work to get you back on track. Good luck!

RTFM: Read the Flippin' Manual!

You might be surprised by all the information people have put in those books and help files that came with your Web server and the .NET Framework. So use them!

Check the online help first. (Searching for the help you need is easier and usually much faster than flipping through the index of a huge manual.) The online help that comes with the .NET Framework offers a wealth of information on ASP.NET 2.0, server controls, Visual Basic 2005, and lots more. In addition, the

.NET Framework comes with an ASP.NET Quick Start tutorial, lots of examples, and answers to many common questions. Check the IIS online help and manuals for Web server configuration issues and scalability questions.

Visit the Bookstore

In this book, you get a good introduction to ASP.NET development topics as well as answers to the questions you need to get started with ASP.NET 2.0. But this is just the beginning! After you take the leap into ASP.NET development, you're bound to run into more complex topics that you need to understand better. So check out these great intermediate/advanced ASP.NET books:

- *ASP.NET 2.0 Everyday Apps For Dummies,* by Doug Lowe
- *Beginning ASP.NET 2.0,* by Chris Hart, John Kauffman, David Sussman, and Chris Ullman
- *Professional ASP.NET 2.0,* by Bill Evjen, Scott Hanselman, Farhan Muhammad, Devin Rader, and Srinivasa Sivakumar
- *Professional Web Parts and Custom Controls with ASP.NET 2.0,* by Peter Vogel

If you run into Web development problems that aren't specifically ASP.NET-related, these books may help:

- *HTML 4 For Dummies,* 5th Edition, by Ed Tittel, et al.
- *JavaScript For Dummies,* 4th Edition, by Emily A. Vander Veer
- *Visual Basic 2005 For Dummies,* by William A. Sempf
- *Visual Basic 2005 Express Edition For Dummies,* by Richard Mansfield
- *Visual Basic .NET For Dummies,* by Wallace Wang
- *Visual Web Developer 2005 Express Edition For Dummies,* by Alan Simpson

Review Technical Journals and Magazines

Are you looking for source code and articles squarely focused on Microsoft development technologies, delivered every month? *Visual Studio .NET Developer* is a technical journal published by Pinnacle Publishing. Edited by yours truly, it focuses on real-world development in all aspects of programming with the .NET Framework.

Other technical magazines you should check out include

- ✔ asp.netPRO (www.aspnetpro.com)
- ✔ CoDe (www.code-magazine.com)
- ✔ Visual Studio Magazine (www.fawcette.com/vsm)
- ✔ MSDN Magazine (http://msdn.microsoft.com/msdnmag)

Strike Up a Discussion at Online Forums and Newsgroups

Discussion forums are Web sites designed to allow you to post messages to ask questions and make comments. Postings are made from developers around the world and are organized into *topics* and then into *discussions*. This is an excellent way to get help from others and to offer help as you gain more experience yourself. I recommend the following forums:

- ✔ http://forums.asp.net
- ✔ www.dotnetspider.com/technology/qa/ASPQuestions.aspx
- ✔ http://forums.devx.com/forumdisplay.php?s=&forumid=111
- ✔ http://discuss.develop.com
- ✔ www.vbcity.com/forums/forum.asp?fid=37

Newsgroups are like discussion forums, but they typically use special software called a newsgroup reader. You can use Outlook Express, which comes with Windows XP, to read newsgroups.

Microsoft hosts numerous newsgroups on its server:

```
news://msnews.microsoft.com
```

If you'd rather access these Microsoft groups from your browser, you can do that at:

```
www.microsoft.com/communities/newsgroups/en-us/
          default.aspx
```

Here are some of the newsgroups you should check out:

The first of those in the following list is by far the most active and a good spot to post any questions related to ASP.NET. The following groups are, obviously, designed to address more specific concerns within the context of ASP.NET.

- ✔ `microsoft.public.dotnet.framework.aspnet`
- ✔ `microsoft.public.dotnet.framework.aspnet.announcements`
- ✔ `microsoft.public.dotnet.framework.aspnet.buildingcontrols`
- ✔ `microsoft.public.dotnet.framework.aspnet.caching`
- ✔ `microsoft.public.dotnet.framework.aspnet.security`
- ✔ `microsoft.public.dotnet.framework.aspnet.webcontrols`
- ✔ `microsoft.public.dotnet.framework.aspnet.mobile`
- ✔ `microsoft.public.dotnet.framework.aspnet.webservices`

The following groups are on topics related to the .NET Framework: the class libraries, database access, performance and the Visual Basic language. You'll see posts there from people working on both Web and Windows applications. However since many of the concerns discussed are shared by all .NET applications, you're sure to find a lot of interesting information and discussions here.

- ✔ `microsoft.public.dotnet.framework`
- ✔ `microsoft.public.dotnet.framework.adonet`
- ✔ `microsoft.public.dotnet.framework.performance`
- ✔ `microsoft.public.dotnet.languages.vb`

These newsgroups, as their names suggest, are designed to address the concerns of Visual Studio developers:

- ✔ `microsoft.public.vsnet.general`
- ✔ `microsoft.public.vsnet.ide`
- ✔ `microsoft.public.vsnet.setup`
- ✔ `microsoft.public.vsnet.servicepacks`

Browse Blogs by the Brightest and Best

Blogs (short for *web logs*) are something like public, online diaries. Writers add entries to their blogs on a regular basis, and the entries are published to a site where anyone can read it. Topics for blogs range from boy bands to biotechnology. The kinds of blogs I recommend here, though, are those written by .NET developers for other .NET developers. Everyone from book authors to industry pundits to Microsoft product-leads can be found blogging for your consumption. Blogs are a great way to find new tips and techniques, discover best practices, and keep abreast of where the industry is headed.

Here are a few blogging sites that host many .NET bloggers:

- http://weblogs.asp.net
- http://blogs.msdn.com
- www.geekswithblogs.net

Here are blogs from the team at Microsoft responsible for creating ASP.NET:

- **Scott Guthrie,** Product Unit Manager for ASP.NET, IIS, and Visual Web Developer: http://weblogs.asp.net/scottgu
- **Nikhil Kothari,** Development Lead, ASP.NET: www.nikhilk.net
- **Brian Goldfarb,** Product Manager, ASP.NET and Visual Web Developer: http://blogs.msdn.com/bgold
- **Shanku Niyogi,** Group Program Manager, ASP.NET: http://weblogs.asp.net/shankun
- **Betrand Le Roy,** Software Design Engineer, ASP.NET: http://weblogs.asp.net/bleroy

These blogs are by prominent industry figures in .NET development who are not directly employed by Microsoft. You'll find everything from development tips, performance tweaks, and solutions for tough problems to industry rumors, news and gossip.

- **Rob Howard:** http://weblogs.asp.net/rhoward
- **Scott Mitchell:** www.scottonwriting.com/sowblog
- **Alex Lowe:** http://callmealex.com
- **Don Box:** http://pluralsight.com/blogs/dbox
- **Bill Evjen:** http://geekswithblogs.net/evjen
- **Christoph Wille:** http://chrison.net
- **Steven Smith:** http://weblogs.asp.net/ssmith
- **Danny Chen:** http://weblogs.asp.net/dannychen
- **The Wintellect Team:** www.wintellect.com/weblogs/wintellect

Stay Up for Popcorn and a Movie: ASP.NET Webcasts

Microsoft provides access to free presentations made by both Microsoft and non-Microsoft trainers and presenters. Topics run the gamut of .NET technologies and you'll find plenty on ASP.NET and related technologies. You see the slides and hear the voice of the presenter. It's an excellent way to get the benefits of many conference sessions without the time and expense of going to the conference!

You can find these presentations at:

```
http://msdn.microsoft.com/asp.net/support/multimedia
```

Wander the World Wide Web

You can find tutorials, source code, answers to common questions, discussion groups, and all kinds of other stuff from ASP.NET Web sites. And there are *lots* of them! So many, in fact, that I dedicate a whole Part of Tens chapter to them. Flip over to Chapter 26 for the "Ten Coolest Web Sites for ASP.NET 2.0 Developers."

Call Microsoft Web Technical Support

Microsoft provides online access to the same documents and source material that the telephone technical support people use. Chances are good that if you're persistent, you can get as much help using this Web site as you would by calling the telephone support line. And the Web site is free! Just go to

```
http://search.support.microsoft.com/search/?adv=1
```

First, select the appropriate product for your question from a drop-down list. Next, choose a search type: Title Only, Full Text, Article ID, or Error Message. Finally, type in your question or keywords in the For text box and click the button to run the search. The Web site presents you with a list of articles that it thinks match your question. If you aren't getting any hits or you're getting hits for the wrong kind of thing, try rewording the question or using different terms.

Make Friends with ASP.NET Geeks and Visit Their User Groups

Programming geeks are hard to miss. You often see them in their native habitat — surrounded by computers, computer parts, and books and manuals stacked to the ceiling. If you work in a large company you may want to wander down to the IT department or help desk to meet them. If not, you'll often find them at computer conferences, computer stores and, of course, gaming and comic book stores. If you find an ASP.NET programming geek near you, I strongly suggest that you strike up a relationship with this person. Your time will be well spent, because ASP.NET geeks often can be your best resource for quick answers and explanations. If your resident geek needs a little encouragement to share his or her prized information, you'll find that high-caffeine beverages, pizza, and munchies work best. But no matter how you add it up, it's cheaper than a telephone call to tech support.

If you don't have your own geek handy, you have to go where they hang out: user groups. A *user group* is a place where computer people who are interested in a particular technology can come together and share their knowledge. Most major cities have a .NET user group. For a list, check out this page:

```
http://www.gotdotnet.com/community/resources/
    default.aspx?ResourceTypeDropDownList=User%20groups
```

Cavort at Conferences

Conferences are great places for getting answers to your questions and discovering more about specific topics. And don't skip the social activities! I've found that the value you get at a good conference comes as much in the people you meet and the discussions you have as it does from the formal conference sessions.

Each conference that I list in this section is presented at least once a year. Go to the Web sites listed to find out when the next conference is coming around and where it will be held.

Microsoft Tech-Ed

Where else can you hear Bill Gates himself speak, get special-release software, get in-depth technical information on a broad range of technologies, and hit the legendary Tech-Ed party and Jam session all in one week?

```
www.msdn.microsoft.com/events/teched
```

Microsoft Professional Developers Conference (PDC)

If you're looking for serious, hardcore development information, tools, and techniques, visit the Microsoft Professional Developers Conference (PDC). Get your information direct from the horse's mouth!

```
www.msdn.microsoft.com/events/pdc
```

VSLive!

If you use Visual Studio for your Web application or desktop development, check out VSLive! This conference is usually held several times throughout the year in different locations:

```
www.vslive.com
```

ASP.NET Connections

If you want a conference that's 100-percent dedicated to ASP.NET technology, you can't go wrong with ASP.NET Connections:

```
www.asp-connections.com
```

Others

You can keep up with upcoming ASP.NET events and other developer-oriented conferences all in one place:

```
www.msdnevents.com
```

Chapter 26

The Ten Coolest Web Sites for ASP.NET 2.0 Developers

In This Chapter

▶ Finding ASP.NET articles, tips, and tricks

▶ Downloading free server components

▶ Getting up-to-date Web news

The Web is a great place to browse, but it isn't exactly the best place to go when you're looking for something specific — unless you already know where to look. Between wading through the random results you get from search engines and the recommended links on sites that you find, you can eventually tell the fool's gold from the real stuff. But that effort takes precious time you might not have.

I include this chapter to save some of that time for you. I've already done all the footwork and come up with the best sites on the Web. Isn't it odd that I found exactly ten?

It's Official: Microsoft's MSDN ASP.NET Developer Center

The official home for all ASP.NET developers is the MSDN ASP.NET Developer Center. Here you can find a wealth of articles, complete application source code, pre-recorded Web presentations by famous people inside and outside Microsoft, newsgroups, ASP.NET event listings, free custom .NET components, and a whole lot more. This should definitely be your first stop.

```
http://msdn.microsoft.com/asp.net
```

Microsoft's ASP.NET

Another site Microsoft created to directly support ASP.NET developers is
www.asp.net. (No one would ever suspect . . .) In addition to listing many,
many articles (new ones virtually every day), this site provides a great springboard for finding out what else is out there on the Web for Microsoft Web
developers:

```
www.asp.net
```

Microsoft's GotDotNet.com

Although not ASP.NET-specific, this Microsoft-supported site provides a
wealth of news, information, links, and user-contributed source code examples. It's definitely worth a look!

```
www.gotdotnet.com
```

DotNetJunkies.com

This is a repository of high-quality articles on a huge variety of .NET-related
topics. If you need to know how to do it, chances are good that you can find
out how to here. It's also the home of some famous .NET bloggers and a big
discussion forum.

```
www.dotnetjunkies.com
```

.netWire

Find news, product releases, information on new postings from other sites,
and lots more. It's your one-stop destination for keeping up on what's hot:

```
www.dotnetwire.com
```

Tek-Tips ASP.NET Forum

You can quickly get answers to your development questions at this very active forum and help others solve their problems. This site also offers forums on a variety of other Microsoft technologies. Membership is free!

```
www.tek-tips.com/threadminder.cfm?pid=855
```

ASP.NET at 4GuysFromRolla

4GuysFromRolla has been a favorite since the Classic ASP days. Today, its support of ASP.NET (2.0 and earlier) is one of the best. Forums, message boards, FAQs, sample chapters from ASP.NET books, tutorials, and a well-categorized list of articles make this a "can't miss" site!

```
http://aspnet.4guysfromrolla.com
```

developer.com

Known for its active discussion forums and regularly updated content, developer.com is a must-see. Don't miss the Microsoft .NET Glossary — it helps make sense of all that Microsoft-speak.

```
www.developer.com/net/asp
```

DevX.com

DevX is an excellent source for articles, news, and discussions on ASP.NET and a variety of other topics such as VB, database access, and security. Be sure to check out the TopCoder Challenges — it's an interesting way to test your coding skills and discover clever solutions from others.

```
www.devx.com/asp
```

ASPAlliance.com

With a vast library of articles and tutorials on ASP.NET, Visual Basic, ADO.NET and many other ASP.NET-related topics, this site is bound to have the answers to your questions. They also have quite a selection of book reviews!

www.aspalliance.com

Appendix

About the CD

*T*he CD in the back of this book is a valuable resource. It not only saves your typing fingers when it comes to book examples, but it also provides you with real-world applications that demonstrate the concepts in this book, as well as a whole Bonus Part with seven chapters to extend, explain, and supplement the content in the book. In this appendix, you discover all the content on the CD and how to use it.

System Requirements

Because ASP.NET 2.0 is a technology and not a software package that you can just drop by your local store and buy, it's a little tricky trying to pin down exactly what the system requirements for it are. The biggest question to resolve is what Web server you want to use to run and test your pages. There are two options: the Web server that's built into Visual Web Developer 2005 Express and Internet Information Server (IIS) which comes with many of the Microsoft operating systems.

In the next three sections, I describe three options you have and spell out the requirements for each.

Using Visual Web Developer 2005 Express' built-in Web server

If you use VWDE, you can use its built-in Web server to test your pages. In this case, your system requirements are the same as the system requirements for VWDE:

- A PC with 600 MHz or faster Pentium-compatible CPU (I recommend 1 GHz or faster)

- At least 128MB of total RAM installed on your computer (I recommend 256MB)

- Windows 2003 Server, Windows XP Professional (with Service Pack 2) or Windows 2000 Server/Professional (with Service Pack 4)

- The .NET Framework 2.0. (See Chapter 1 for information on getting the .NET Framework 2.0 for free from Microsoft)

- Visual Web Developer 2005 Express (which comes with its built-in Web server)

This is an excellent option if you are planning to use VWDE to create your ASP.NET 2.0 applications.

When your application is complete, you need to copy it to another machine that's running IIS (see the next two sections) before you can make it available to the world (or even to your department). That's because VWDE's built-in Web server doesn't serve up pages to other machines — only to the machine on which it's running.

Using IIS on your machine

If you want to use IIS to test your pages (with or without VWDE), you need to have a server machine powerful enough to handle it. Here's the minimum software and hardware setup you need to create an ASP.NET 2.0 Web server for use locally, on an intranet, or on the Internet:

- A PC with an 800 MHz or faster Pentium-compatible CPU (I recommend 1 GHz or faster)

- At least 128MB of total RAM installed on your computer (I recommend 256MB)

- Windows 2003 Server, Windows XP Professional, or Windows 2000 Server/ Professional

✔ Internet Information Server (which comes with all the preceding operating systems)

✔ The .NET Framework 2.0 (see Chapter 1 for information on getting the .NET Framework 2.0 for free from Microsoft)

With this configuration, plus a network or Internet connection of some type, you can also make your page available on the Internet or on your corporate intranet. IIS is a powerful Web server that can ably handle virtually any Web site's requirements.

Using IIS on a corporate or hosted machine

You don't necessarily need to own a machine with the requirements outlined in the preceding sections to use this book or explore ASP.NET 2.0. You might have an intranet server at work running ASP.NET 2.0. Or you might subscribe to a hosting service that supports ASP.NET 2.0. In either case, you can use virtually any machine you like (as long as it has a network or Internet connection and can run a browser) to access the IIS Web server machine, send your files to it, and test them in your browser. (For more information on the hosting service option, see Chapter 1.)

How do I choose?

As you can see, whether you use the VWDE Web server or IIS, the requirements are similar. There are a few key factors to keep in mind:

✔ VWDE will run on Windows XP Home while IIS requires Windows XP Professional, Windows 2000, or Windows 2003.

✔ VWDE requires a separate purchase of VWDE itself (although the price is very reasonable), whereas Windows XP Professional, 2000, and 2003 all include IIS for free.

✔ A hosting service may have both up-front costs for setup and monthly costs. However many hosting companies provide free setup and very reasonable monthly fees for a simple ASP.NET 2.0 site.

✔ A corporate Web server may be available to you for free, but there are often restrictions and standards associated with its use. Be sure you understand these terms before you begin.

Using the CD

To install items from the CD to your hard drive, follow these steps:

1. **Insert the CD into your computer's CD-ROM drive.**

2. **Choose Start⇨Run.**

3. **In the dialog box that appears, type** d:\start.htm.

   Replace *d* with the proper drive letter for your CD-ROM if it uses a different letter. (If you don't know the letter, double-click My Computer on your desktop and see what letter is listed for your CD-ROM drive.)

   Your browser opens, and the license agreement is displayed.

4. **Read through the license agreement, nod your head, and click the Agree button if you want to use the CD.**

   After you click Agree, you're taken to the main menu, where you can browse through the contents of the CD.

5. **To navigate within the interface, click a topic of interest to take you to an explanation of the files on the CD and how to use or install them.**

6. **To install software from the CD, simply click the software name.**

   You see two options: to run or open the file from the current location or to save the file to your hard drive.

7. **Choose to run or open the file from its current location, and the installation procedure continues.**

8. **When you finish using the interface, close your browser as usual.**

Note: These HTML pages include an "easy install" option. If your browser supports installations from within it, go ahead and click the links of the program names you see. You see two options: Run the File from the Current Location and Save the File to Your Hard Drive. Choose to Run the File from the Current Location, and the installation procedure continues. A Security Warning dialog box appears. Click Yes to continue the installation.

To run some of the programs on the CD, you might need to keep the disc inside your CD-ROM drive. This is a good thing. Otherwise, a very large chunk of the program would be installed to your hard drive, consuming valuable hard drive space and possibly keeping you from installing other software.

What You Can Find on the CD

The following sections provide a summary of the software and other goodies on the CD. If you need help with installing the items provided on the CD, refer to the installation instructions in the preceding section.

Napoleon Bonus Part (Get It?)

The CD includes seven important bonus chapters. They provide detailed, blow-by-blow descriptions on how each page of the Café Chat Room and Classy Classifieds applications works. You also get a Guestbook application and a detailed description of how that application is constructed.

Two chapters are full of topics I didn't have room to cover in the book but still wanted to include. Another chapter is specifically for Classic ASP developers. This bonus chapter provides a fast-paced overview of all the key changes Classic ASP developers need to consider. Finally, you get a chapter that covers all the fundamental concepts for databases and database management systems (DBMSs). This final bonus chapter is a great place to stop before you tackle Chapters 19, 20, and beyond.

In all, the CD includes seven chapters of information that show you all the tricks you need to make ASP.NET 2.0 sing.

Source code from the book

This CD includes several major examples: the ASP.NET TipVault, the MyNewsNow portal, Classy Classifieds, the Café Chat Room, and the Guestbook — each of which I describe in the following list. In addition, the CD provides source code from numerous smaller examples from individual chapters — primarily to help you avoid carpal tunnel syndrome. The source code included on the CD is organized into folders that are named according to the chapter number in which the example appears in the book: for example, `Author\Chapter01`, `Author\Chapter02`, and so on.

✔ The **ASP.NET TipVault** demonstrates the new ASP.NET 2.0 Login controls. It offers exclusive tips and tricks for ASP.NET programmers — but only to registered users. It has a public welcome page that links to a registration page and a login page. On the registration page, new users enter essential information to join the site. On the login page, users type their user ID and password. After they do, they access the members-only section where they can browse all they like. However, if a user tries to access the members-only section without logging in (even if they happen to have a Favorite set up to take them there), they will be kicked back to the login page automatically. This is a very common scenario for public Web sites, and it allows you to easily create both public pages and private pages that can only be accessed by registered users. For a detailed walkthrough of the code for this application, see Chapter 22.

✔ The **MyNewsNow portal** demonstrates another new ASP.NET 2.0 feature called Web Parts. MyNewsNow is a user-customizable application that presents information in the form of small panels or Web parts. These panels can be added, removed, minimized or moved around on the page so that the user can create exactly the kind of interface they want to see.

✔ **Classy Classifieds** demonstrates the new ASP.NET 2.0 SQL data provider as well as the new grid and details view controls. It demonstrates how you can do simple queries, complex, user-defined queries and how to update, insert and delete database rows. Classy is a classified ads site. Users browse ads by category or search for specific ads. Then they can respond to an ad via e-mail. Users also can place their own ads and update or delete their ads, as necessary. For the details on this application, see Bonus Chapter 2 on the CD. For all the source code, see the \Author\Classy2 folder on the CD.

✔ The **Café** demonstrates the appropriate use of application variables and session variables in an application to share global information across pages and across sessions. Café is a real-time chat room. After the user selects a nickname, they enter the primary window, where they can type messages and see messages typed by others. There's even a list down the right side of the window of all the users currently in the Café. For a detailed examination of this application, see Bonus Chapter 1 on the CD. The \Author\Cafe folder contains all the source code.

✔ The **Guestbook** demonstrates VB 2005's new My keyword, showing how it can be used to save and retrieve files from the server's hard drive. Guestbook provides a place where visitors can check in with you and tell you a little about themselves. It stores this information in a text file and then retrieves the entries to view. Maintenance functions are also provided to perform a backup, to delete the current list and to restore the list from a backup. For an overview of some of the techniques used in this application, see Chapter 17. For a detailed examination of this application, see Bonus Chapter 3 on the CD. For complete source code, see the \Author\Guestbook folder on the CD.

Troubleshooting

I tried my best to compile programs that work on most computers with the minimum system requirements. Alas, your computer might differ, and some programs might not work properly for some reason.

The two likeliest problems are that your computer doesn't have enough memory (RAM) for the programs you want to use, or you have other programs running that are affecting installation or running of a program. If you get an error message such as `Not enough memory` or `Setup cannot continue`, try one or more of the following suggestions and then try using the software again:

- ✔ **Turn off any antivirus software running on your computer.** Installation programs sometimes mimic virus activity and might make your computer incorrectly believe that it's being infected by a virus.

- ✔ **Close all running programs.** The more programs you have running, the less memory is available to other programs. Installation programs typically update files and programs, so if you keep other programs running, installation might not work properly. This might include closing the CD interface and running a product's installation program from Windows Explorer.

- ✔ **Reference the ReadMe:** Please refer to the ReadMe file located at the root of the CD-ROM for the latest product information at the time of publication.

- ✔ **Have your local computer store add more RAM to your computer.** This is, admittedly, a drastic and somewhat expensive step. However, adding more memory can really help the speed of your computer and enable more programs to run at the same time.

If you have trouble with the CD-ROM, please call the Wiley Product Technical Support phone number at 800-762-2974. Outside the United States, call 317-572-3994. You can also contact Wiley Product Technical Support at `www.wiley.com/techsupport`. John Wiley & Sons will provide technical support only for installation and other general quality control items. For technical support on the applications themselves, consult the program's vendor or author.

To place additional orders or to request information about other Wiley products, please call 877-762-2974.

Index

Wiley Publishing, Inc.
End-User License Agreement

READ THIS. You should carefully read these terms and conditions before opening the software packet(s) included with this book "Book". This is a license agreement "Agreement" between you and Wiley Publishing, Inc. "WPI". By opening the accompanying software packet(s), you acknowledge that you have read and accept the following terms and conditions. If you do not agree and do not want to be bound by such terms and conditions, promptly return the Book and the unopened software packet(s) to the place you obtained them for a full refund.

1. **License Grant.** WPI grants to you (either an individual or entity) a nonexclusive license to use one copy of the enclosed software program(s) (collectively, the "Software," solely for your own personal or business purposes on a single computer (whether a standard computer or a workstation component of a multi-user network). The Software is in use on a computer when it is loaded into temporary memory (RAM) or installed into permanent memory (hard disk, CD-ROM, or other storage device). WPI reserves all rights not expressly granted herein.

2. **Ownership.** WPI is the owner of all right, title, and interest, including copyright, in and to the compilation of the Software recorded on the disk(s) or CD-ROM "Software Media". Copyright to the individual programs recorded on the Software Media is owned by the author or other authorized copyright owner of each program. Ownership of the Software and all proprietary rights relating thereto remain with WPI and its licensers.

3. **Restrictions On Use and Transfer.**

   (a) You may only (i) make one copy of the Software for backup or archival purposes, or (ii) transfer the Software to a single hard disk, provided that you keep the original for backup or archival purposes. You may not (i) rent or lease the Software, (ii) copy or reproduce the Software through a LAN or other network system or through any computer subscriber system or bulletin-board system, or (iii) modify, adapt, or create derivative works based on the Software.

   (b) You may not reverse engineer, decompile, or disassemble the Software. You may transfer the Software and user documentation on a permanent basis, provided that the transferee agrees to accept the terms and conditions of this Agreement and you retain no copies. If the Software is an update or has been updated, any transfer must include the most recent update and all prior versions.

4. **Restrictions on Use of Individual Programs.** You must follow the individual requirements and restrictions detailed for each individual program in the About the CD-ROM appendix of this Book. These limitations are also contained in the individual license agreements recorded on the Software Media. These limitations may include a requirement that after using the program for a specified period of time, the user must pay a registration fee or discontinue use. By opening the Software packet(s), you will be agreeing to abide by the licenses and restrictions for these individual programs that are detailed in the About the CD-ROM appendix and on the Software Media. None of the material on this Software Media or listed in this Book may ever be redistributed, in original or modified form, for commercial purposes.

5. Limited Warranty.

(a) WPI warrants that the Software and Software Media are free from defects in materials and workmanship under normal use for a period of sixty (60) days from the date of purchase of this Book. If WPI receives notification within the warranty period of defects in materials or workmanship, WPI will replace the defective Software Media.

(b) WPI AND THE AUTHOR(S) OF THE BOOK DISCLAIM ALL OTHER WARRANTIES, EXPRESS OR IMPLIED, INCLUDING WITHOUT LIMITATION IMPLIED WARRANTIES OF MERCHANTABILITY AND FITNESS FOR A PARTICULAR PURPOSE, WITH RESPECT TO THE SOFTWARE, THE PROGRAMS, THE SOURCE CODE CONTAINED THEREIN, AND/OR THE TECHNIQUES DESCRIBED IN THIS BOOK. WPI DOES NOT WARRANT THAT THE FUNCTIONS CONTAINED IN THE SOFTWARE WILL MEET YOUR REQUIREMENTS OR THAT THE OPERATION OF THE SOFTWARE WILL BE ERROR FREE.

(c) This limited warranty gives you specific legal rights, and you may have other rights that vary from jurisdiction to jurisdiction.

6. Remedies.

(a) WPI's entire liability and your exclusive remedy for defects in materials and workmanship shall be limited to replacement of the Software Media, which may be returned to WPI with a copy of your receipt at the following address: Software Media Fulfillment Department, Attn.: ASP.NET 2.0 For Dummies, Wiley Publishing, Inc., 10475 Crosspoint Blvd., Indianapolis, IN 46256, or call 1-800-762-2974. Please allow four to six weeks for delivery. This Limited Warranty is void if failure of the Software Media has resulted from accident, abuse, or misapplication. Any replacement Software Media will be warranted for the remainder of the original warranty period or thirty (30) days, whichever is longer.

(b) In no event shall WPI or the author be liable for any damages whatsoever (including without limitation damages for loss of business profits, business interruption, loss of business information, or any other pecuniary loss) arising from the use of or inability to use the Book or the Software, even if WPI has been advised of the possibility of such damages.

(c) Because some jurisdictions do not allow the exclusion or limitation of liability for consequential or incidental damages, the above limitation or exclusion may not apply to you.

7. U.S. Government Restricted Rights. Use, duplication, or disclosure of the Software for or on behalf of the United States of America, its agencies and/or instrumentalities "U.S. Government" is subject to restrictions as stated in paragraph (c)(1)(ii) of the Rights in Technical Data and Computer Software clause of DFARS 252.227-7013, or subparagraphs (c) (1) and (2) of the Commercial Computer Software - Restricted Rights clause at FAR 52.227-19, and in similar clauses in the NASA FAR supplement, as applicable.

8. General. This Agreement constitutes the entire understanding of the parties and revokes and supersedes all prior agreements, oral or written, between them and may not be modified or amended except in a writing signed by both parties hereto that specifically refers to this Agreement. This Agreement shall take precedence over any other documents that may be in conflict herewith. If any one or more provisions contained in this Agreement are held by any court or tribunal to be invalid, illegal, or otherwise unenforceable, each and every other provision shall remain in full force and effect.